Living With Grief

CHILDREN, ADOLESCENTS, AND LOSS

Edited by Kenneth J. Doka

Foreword by Jack D. Gordon, President
Hospice Foundation of America

Living With Grief

CHILDREN, ADOLESCENTS, AND LOSS

Edited by Kenneth J. Doka

Foreword by Jack D. Gordon, President
Hospice Foundation of America

To order, contact:
Hospice Foundation of America
800-854-3402
www.hospicefoundation.org
E-mail: hfa@hospicefoundation.org

Library of Congress Catalog Card #: 99-075855

ISBN #: 1-893349-01-2

In Celebration of New Beginnings

To

My son, Michael, and his fiancee, Angelina
On their engagement

To Lisa and Dan
On the birth of their son

To Linda and Russell
On the birth of their son Ryan

Contents

Foreword

Jack D. Gordon, President
Hospice Foundation of America

Upon reading the title of this book, many people may be struck by reminders of traumatic events involving children and loss. The images of teens sobbing after tragic school shootings in Littleton and Jonesboro, or young children being led away from a day care center after a random attack, are forever burned into our memories. These events are indeed powerful reminders of the uncertainty that faces all of us every day. While the number of children and adolescents directly affected by these random incidents is relatively small, the impact on the nation's consciousness has been enormous.

If something positive can be learned from these events, it may be that these situations help people begin to understand what death educators and hospice professionals have always known: Children and adolescents, as well as adults, face a myriad of losses every day, and they do grieve these losses. Of course, loved ones die—grandparents, parents, siblings, schoolmates. So do beloved pets—often a child's first real experience with death.

Other losses do not involve death, but can generate grief reactions. One of the most significant loss situations facing children in our society is divorce. Children also may have to relocate, or go to a new school. And, as children move into adolescence, there are the more subtle but important losses—loss of identity, loss of roles, loss of self-esteem.

We are focusing on the topic of children, adolescents, and loss in this book, and in our 7th annual National Bereavement Teleconference, to help people recognize that loss does impact children and adolescents, and that they do grieve. We feel that it is important to include more than an adult perspective on these issues, so throughout the book you'll find essays called "Voices"—articles written by children and adolescents, conveying their perspectives on loss in their own words.

The book and the teleconference both emphasize another critical factor grounded in more current conceptions of the grief process—that grief is not something that you "get over." This understanding has especially important ramifications for young people. Losses that they experience early in life may be revisited at critical developmental stages or during important life events. The more that educators, counselors, school administrators, parents, and anyone else who works with children and adolescents realize this, the more equipped they will be to help young people cope with grief and incorporate loss in their lives in ways that are mentally and physically healthy.

Hospice, as the only medical system of care that deals with the emotional and spiritual aspects of death and dying, has always understood the impact of grief and loss on children and adolescents. Many hospices offer support groups for children. In addition, more and more communities now have independent children's grief centers. While traumatic images of young people and loss may linger in our collective memory, the best way to help and prepare children for the future is through education and understanding of the day-to-day ramifications that loss and grief have on them. This book is designed to help the adults involved with children and adolescents to provide that education and understanding.

Acknowledgments

It seems appropriate to begin this section by expressing appreciation to the contributing authors. Each of them willingly undertook the challenge of writing a chapter and responding to tight deadlines. I would especially like to thank all the young authors who contributed to our *Voices* pieces. Each of them, in their own voice, reminds us of the many ways that children and adolescents respond to and adapt to loss. I also thank those adults who called these pieces to our attention.

Naturally, too, I need to recognize and salute the Hospice Foundation of America. Each year, they manage not only to produce an annual teleconference but also to produce a variety of educational resources, including this book. Jack Gordon, the Foundation's president, offers not only a guiding vision but thoughtful ideas as well. And he constantly battles against anything he sees as meaningless jargon. His vision becomes a reality through the work of an incredible staff that includes David Abrams, Sophie Viteri Berman, Lisa McGahey Veglahn, Jon Radulovic, Michon Lartigue, and Tiponya Gibson. Cokie Roberts adds so much to making the teleconference the remarkable event it has become. I need to especially acknowledge the editorial role of Lisa McGahey Veglahn, who labored on this book even in the last month of pregnancy. Chris Procunier, who has moved on from the Foundation to head his own business, was a great help, and he will be missed. I also want to acknowledge Joyce Davidson, a former co-editor, who stepped in to help. I hope that in future years, Joyce will again agree to co-edit this series.

I also need to thank the College of New Rochelle for its ongoing support. President Steve Sweeney, Vice President Joan Bailey, and Dean Laura Ellis all contribute to maintaining a wonderful environment in which to work and to teach. Students and colleagues provide both stimulation and support. And secretaries such as Rosemary Strobel and Vera Mezzacuella, as well as my research assistant, Susan McVicker, all work their own magic.

And finally, I want to acknowledge the ongoing support of all my family, friends, and neighbors. They remain a great gift.

Kenneth J. Doka

Part I

Theoretical Overview

In a 1972 seminal article, revised and reprinted in this volume, Robert Kastenbaum suggested that we like to think of childhood as "the kingdom where nobody dies." Yet much as we like to think we can protect children and adolescents from loss and death, the power to do so eludes us. As Kastenbaum notes, from early ages, children are constantly exposed to dying, death, loss, and grief in many ways—from games, music, and television, to their own experiences and concerns. The question of "how can we protect" is moot. The meaningful question is, "How can we prepare and support children and adolescents as they cope with loss?"

It is this question that guides this book, much as it guides the Hospice Foundation of America's Seventh Annual National Bereavement Teleconference on *Living With Grief: Children, Adolescents, and Loss.* Both the teleconference and this book strive to offer sound theoretical underpinnings, as well as practical clinical suggestions in helping children and adolescents cope with loss.

This opening section attempts to establish a theoretical base. The chapters and *Voices* pieces trace the development of children and adolescents, emphasizing the ways in which this developmental process contributes to how children and adolescents experience, express, and adapt to loss. Throughout these chapters, certain themes emerge.

Children and Adolescents Experience a Wide Range of Losses

We can make a critical error in assuming that losses through death are the only losses children and adolescents experience. Gordon notes in the foreword that, as with adults, the range of losses that children and adolescents grieve can be extensive. As they age, children and adolescents must adapt to a variety of developmental losses, including, for example, the loss of childhood. Even transitions such as graduation may include elements of grief. Friendships change. People move. In adolescence, they may experience the loss of romantic relationships. Dreams may die, too, as adolescents realize they may not become the actor or athlete they hoped to be. Illness and disability both involve loss.

There may be other losses as well. Death may strike family, friends, or pets. Parents may be separated, divorced, or incarcerated. Young people may be placed in foster care or sent away to different institutions. As Kastenbaum well emphasizes, children and adolescents are not strangers to loss.

Children and Adolescents Are Constantly Developing

Kastenbaum, Corr, and Balk emphasize the continued development that takes place as children grow into late adolescence. This development proceeds on all levels. They develop cognitively, mastering, over time, more mature understandings of complex concepts such as death or loss. Yet they develop in other ways as well.

As children age, they learn to manage affect. Young children, for example, often have a "short feeling span." They are unable to sustain strong feelings for long periods of time. Mood shifts are frequent. Children and adolescents develop socially, gradually moving from an egocentric perspective that looks at any loss through a very personal lens, to one that sees the broader relational aspects of loss. The child who wonders who will take him fishing now that Grandpa has died is able, at an older age, to empathize with his grandmother's loss. Children develop spiritually as well. At early ages, Coles (1990) reminds us, children still grapple with spiritual issues as "spiritual pioneers," struggling to explore what to them is unmapped territory. Later, they will both develop and continually reevaluate their spiritual beliefs. Yet as we attempt to understand this developmental process, Suarez and McFeaters add a further caution. The filters—cultural and experiential—that frame their lives always affect this process.

This developmental process affects grief and mourning. An early question of research asked, "At what age can children be said to grieve?" The articles in this section answer clearly: At any age, but in ways that are both similar to and different from the ways grief and mourning manifests itself in adults.

Support is Critical

All the chapters in this section emphasize the critical nature of understanding and support. Children and adolescents are helped when adults around them recognize that they grieve and support them as they mourn. Yet there may be limits to that support. Parents may be coping with loss themselves, limiting their own energy and ability to help.

Johns' chapter emphasizes the critical role that schools can offer. Schools, he reminds us, play many roles in the lives of youth. Here a range of supportive adults can assist children and adolescents as they cope with loss. But our *Voices* pieces add a note of caution. The anonymous piece sadly reminds us that teachers too are human and some may lack sensitivity and empathy. The dialogue between Whitehead and Atkins expresses the many hesitations that adolescents have in reaching for support from their schools. And Janczuk's *Voices* piece stresses a critical point—that students away at school may also be away from critical sources of support. These pieces do not belie Johns' contention that schools can be a vital resource, but they emphasize both barriers and the need for effort, education, and training.

Finally, the anonymous piece hints at the value of other sources of support such as counseling. It is this theme that will be emphasized in the next section.

1

The Kingdom Where Nobody Dies

This is an updated version of an article that first appeared
in *Saturday Review of Literature* (December 23, 1972).

Robert Kastenbaum

Children are playing and shouting in the early morning sunshine near
the end of Alban Berg's opera *Wozzeck*. They are chanting a variant
of the very familiar rhyme: "Ring-a-ring-a roses, all fall down! Ring-a-
ring-a roses, all...." The game is interrupted by the excited entry of other
children, one of whom shouts to Marie's child, "Hey, your mother is
dead!" But Marie's child responds only by continuing to ride his hobby-
horse. "Hop, hop! Hop, hop! Hop, hop!" The other children exchange a
few words about what is "out there, on the path by the pool," and run off
to see for themselves. The newly orphaned child hesitates for an instant
and then rides off in the direction of his playmates. End of opera.

What begins for Marie's child? Without knowing the details of his
fate, we can sense the confusion, vulnerability, and terror that mark this
child's entry into the realm of calamity and grief. Adult protection has
failed. The grown-ups, as it has turned out, couldn't even protect themselves. The reality of death has shattered the make-believe of childhood.

Children often are exposed to death in ways much less dramatic than
the sudden demise of a parent. A funeral procession passes by. A pet dies.
An innocent question is raised at the dinner table: "This didn't come from
a real live cow, did it, like Elsie, the one we saw at school today?" Many of

the questions children ask about death make parents uncomfortable. During research interviews, mothers of young children clearly identified a reason for this discomfort. One woman recalled that, "We never spoke about dying or death in my house, even when there was a funeral. If my parents ever did talk about it, they made sure that the kids weren't around." Another remembered being told that God wanted her older sister. "I didn't think God was so nice after that, and I worried a lot about getting older and that God might want me, too."

With few exceptions, the mothers agreed that the subject of death had been locked in silence and tension. In consequence, they felt unprepared and insecure when it was their turn to respond to a child's curiosity about death. "I wanted to find just that one thing to say that would put Jeff's mind at ease and I guess, really, just get him off the subject. But—and this is going to sound terrible—I heard myself sounding just like my mother, talking in a forced and fakey voice. I don't think she convinced herself when she was trying to convince me, and she didn't, and I couldn't when it was my turn."

The intrusion of death, even in words alone, can make loving and capable parents feel awkward. They are not able to relax and observe, much less *appreciate*, how resourcefully children attempt to comprehend the mysteries of loss, discontinuity, absence, and death. Adults do have the responsibility to protect their children from stress and harm. Yet much can be learned if we are able to drop our guard on occasion and participate in the child's discovery of death. Nobody comes to an understanding of life without coming to some kind of understanding of death, and this process begins earlier than most of us have imagined. In observing children's efforts to comprehend death we are granted the opportunity to witness sparks of creativity and surges of courage that can only enhance our respect for their spirits.

Death in the Everyday Life of Children

A child's fascination with death can demonstrate itself almost at any time and place. Mortality is a theme that finds its way into many of the child's activities, whether solitary or social, and so it has been for as long as history has had a voice. Consider games, for example. "Ring-around-the-rosey" has been a popular childhood play theme throughout much of the world. Our grandparents delighted in "all fall down," as did their ancestors all the way back to the fifteenth century. The origin of this game, however, was anything but delightful.

Medieval society was almost totally helpless against bubonic plague—the Black Death. It has been estimated that at least one-fourth of the Asian and European populations perished during the most intense plague years. If adults could not ward off death, what could children do? They could join hands. They could form a circle of life. They could chant ritualistically and move together in a reassuring rhythm of unity. This demonstration of safety in numbers and human contact would not persist, though. The children also had to recognize their peril by enacting death. One child would drop out of the slowly moving circle and spin lifelessly to the ground. The circle would then tighten and close again, small voices still chanting. A few minutes later another child would drop to the ground, and the circle would contract again. And so it went, until only one child remained standing to chant plaintively, "All fall down." This game of childhood was not so simple after all. It not only recognized the peril of imminent death and loss but also provided comfort through a bonding ritual. Furthermore—and perhaps most subtly—death had been made to follow the rules of the game. Ring-around-the-rosey had another distinct advantage over its model—one could arise to play again. How joyous it must have been to laugh and leap up from the ground. True, one might fall again, and this time for real. But even a little triumph over death was a triumph.

In their own way the children were participating in medieval Europe's response to devastation by capturing and mocking death through dramatic enactments, songs, and caricatures. Young children were not too young to apply themselves to this enterprise, just as vulnerable children in violent environments today find ways to incorporate death into their lives as a sort of immunization. In Northern Ireland, for example, children have played "soldier and terrorist" instead of "cops and robbers."

Death has been ritualized in many other children's games as well. In the playful romping of "tag," what is the hidden agenda or mystery, that makes the chaser it? Folklorists (Opie and Opie, 1969) have amassed evidence strongly suggesting that it is death's stand-in. Death (or The Dead Man) is sometimes the actual name given to the chaser. In the

English game "Dead Man Arise," the central player lies prostrate on the ground while other children either mourn over him or seek to bring him back to life. When least expected, up jumps John Brown, The Dead Man, the Water Sprite, Death Himself, or whatever name local custom prefers. The children flee or freeze in pretend surprise as the chaser whirls toward them for a tag that will bestow Dead Man status upon the victim.

In her pioneering studies of children's thoughts of death, Sylvia Anthony (1948/1972) identified a phenomenon she called *oscillation*. Her respondents, mostly happy and normal children, often spontaneously reversed roles in death games. Now they would be the poor, sad victim of a terrible accident or murder. Now they would be the person causing the "accident," or even the cold-blooded killer. Anthony concluded that children take all possible roles in death as a way of getting their minds around this challenging problem. She likened this process to the delight that very young children take in feeding the person who is feeding them. Spontaneous experiential learning is a talent that seems to develop early and that is quickly put to use. The findings of Anthony and other researchers should provide a little comfort to parents. If we observe a touch of sadism in our children, this probably does not mean that we have been raising monsters. It is far more likely that they are attempting to transform some of their sense of vulnerability to the active mode, a counterphobic move that has adaptive value if not taken too far. Similarly, when children play dead they are not necessarily demonstrating pathological morbidity. They are probably a lot more like the kids I've watched scrambling around rocks and trees enacting occasional melodramatic deaths that are reversed by a tickle. They arise, literally tickled to be alive again, having survived a micro-simulation of what it might be like to be really and truly dead.

Children's games that have been passed on from generation to generation may themselves be on the endangered list. There are fewer neighborhoods in which children play their traditional street games. Children's games have become influenced significantly by movies, television, and computer systems at the same time that "keeping kids off the streets" has been replacing the outdoor neighborhood experience. Death continues to have its place, although the forms may vary. "Bang, bang, you're dead!" became the up-to-date variant of tag games as Western and gangster movies became popular. Today many young fingers are destroying aliens or playing other computer games of more remarkable savagery. Up to this point, computer-mediated culture has offered much less opportunity to develop compassion, healing, memorialization, and that entire spectrum of death-related experiences that does not feast on violence.

No matter what might be available in the way of existing death-related games, children sometimes must create their own. This is often the case when children are alone with feelings of foreboding and vulnerability. Again, these actions are subject to misinterpretation if viewed exclusively from an adult perspective. For example, a parent might scold or tease a child who is suffocating and burying a doll. If adult anxieties can be set aside for a moment, much could be learned here from a low-key conversation. It might be discovered that the child has heard something on the news about a person suffocating, or has himself had a moment of respiratory panic. The burial could also be an experiment to prove that the dead can return if one knows the right things to say and do. Similarly, a child may arouse adult ire by a noisy game of repeatedly crashing toy cars into each other. I remember one small boy who provided an astoundingly effective soundtrack for the repeated crashing of his model plane. In a sense these children are being rude and destructive. But in a deeper sense they may be testing out feelings that have been aroused by observations of loss, change, and abandonment. Incidentally, the boy who was specializing in air disasters comforted the adult onlooker, saying shyly, "Nobody gets killed bad."

How death becomes a vital element in what we call child's play was illustrated when one of my sons (eight years old at the time) marched himself over to the piano and started to improvise. This was not his usual style of moderated keyboarding, but loud, clangorous thumps. A few minutes later he moved to the floor near the piano and started to stack his wooden blocks. These two sets of spontaneous actions did not have any relationship to each other that I could see, nor did they bear an apparent mark of death awareness. Yet the only way to appreciate David's behavior was in terms of his response to death and loss. The piano playing and block building occurred within a half-hour of the time David and I had discovered our family cat lying dead on the road. Together we had acknowledged the death, discussed the dangers of the all-too-busy street (we moved not long afterward), shared our sorrow, and removed the body for burial in the woods. David had then gone his own way for a while, which eventually included the actions already mentioned.

When I asked what he was playing on the piano, David answered, "Lovey's life story." He patiently explained how the various types of music he had improvised represented memorable incidents in the life of his cat (e.g., "This is music from when she scratched my arm"; "This is Lovey curling up to sleep"). The wooden blocks turned out to be a monument for Lovey. A close look revealed that the entire structure was constructed in an L shape, with several other L's at salient points.

If there had been no sharing of the death encounter when it first occurred, I probably would not have guessed that David's play had been inspired by an encounter with mortality. Adults sometimes fail to fathom the implications of their children's play because they have not had the opportunity to perceive the stimulus. The fact that a particular behavior does not seem to be death-related by no means rules out the possibility that it must be understood at least partially in those terms.

How Do Children Develop an Understanding of Death?

The more we understand about the child's understanding of death, the more prepared we are to provide guidance and comfort. Interest in death is a normal part of cognitive, social, and personality development. This development will take place whether guided, distorted, or neglected by adults. We tend to filter our responses to children's encounters with death through our own experiences, which frequently include fears, doubts, and unresolved issues. Most counselors and therapists recognize the general principle that we need to have our own issues under control before we can be helpful to others; this principle certainly applies to supporting the child's discovery and interpretation of death.

Death themes engage the mind very early in life. It was once a mainstream assumption that young children are oblivious to death because they are *pre-conceptual* (or *pre-operational*, in Piaget's terminology). This assumption does not hold up. A young child does not have to understand death in a philosophical or conceptual sense in order to feel frightened by separation or puzzled and distressed by loss. Separation anxiety remains at the core of adult interpretations of death, an anxiety that is experienced repeatedly by even the most secure child when parents are temporarily absent. In fact, the limited conceptual development and life experience of the young child can make separation episodes even more disturbing. Similarly, recognition that something is gone comes very early in the developmental process. Many a toddler has been almost inconsolable when a favorite blankie has disappeared into the laundry or a cuddly toy left behind on a trip. Adult anxieties when some small item has disappeared may have originated in early childhood distress at the loss of a comforting presence. Children are alert to separations, losses, absences, and changes. In trying to understand a world in which people and things come and go, they are also working toward the comprehension of mortality.

There are two different, although related, realizations that children must eventually develop:

1. Other people die.
2. I will die.

One of the earliest inquiries into the psychology of death touched upon the child's exposure to the death of others. G. Stanley Hall, one of the most distinguished of the first generation of American psychologists, and one of his students obtained adult recollections of childhood (Hall and Scott, reported in Hall, 1922). Many of the earliest memories involved some form of death, and practically all respondents vividly recalled their first encounters with mortality. Hall later wrote that:

> The first impression of death often comes from a sensation of coldness in touching the corpse of a relative and the reaction is a nervous start at the contrast with the warmth that the contact of cuddling and hugging was wont to bring. The child's exquisite temperature sense feels a chill where it formerly felt heat. Then comes the immobility of face and body where it used to find prompt movements of response. There is no answering kiss, pat, or smile...often the half-opened eyes are noticed with awe. The silence and tearfulness of friends are also impressive to the infant, who often weeps reflexively or sympathetically. (Hall, 1922, 439-440)

Taking careful note of mental reactions to the elaborate funerals of the era, Hall observed that:

Little children often focus on some minute detail (*thanatic fetishism*) and ever after remember, for example, the bright pretty handles or the silver nails of the coffin, the plate, the cloth binding, their own or others' articles of apparel, the shroud, flowers, and wreaths on or near the coffin or thrown into the grave, countless stray phrases of the preacher, the fear lest the bottom of the coffin should drop out or the straps with which it is lowered into the ground should slip or break, a stone in the first handful or shovelful of earth thrown upon the coffin, etc. The hearse is almost always prominent in such memories and children often want to ride in one. (op. cit., 440-441)

Some adult memories of death went back to age two or three. A child that young could not interpret or symbolize death in anything approaching the adult mode. Yet the exposure to death had made a special impression that had to be preserved in some way. It is most likely that the memory is preserved in details of the perception. Elements of the scene that are easily overlooked by an adult may remain charged with emotion and vividly etched in the child's mind. We still do not know very much about the process through which these early death portraits affect individual development, although there are numerous anecdotal reports to suggest this is neither an uncommon nor an insignificant phenomenon. One could compile a book devoted to "kiss of death" memories alone and the enduring effects reported by adults who were forced to press their lips to the face of a dead relative. Likewise, we could use more knowledge regarding the circumstances that evoke these childhood memories in adulthood. Nevertheless, there is enough evidence to suggest that many of us have death perceptions engraved at some level in our memory that predate our ability to preserve experiences in the form of verbal concepts. It is perhaps unnecessary to mention to therapists and counselors that fishing around for these childhood memories in other people is not a pastime that should be pursued for idle amusement.

A more direct way to study the impact of death upon young children is to learn how they respond to the loss of people close to them. Findings that have held up well over time emerged from a series of studies by Albert Cain and his colleagues at the University of Michigan. They observed that a pattern of disturbed behavior often follows a death in the family. The symptoms can become part of the child's personality from that time forward. One of the studies focused upon responses to the death of a sibling (Cain, A., Cain, B., and Fast, I., 1964). As might be expected, guilt was one of the more frequent reactions, occurring in about half the cases, and still being evident five years after the sibling's death.

> Such children felt responsible for the death, sporadically insisted that it was all their fault, felt they should have died, too, or should have died instead of the dead sibling. They insisted they should enjoy nothing, and deserved only the worst. Some had suicidal thoughts and impulses, said they deserved to die, wanted to die—this being also motivated by a wish to join the dead sibling. They mulled over and over the nasty things they had thought, felt, or said to the dead sibling, and became all the guiltier. They also tried to recall the good things they had done, the ways they had protected the dead sibling, and so on. (op. cit., 747)

Trembling, crying, and sadness were also common. Some young children developed distorted ideas of what is involved in both illness and death. This heightened their death anxiety—something bad might happen to them at any time. A slight illness might prove fatal. There were even some fantasies that adults had killed their siblings, fantasies often fed by misinterpretations of emergency procedures such as resuscitation efforts. The surviving children sometimes became very fearful of physicians and hospitals or resented God as the murderer of their siblings. A few children also developed major problems in mental functioning; they suddenly appeared "stupid," did not even know their own age, and seemed to lose their sense of time and causation. These were dramatic illustrations of temporary effects of a bereavement experience in childhood. Retrospective studies conducted by other investigators indicate that long-term effects also may occur (in fact, childhood bereavement is reported more frequently among people who have required psychiatric care in adult life).

In an important ethnographic study, Myra Bluebond-Langner (1996) found many signs of stress among the siblings of terminally ill children. Along with the guilt feelings noted by earlier researchers, she reported sleep disturbances, outbursts of anger, and many other indices of a stress experience affecting the entire family. The children were also well aware of the ordeal being experienced by their parents. There was no doubt that children respond powerfully to the stress occasioned by family terminal illness and bereavement whether or not they share the adult conception of death.

The loss of an expected family member also proved unsettling to many of the children observed by Cain. Although young children had a difficult time understanding miscarriage, it was clear to them that something important had gone wrong. Evasive answers by anxious parents increased the problem for some children. In the absence of accurate knowledge they created fantasies that the fetus had been abandoned or murdered. One child insisted that his mother had thrown the baby into a garbage can in a fit of anger; another associated the miscarriage with guppies that eat their young. At times the insistent questioning by the child had the effect of further unsettling parents who were trying to deal with their own feelings about the miscarriage.

Fortunately, not all children become permanently affected by a death in the family. Some weather the loss with the strong and sensitive help of others. One woman remembers being encouraged by her parents to arrange a photograph and picture album that would help them all to think of the good times they had with their grandmother. "I realize now that this was a way to let me express my own feelings and not keep all the sadness inside me. I think it helped; I know it did."

There is no way of knowing for sure which death will make the greatest impact upon which child. The death of an animal companion sometimes affects a youngster more than the death of a person. This is more likely to happen when the animal's death is the first the child has encountered and the adult has been a somewhat distant part of the child's life. What children take from a death also depends on the circumstances. A social worker recalls her shock and anger at adult indifference to the death of her dog under the wheels of a visitor's truck. She feels certain that her career in child services was prefigured in this painful episode.

Whatever the impact of other deaths, however, the loss of a parent generally has the most profound and enduring influence on children. Bereavement in early childhood has been implicated as an underlying cause of depression and suicide attempts in later life. Some counselors and therapists have learned to be alert to the possible intensification of suicide ideation when a person reaches the age at which a parent died— especially if that death was by suicide or other violent means. Many case studies have found that a child may be growing up with suicidal ideation that will later be transformed into action because other family members had already taken that route (e.g., Heckler, 1994). The connection between early bereavement experiences and later anxiety, depression, and suicidality can be difficult to detect because there is a kind of timing mechanism involved: The emotional bomb does not explode until a particular time or situation arises. For example, a woman became panicked and acutely suicidal when she reached the age at which her mother had died. She could not help but believe that she would have to die as well, so it would be better to kill herself and get it over with.

This phenomenon can extend far into the adult years. Many healthy and active people in their middle years have told me of the suicidal plans they have in mind to avoid experiencing "old age." As one woman vehemently put it, "I saw my grandmother die inch by inch, lying in her own filth. I don't want my children to see me that way. Give me a quick, clean death or I'll take it myself." The puzzled, frightened, and hurt child remains in many an adult.

Of all the methods used to piece together the meaning of death during childhood, none can replace the sharing of a direct experience with a young child. In such moments we are granted a clear view of the child's face-to-face encounter with death. I recall, for example, David's first encounter with death.

David, at eighteen months, was toddling around the back yard. He pointed at something on the ground. I saw the dead bird. David appeared uncertain, puzzled, and curious, but made no effort to touch the bird. This was unusual hesitancy for a child who characteristically engaged physically with practically everything he could reach. David then crouched over and moved slightly closer to the bird. His face changed expression. To my astonishment, his face was now set in a frozen, ritualized expression resembling nothing so much as the stylized Greek theatrical mask of tragedy. I said only, "Yes, bird...dead bird." In typically adult conflict, I was tempted to add, "Don't touch," but then decided against this injunction. In any event, David still made no effort to touch.

That incident proved to be just the beginning. Every morning for the next several days he would begin his morning explorations by toddling over to the dead-bird place. David no longer assumed the ritual mask expression but still restrained himself from touching. The bird was allowed to remain there until greatly reduced by decomposition. I reasoned that he might as well have the opportunity of seeing the natural processes at work. This was, to the best of my knowledge, David's first exposure to death. No general change in his behavior was noted, nor had any been expected. The first small chapter had closed.

But a few weeks later a second dead bird was discovered. David had a different reaction this time. He picked up the bird and gestured with it. He was "speaking" with insistence though without an adequate vocabulary. When he realized that I did not comprehend his wishes, he reached up toward a tree, holding the bird above his head. He repeated the gesture several times. I tried to explain that being placed back on the tree would not help the bird. David continued to insist, accompanying his command now with gestures indicating a flying bird. What could I do but put the bird back on the tree? The bird, of course, did not fly or even stir. David insisted that I try again. After several more failed efforts, David lost interest in the bird that could not be made to fly again.

There was another sequel a few weeks later—by now autumn. David and I were walking in the woods, sharing small discoveries. After a while, though, his attention became thoroughly engaged by a single fallen leaf. He tried to place it back on the tree himself. Failure. He gave the leaf to me with "instructions" that it be restored to its rightful place. Failure again. When I started to try once more, he shook his head no, looking both solemn and convinced. Although other leaves were seen to fall and dead animals were found now and then, he made no further efforts to reverse their fortunes.

David's look of puzzlement and his repeated efforts to reverse death suggest that even the very young child recognizes a problem when he sees one. Indeed, the related problems of death-loss-absence might be the prime challenge that sets into motion the child's curiosity and mental questing. Piaget's (1973) influential view of cognitive development emphasizes the child's construction of invariance or constancy. What changes or melts away is of little interest. This model misses the point that children must be aware of changes, losses, and disappearances if they are to understand that which endures. Even more significantly, change, loss, and death are part of reality. A construction of the world that ignores mortality can only be a form of institutionalized denial.

Adah Maurer (1966) has offered a view of early development based on her experiences as a school psychologist. Is her position too extreme? Judge for yourself as she describes the behavior of a three-month-old whose daily experiences alternate between frequent sleeping and waking states:

> The healthy baby is ready to experiment with these contrasting states. In the game of peek-a-boo, he replays in safe circumstances the alternate terror and delight, confirming his sense of self by risking and regaining complete consciousness. A light cloth spread over his face and body will elicit an immediate and forceful reaction. Short, sharp intakes of breath, and vigorous thrashing of arms and legs removes the erstwhile shroud to reveal widely staring eyes that scan the scene with frantic alertness until they lock glances with the smiling mother, whereupon he will wriggle and laugh with joy....To the empathic observer, it is obvious that he enjoyed the temporary dimming of the light, the blotting out of the reassuring face and the suggestion of a lack of air which his own efforts enabled him to restore, his aliveness additionally confirmed by the glad greeting implicit in the eye-to-eye oneness with another human. (op. cit., 36)

Babies a few months older often delight in disappearance-and-return games. Overboard goes a toy, somebody fetches it, then overboard again. The questions, "When is something gone?" and, "When is it gone and not going to come back?" seem very important to the precocious explorer. Maurer observes that young children devise many experiments for determining under what conditions something is "all gone," including, for example, blowing out a candle with demonic glee and giving various objects burials at sea via the toilet bowl.

Maurer's interpretations are difficult to test, but the kind of behavior she describes is widely available for observation. Furthermore, once children have developed a verbal repertoire we usually hear key death-related observations from their own lips. I remember hearing a four-year-old girl spontaneously lecturing her 84-year-old great-grandmother about death. "You are old. That means you will die. I am young, so I won't die, you know." However, a moment later she added, "But it's all right,

Gran'mother. Just make sure you wear your white dress. Then, after you die, you can marry Nomo (great-grandfather) again, and have babies." Although this child's cognitive mastery was not without its flaws, it is clear that death had become a salient topic to which she was devoting her avid attention.

The bedrock study of children's cognitions of death was reported by Maria Nagy (1948), her respondents being normal Hungarian children between the ages of three and ten. Even the youngest children were aware that "dead" was much different than "alive." Their thoughts about "dead" and "death" were based largely on realistic and concrete perceptions. Nagy (affectionately dubbed "Auntie Death" by the children who answered her questions and drew pictures) found three stages in the development or acquisition of death concepts.

Stage one included mostly children between the ages of three and five. These youngest of the young were full of questions about funerals, coffins, cemeteries, and everything that seemed to be related to death. They saw death as a continuation of life but in a diminished form: the dead are much less alive. Furthermore, death could be temporary.

Stage two included mostly children from ages five or six to nine. These children recognized that death was final: the dead do not return. Some of these children also personified death, for example, as a skeleton or some other mysterious human-like figure. A few adventurous children at Stage two revealed their plan to "Kill the death-man so we will not die."

Stage three started for most children around age nine or ten and was thought to continue through the adult years. Older children recognized that death is personal, universal, final, and inevitable. They, too, would die some day, and there would be no getting around it.

Later studies have found few personifications of death (these may have faded from children's awareness as folk cultures have given way to technologies and mass media). It is also clear that the child's level of maturation is an important factor: chronological age is still a useful index, but we should also attend to the particular child's general level of cognitive and emotional development (Kenyon, in press). Nagy's stages offer a useful guide to the development of the child's concept of death, but not all observations fit neatly into these categories. For example, there are instances in which personal inevitable mortality is spontaneously grasped by children who might be thought too young to have such a concept. A six-year-old boy worked out for himself the certainty of death. In a shocked voice he revealed, "But I had been planning to live forever, you know." A five-year-old reasoned aloud: "One day you (father) will be died. And one day Mommy will be died...and one day even Cynth (younger sister), she will be died. I mean dead, too. [Pause]. And one day I will be dead. [Long pause]. Everybody there is will be dead. [Long, long pause]. That's sad, isn't it?"

It is possible that children can spontaneously grasp or work out the basic facts of death for themselves at an early age, but then retreat from this realization. The compulsion to avoid holding opposite or contradictory ideas at the same time is a requirement that even many adults fail to honor on all occasions. Children may have a more situational conception of death, sometimes "childish" and wishful, other times absolutely on target.

Sooner or later most children do come to understand that death is final, universal, personal, and inevitable (Kastenbaum, 2000). Parents might prefer otherwise. We might hope for our children to remain innocent of both sexual and mortal matters until they have further ripened. But it is our own make-believe, not theirs, if we persist in behaving as though children are not attuned to the prospect of mortality. This awareness is further heightened by experiences with illness and encounters with lethal violence—even in our schools. Many children have survived into adulthood with few illusions about security and permanence.

"The kingdom where nobody dies," as Edna St. Vincent Millay once described childhood, is the fantasy of grownups. We want our children to be immortal—at least temporarily. We can be more useful to children, though, if we can share with them realities as well as fantasies about death. This means some uncomfortable moments. Part of each child's adventure into life is the discovery of loss, separation, nonbeing, death. No one else can have this experience for the child, nor can death be locked into another room until a child comes of age. At the beginning children do not know that they are supposed to develop a fabric of evasions to protect themselves—and us—from this hard reality. Most children are ready to share their discoveries with us. Are we?

Robert Kastenbaum has been studying lifespan development and the human encounter with death for four decades. He founded The International Journal of Aging and Human Experience *and* Omega, Journal of Death and Dying. *He is an author and professor emeritus at Arizona State University.*

2

What Do We Know About Grieving Children and Adolescents?

Charles A. Corr

How do children and adolescents grieve? What are their grief and mourning like? Do children and adolescents grieve in ways that are different from adults? What do we know or think we know about grieving children and adolescents?

This chapter offers answers to such questions by drawing on the best theoretical literature from clinicians, researchers, and other scholars writing for professionals and other adults who work with bereaved children and adolescents. Quite a large body of literature is now at hand, including, in recent years, articles in professional journals that are too numerous to mention here; broad overviews of death, dying, and bereavement that include discussion of children and adolescents (e.g., Corr, Nabe, and Corr, 2000); books that focus specifically on issues related to children and death (e.g., Adams and Deveau, 1995; Corr and Corr, 1996; Doka, 1995) or adolescents and death (e.g., Corr and Balk, 1996); and books with a special concentration on bereavement in childhood and adolescence (e.g., Silverman, 1999; Webb, 1993; Worden, 1996).

Despite many variations in the language and concepts that are used to describe any bereaved persons, the professional literature sensitizes us to the difference between *bereavement* (the objective state of having suffered a significant loss), *grief* (the subjective reaction to loss), and *mourning* (the conscious and unconscious intrapsychic processes, together with the cultural, public, or interpersonal efforts, that are involved in attempts to cope with loss and grief) (Corr, Nabe, and Corr, 2000; Rando, 1984, 1993).

From this professional literature, we can identify four central questions for this chapter: What is grief? How do children and adolescents experience grief? How do children and adolescents express their grief? How do children and adolescents mourn or try to cope with loss and grief?

In addition to the professional literature, there is another quite different body of literature which is helpful, composed of books that address death-related topics and designed to be read by or with young readers. The creativity of the authors of such literature, along with the imagination of their illustrators in many cases, can help to enrich appreciation of bereavement and grief in children and adolescents. In this chapter, 60 citations to works intended to be read by children and adolescents appear in italics (by contrast with the standard typeface used for citations to the professional literature) and are meant to refer to entries in the bibliography of this book.

What Is Grief?

When we inquire about "grieving" children and "grief" in children, it helps to be clear about the language and the concepts that are used to describe all bereaved persons. Even a brief acquaintance with the professional literature on bereavement shows that they are used in different ways and mean different things to different authors and speakers.

The term "grief" is often defined as "the emotional reaction to loss." That is not a bad definition, but it can be overly limiting if not understood correctly. Grief certainly is the term that is commonly used to identify a bereaved person's reaction to loss. Thus, if "bereavement" is the objective situation of someone who has experienced a significant loss, then "grief" is the subjective or personal reaction to that situation. When anyone experiences the loss of someone or some thing that is valued, he or she is harmed. Something important is taken away, often abruptly and in a hurtful way. It would be surprising if a bereaved person did not react to what he or she has experienced.

Feelings and emotions are a prominent part of most grief reactions. As part of the grief reaction, one experiences pain, sadness, anger, bewilderment, and many other feelings. Bereaved persons are all too familiar with these affective reactions to loss. But while feelings are an important part of the grief reaction, they are not the whole story. Feelings represent human sentiment, sensibility, and passion. In addition to feelings, a bereaved person may experience reactions that are distinctively cognitive, physical, behavioral, social, or spiritual in nature. For example, many bereaved persons experience confusion or an inability to focus on school work and other activities, lack of energy or a lump in the throat, tightness in the chest or hollowness in the stomach, sleep or appetite disturbances, upsetting dreams, restless overactivity or loss of interest in activities that had previously been enjoyed, problems in interpersonal relationships, hostility toward God, or a search for a sense of meaning. In children, cognitive disturbances associated with grief may be misconstrued as learning disabilities, while regression to bedwetting or thumbsucking may be misinterpreted, and sometimes punished, as simple misbehavior.

This is another way of saying that grief is a holistic reaction to loss on the part of all human beings. It would be surprising and incomplete to insist that any bereaved person could only react to a significant loss in one or two ways, reflecting just one or two aspects of his or her whole humanity. Grief is or can be a reaction to loss that involves all of the dimensions of a bereaved individual's being.

How Do Children and Adolescents Experience Grief?

Some scholars have argued that children are not able to experience grief. Such claims go wrong because they depend on false premises. If one simply asks, "Can children react to loss?" or "Do children react to loss?", surely there would be no temptation to reply in the negative.

Consider what some children's books have to offer on this matter. In *Tough Boris* (*Fox, 1994*) children learn that even fearsome pirates cry when they experience a loss. By contrast, in *Why Did Grandpa Die?* (*Hazen, 1985*), young Molly is unable to cry when her grandfather dies, even though she feels frightened and awful. That is, she responds to her encounter with death in some ways, but not in other ways. Whether or not she cries, is Molly reacting to the loss that she has experienced? Is she experiencing grief? Certainly.

In two books about the death of friends in automobile accidents, *Dusty Was My Friend* (*Clardy, 1984*) and *I Had a Friend Named Peter*

(*Cohn, 1987*), eight-year-old Benjamin and a young girl named Beth share different experiences. Each of these youngsters is surprised and challenged by his or her unexpected reactions to the death of a friend, but both do react and struggle to understand their feelings.

In *The Dead Bird* (*Brown, 1958*), the first reaction of a group of children who find a wild bird that has just died is curiosity. They hold and touch the bird, leading them to discover that its heart is no longer beating, its body is growing cold, and it is becoming stiff. And in *Nana Upstairs and Nana Downstairs* (*De Paola, 1973*), when young Tommy is told that his beloved great-grandmother has died, his first reaction is disbelief. He finds it difficult to accept that she is really gone and he needs to see her empty bed to begin to grasp the hard fact that she has died.

In brief, stories for children about the deaths of grandparents, parents, other adults, siblings, friends, pets, and wild animals all describe a rich and varied panorama of reactions to loss. Much the same can be found in books like *Timothy Duck* (*Blackburn, 1987*), *Thumpy's Story* (*Dodge, 1984*), *Aarvy Aardvark Finds Hope* (*O'Toole, 1988*), *Badger's Parting Gifts* (*Varley, 1992*), and the most famous of all, *Charlotte's Web* (*White, 1952*), in which animals with human characteristics serve as the leading figures in captivating dramas of threats to life, death, bereavement, and grief.

These stories all ring true to child, adolescent, and adult readers because they paint accurate verbal and dramatic portraits of one of the most fundamental of all human experiences—experiencing and reacting to loss. Readers would hardly be attracted to such stories if their central characters did not experience grief related to their losses. One key part of being a grieving child is encountering loss and experiencing a broad range of reactions to such loss. In any specific encounter with death, the personal grief reactions experienced by a particular child or adolescent will depend upon the individual youngster and other characteristics that define the bereavement situation.

How Do Children and Adolescents Express Grief?

In addition to encountering loss and experiencing grief reactions, children and adolescents also express their grief in a variety of ways. What forms do children's and adolescents' expressions of grief usually take? Do children and adolescents always express their grief? Are children's and adolescents' expressions of grief similar to those of adults?

If a needle were to prick the skin of a child, one would expect that child both to experience the pain of such an unwelcome violation of bodily integrity and then to give vent to what he or she is feeling in that experience—perhaps by recoiling from the needle, yelling "ouch," or shedding tears. Similarly, if a child were to experience a death or other significant loss, one would expect that child first to react to that experience in the form of grief and then to give vent in some way or other to the reactions that he or she is experiencing. How children do or do not give vent to or share their reactions to loss depends upon the personality of the individual child, his or her ability to communicate what he or she is experiencing, and what the immediate environment (circumstances, family, culture, etc.) does or does not permit (Corr and Corr, 1996). But it would be surprising (and perhaps a source of concern) if over a reasonable period of time a bereaved child did not express any grief reactions to a significant loss.

Some grief reactions are expressed in familiar ways. For example, in *The Accident* (*Carrick, 1976*), Christopher's dog, Bodger, is accidentally killed by a truck. Almost immediately, Christopher lets everyone around him know that he is angry at the truck driver. He also makes clear that he is angry at his father for not getting mad at the driver. (In addition, Christopher is angry at himself for not paying attention and allowing Bodger to wander to the other side of the road as they walked, but that aspect of his grief is not so openly displayed at first.)

Many children share their grief reactions with parents or other available adults. For example, in *Tell Me About Death, Tell Me About Funerals* (*Corley, 1973*), a funeral director describes an imaginary dialogue in which a young girl poses and discusses with her father many grief-related questions (e.g., about guilt, abandonment, and choices about funerals and bodily disposition) after the death of her grandfather. Some children share their grief with siblings or peers who are experiencing similar losses as in *Geranium Morning* (*Powell, 1990*) when a boy whose father has died suddenly in an accident and a girl whose mother is in the process of dying share their strong feelings, memories, and guilt.

Sometimes, a teacher, clergy person, or other empathetic adult can help a child express his reactions to loss. For instance, when a mischievous boy called Jamie dies suddenly of an allergic reaction to a bee sting, the unnamed narrator of a *Taste of Blackberries* (*Smith, 1973*) brings his questions to an adult neighbor: Did Jamie really die or is this just another one of his pranks? Could his death have been prevented? Is it disloyal to go on living when Jamie is dead? In this book, the lesson from these reflections is that "some questions just don't have answers," but the point for our purposes is the very occurrence of the dialogue in which a child gives expression to these puzzling grief-related reactions.

Grief reactions are expressed and explored in literature for children in many ways: through books like *Saying Goodbye* (*Boulden, 1989*) that permit drawing pictures, coloring images, or inserting personal thoughts on their pages; via journaling and art in *The Last Goodbye* (*Boulden and Boulden, 1994*), *My Memory Book* (*Gaines-Lane, 1995*), and *When Someone Very Special Dies* (*Heegaard, 1988*); with friends and through ritual in *When Violet Died* (*Kantrowitz, 1973*); even just by telling and recording stories that make up the literature for children and adolescents with which bereaved children can identify.

Some children are not permitted or given opportunities to express their grief. Others may not feel secure in doing so, perhaps because they are afraid of their own powerful reactions, or because they blame themselves for what has happened and are unwilling to acknowledge their perceived guilt to others. For some children, grief is a new event in their lives—they lack prior experience with such strong and difficult reactions, the conceptual ability to identify and understand what they are experiencing, or the communicative skills with which to articulate and share their grief reactions.

Adolescent expressions of grief are similar to those of children, although inevitably influenced by the additional life experiences, enhanced communication skills, and personal situations of bereaved adolescents, together with the normative developmental tasks they face (Corr and Balk, 1996). Thus, thirteen-year-old Kate and her family are flooded with grief when her eleven-year-old sister Joss is unexpectedly killed in a fall from a tree in *Beat the Turtle Drum* (*Greene, 1976*). Bewilderment and guilt are openly expressed by fifteen-year-old Anthony's friends, teacher, and family members after he hangs himself in *Tunnel Vision* (*Arrick, 1980*). By contrast, the bereaved youngsters in *Grover* (*Cleaver and Cleaver, 1970*) and *There Are Two Kinds of Terrible* (*Mann, 1977*) must struggle to share their suffering and their memories with "cold fish" fathers who initially cannot face their own grief or that of their sons in the aftermath of a spouse's death. A special challenge for many bereaved adolescents is their need not to feel out of control and not to embarrass themselves in front of their peers.

Children's and adolescents' expressions of grief are both similar to and different from those of adults. In the aftermath of a significant loss, it is normal to expect that all human beings will experience and express grief reactions. But adults in our society have often been socialized not to express their grief in certain contexts (e.g., in public settings after the funeral, at work, or when some time has passed since the death) or roles (e.g., as a male or as the individual designated as the "strong" person in a family). Some children are unaware of such adult inhibitions or are not restrained by them. Thus, when family members are unavailable to them, children may speak freely of their loss and grief to strangers, or unexpectedly pose questions and ideas that are on their minds.

Of course, older children and adolescents sometimes find themselves in situations that suppress the expression of their grief. For example, *The Mother Tree* (*Whitehead, 1971*) describes the consequences of a mother's death on a farm in the early 1900s. Almost immediately, eleven-year-old Tempe has to take over her mother's duties, including the responsibility of caring for her four-year-old sister, Laura. Tempe is not really able to share her grief with anyone other than a large old tree in the backyard. While some new responsibilities may be unavoidable, all too often adults unnecessarily add to the pressures on bereaved children by telling them, "Now you are the big man of the family," or, "You need to be strong for your surviving parent."

Some children, especially those who are younger, may find that their grief is disenfranchised or not socially recognized, supported, and validated (Doka, 1989). This occurs when adults say to each other that a child is not able yet to understand fully what death means, or that she is too young to appreciate the depth of her loss. This is seen in *Mama's Going to Buy You a Mockingbird* (*Little, 1984*), when the children do not learn that their father is dying until they overhear people talk about it. The situation is made even more difficult for them when they are allowed only limited contact with him and given little information while he is in the hospital before his death. This is quite different from the behavior of Michael's grandfather in *So Long, Grandpa* (*Donnelly, 1981*) who helped prepare the boy for his anticipated death by taking him to an elderly friend's funeral.

Recent research (e.g., Silverman, 1999; Worden, 1996) suggests that children and adolescents do experience and express grief, but often in ways that may be more intermittent and drawn out over a longer period of time than is typical for most adults. In part, this seems to occur because most bereaved youngsters are only able to tolerate strong grief reactions for brief periods. When they feel able to confront their grief, they may limit their exposure to grief or only permit themselves a small "dose" of that experience before turning back to play, silence, or some other safer arena. Another key variable is whether or not their social situation recognizes, tolerates, and supports bereaved youngsters in their expression of grief. If not, such youngsters are usually less able to influence their social environments than are most bereaved adults.

It is also important to note that both the experience and the expression of grief in children and adolescents are inevitably influenced over time by new challenges in the form of normative developmental tasks (and perhaps also non-normative situational tasks related to other significant life events) that may stimulate renewed grief and new modes of grief expression. For example, a preschool child whose parent has died may experience a new sense of loss at a later date when she is the only one in class who does not have a living mother or father to prepare a card for on Mother's Day or Father's Day. Or a bereaved adolescent may face new challenges several years after the death of a sibling when that special brother or sister is not available for the confidences and guidance they used to offer each other.

How Do Children and Adolescents Mourn or Try to Cope with Loss and Grief?

In addition to how children and adolescents experience their grief reactions and how they give expression to their grief, a third key element in understanding grieving youngsters is how they mourn. Here, *mourning* means how bereaved youngsters try to cope with loss and grief. *Coping* refers to the efforts that are made to try to manage or contend with anything in life that is perceived as stressful or taxing one's resources (Lazarus and Folkman, 1984). In cases involving a death, coping may be directed to the primary loss of the person or animal that died, the secondary losses that are associated with the death (e.g., being deprived of someone's company), and the grief reactions that one experiences.

Once upon a time it was thought that children were unable to mourn because of their limited understandings of the concept of death or because they lacked the ego strength to carry their coping through to a successful resolution (Furman, 1973). But this holds children to false standards that would not be valid even for bereaved adults. No one fully understands the concept of death. Everyone copes on the basis of limited understandings. One important facet of all coping is its cognitive focus, through which an effort is made to appraise or understand a stressful situation. Children and adolescents seek to cope with concrete encounters with death in terms of what they actually do understand about the meanings and implications of those experiences.

Similarly, *resolution* (or its analogues, such as *completion* or *recovery*) is too demanding a criterion for most bereaved persons. Coping seeks to manage, not necessarily master, a stressful situation. In bereavement, it involves efforts to find ways to live with, adapt to, or integrate loss and grief into one's life. When such coping is successful or productive, it means that the bereaved person can go on with healthy living and loving. But that need not mean mourning is over for all time, that one's losses and grief will never again be revisited.

Research has shown that bereaved youngsters often maintain a connection of some type to a deceased person whom they loved (Silverman and Worden, 1992; Silverman, Nickman, and Worden, 1992). They are able to draw on inner strengths and external support in order to go on with living, but they are inevitably changed by their encounters with death. They do not "go back to normal"; on the contrary, effective coping is part of the effort to develop "new normals" in their lives.

Much of this can be seen in literature for children and adolescents. For example, in *The Eagle Kite* (*Fox, 1995*) young Liam struggles with cognitive and affective issues such as confusion, anger, and puzzling reactions from the adults around him when his father becomes sick with AIDS and dies. Similarly, two young Chinese-American girls must strive to work out what their mother means when she tells them to expect *The Happy Funeral* (*Bunting, 1982*) after their grandfather dies. *In Tiger Eyes* (*Blume, 1981*), a fifteen-year-old girl, her mother, and her younger broth-er must learn how to rebuild their lives when they each react differently and are initially unable to help each other in their grief after their father is killed during a holdup. And in *With You and Without You* (*Martin, 1986*) four children in one family must each face their own losses and coping challenges when their father becomes ill and dies.

Pet deaths often involve their owners in coping with both grief and some degree of perceived guilt, as in *The Accident* (*Carrick, 1976*) and *Mustard* (*Graeber, 1982*). As part of a different set of coping issues, however, two other boys are wise enough not to try to foreshorten their mourning by accepting a replacement animal too quickly after their elderly pets die in *Growing Time* (*Warburg, 1969*) and *I'll Always Love You* (*Wilhelm, 1985*).

In terms of identifying resources for coping, the youthful protagonists in *The Sunday Doll* (*Shura, 1988*) and *Hunter in the Dark* (*Hughes, 1984*) are able to find strengths within themselves when challenged by life-threatening illness and death. Another group of children turn to each other to engage in commemorative activities when the adult son of their elementary school teacher dies in *We Remember Philip* (*Simon, 1979*). And helpful adults enable still other children to share in the funeral of their beloved grandmother and in the disposition of her property to keep as remembrances of *Nonna* (*Bartoli, 1975*).

Some books pose issues that commonly arise in children's coping with death, such as the questions in *What's Heaven* (*Shriver, 1999*). And *Annie and the Old One* (*Miles, 1971*) describes a world view in which a child is led to see death and life as part of a single natural cycle. Many books carry this a step further to explore various ways of thinking about what happens after death, as in *Losing Uncle Tim* (*Jordan, 1989*), *Liplap's Wish* (*London, 1994*), or *Annie and the Sand Dobbies* (*Coburn, 1964*). One author even tries to imagine animal perspectives on the afterlife in *Dog Heaven* (*Rylant, 1995*) and *Cat Heaven* (*Rylant, 1997*). A number of books like *Blow Me a Kiss, Miss Lilly* (*Carlstrom, 1990*), *Meggie's Magic* (*Dean, 1991*), *My Grandpa Died Today* (*Fassler, 1971*), *Animal Crackers* (*Marshall, 1998*), *My Grandson Lew* (*Zolotow, 1974*), *Winter Holding Spring* (*Dragonwagon, 1990*), and *The Garden Is Doing Fine* (*Farley, 1975*) explore continuing bonds with the deceased and the ongoing legacy that endures within bereaved children after the death of a loved one.

One thing that can assist bereaved youngsters in their mourning is the knowledge that they are not alone, that others have faced and successfully managed similar challenges. In the literature for children and adolescents this perspective is represented by books in which adult editors and compilers enable bereaved children and adolescents to give voice to their own losses, grief reactions, and coping processes. Such books include *How It Feels When a Parent Dies* (*Krementz, 1981*); *There Is a Rainbow Behind Every Dark Cloud* (*Jampolsky and Taylor, 1978*); *Losing Someone You Love: When a Brother or Sister Dies* (*Richter, 1986*); and *Children Facing Grief: Letters from Bereaved Brothers and Sisters* (*Romond, 1989*). For more mature readers, *A Grief Observed* (*Lewis, 1976*) normalizes grief reactions through the author's candid description of his own grief after the death of his wife.

A Brief Conclusion

Adults will be able to understand and assist grieving children and adolescents better if they:

- clarify the differences between grief and mourning
- do not depend upon limited conceptual frameworks
- pay close attention to how bereaved children and adolescents experience grief by reacting to loss
- observe carefully how bereaved children and adolescents express their loss reactions
- examine the efforts that bereaved children and adolescents make to cope with both their losses and their grief
- draw upon useful lessons both from the professional literature and from books written to be read by or with children and adolescents
- remain open to the many lessons that children and adolescents have to teach all of us about bereavement, grief, and mourning.

In *Lifetimes: A Beautiful Way to Explain Death to Children* (*Mellonie and Ingpen, 1983*), readers are told that "there is a beginning and an ending for everything that is alive. In between is living. . . . So, no matter how long they are, or how short, lifetimes are really all the same. They have beginnings, and endings, and there is living in between." Adults who seek to understand and help bereaved children and adolescents will do well to focus not so much on the beginnings and the endings, but on the living in which these youngsters are engaged. When one does that, even sad and difficult events can be turned into ways to help bereaved children and adolescents enhance their appreciation of life and living. Consider the teenage protagonist in the novel, *A Season In-Between* (*Greenberg, 1979*), who learns to cope with the death of her father by drawing on the rabbinical teaching that one should turn scratches on a jewel into a beautiful design, or the eleven-year-old child who writes in *Be a Friend: Children Who Live with HIV Speak* (*Wiener, Best, and Pizzo, 1994*): "I often wonder how other children without AIDS learn to appreciate life. That's the best part about having AIDS" (p. 13).

Charles Corr, PhD, is Professor Emeritus in the Department of Philosophical Studies at Southern Illinois University Edwardsville, a member of the Executive Committee of the National Donor Family Council, and a former Chairperson of the International Work Group on Death, Dying, and Bereavement. Dr. Corr was seen on the Hospice Foundation of America's second annual National Bereavement Teleconference, Children Mourning, Mourning Children.

PRACTICAL SUGGESTIONS

Eight Myths About Children, Adolescents, and Loss

1. Children do not grieve, or only grieve when they reach a certain age.
Children grieve at any age. The ways that grief is manifested will vary, depending on the child's age, development, and experiences.

2. The death of a loved one is the only major loss that children and adolescents experience.
Children and adolescents experience a range of losses. These can include the normal developmental losses incurred when growing older (e.g., giving up childhood activities, school transitions, etc.), losses of pets, losses of dreams, separations caused by divorce or relocations, losses of friends and relationships, losses caused by trauma (such as a loss of safety), as well as losses due to illness or death. All of these losses generate grief.

3. It is better to shield children from loss, as they are too young to experience tragedy.
Much as we like to protect children from loss, it is impossible. It is far better to provide children and adolescents with support as they experience inevitable loss. We can teach and model our own ways

of adapting to loss if we include children and adolescents rather than exclude them. Exclusion only increases fears and breeds feelings of resentment and helplessness.

4. Children should not go to funerals. Children should always attend funerals.

Children and adolescents should have the choice as to how they wish to participate in funeral rituals. For that choice to be a meaningful one, they will need information, options, and support.

5. Children get over loss quickly.

No one gets over significant loss. Children, like adults, will learn to live with the loss, revisiting that loss at different points in their development. Even infants will react to a significant loss and, as they get older, may question the events of the loss and experience a sense of grief.

6. Children are permanently scarred by early, significant loss.

Most people, including children, are resilient. While early significant losses can affect development, solid support and strong continuity of care can assist children as they deal with loss.

7. Talking with children and adolescents is the most effective therapeutic approach in dealing with loss.

There is much value in openly communicating with children and adolescents. But there is also great value in using approaches that allow the child or adolescent other creative ways of expression. Play, art, dance, music, activity, and ritual are examples of creative modes of expression that children and adolescents may use to express grief and adapt to loss.

8. Helping children and adolescents deal with loss is the responsibility of the family.

Families do have a critical responsibility. But it is a responsibility shared with other individuals and organizations such as hospices, schools, and faith communities, as well as the community at large. In times of significant loss, it is important to remember that the ability of family members to support one another can be limited.

3

Adolescents, Grief, and Loss

David E. Balk

The purpose of the chapter is to indicate the unique ways that early, middle, and older adolescents grieve and the ways that their grief affects, and is affected by, developmental issues. The chapter is organized around these topics:

- Brief sketches of three grieving adolescents
- Developmental phases of adolescence
- Bereavement considered as a life crisis that threatens completion of developmental tasks
- Examples of critical life tasks unfolding in the lives of bereaved adolescents
- A discussion of the type of research that is needed and the ways we can help.

Brief Sketches of Three Grieving Adolescents

For this chapter to work, it is important for the reader to be grounded in the experiences that grieving adolescents report. Here are brief sketches from the lives of three grieving adolescents.

Grief during early adolescence

Deborah was thirteen when her brother was killed in a boating accident. She said that she talked often with her mother after the death: "We talked about why. Why did he die? And what am I supposed to do?" She noted that several of her brother's friends wanted to talk to her after the accident: "Mostly about how I was. How I was and how the family was doing. Then next came what did I feel like and what really happened. I wanted to talk with them because they were the people we knew best and how I would react. And I felt comfortable with them. They were like, Ed's friends, because they knew him first."

Two years after Ed's death, Deborah felt very close to her parents and her remaining brother Mike, talked with her mother often, and would have liked to talk with Mike about Ed's death. However, "he keeps a lot of his feelings in and doesn't talk a lot." She wanted to talk "because it still hurts." In the immediate aftermath of the death, Deborah had worried that her family would disintegrate, but they became a major source of support for each other. She said that two years of coping led her to learn a lot more about life and to appreciate that if a brother dies, "all these different stages of feelings you go through are normal. That you are not crazy" (Balk, 1981, 1983, 157-158).

Grief during middle adolescence

Ralph was fifteen when his sister died of cancer. He felt very close to her but distant from his parents. He said, "I never really talked to anybody in my family after Sally died. They thought I was crazy or something. They wanted to bring it up, but I knew she was going to die and there was nothing I could do about it. So I accepted the fact, and when it happened, it happened. They all felt I should feel worse than I did or something. They thought there was something wrong with me because they didn't think I was acting normal. When she died, I sort of moped around. And I didn't talk too much at school. Usually I'm a big mouth in class. I seem to get along better with kids at school now. I don't know why. I guess I appreciated everything more. I'd never really thought about dying. It was just something that happened 80 or 90 years away."

Ralph said the best advice he can give other adolescents whose brother or sister is dying is to be realistic. "You've got to look at it from a reality point. You've got to face the fact. You can't ignore it. Try to live with it, that's the biggest thing. Try to become at peace with yourself about how you felt. Sit down and think it out by yourself" (Balk, 1981, 1983, 158-159).

Grief during later adolescence

Rhonda was nineteen when her father died after four years of struggling with colon cancer. She kept a journal for a few months at the end of his illness and for four years after his death. In addition to the overall theme of a search for self, themes that emerged in her journal entries were (1) her ongoing relationship with her father, (2) problems coping with his death and subsequent events colored by her bereavement, and (3) life lessons. When facing her own problems, she thought about "what a trooper" her father had been during his illness and how that example made her "feel as though I too should fight" (Balk and Vesta, 1998, 35). She noted in an entry addressed to her father on the third anniversary of his death that "I can honestly say it becomes easier with time. The intensity of your death lessens. I don't think of you all the time and can function" (Balk and Vesta, 1998, 34).

The college environment, including her sorority, provided Rhonda little solace and comfort. She had thought she could forget her grief by concentrating on her studies, but instead found that often she just wanted to stop and cry. She noted "I seem to be very, very tired all the time," realized with surprise that "I never thought I would miss you so intensely that it would almost control me," and found with regret that she was removing herself from the other students. "They just don't understand, and I hope that they never have to" (Balk and Vesta, 1998, 35, 38).

Rhonda would agree that grief has left an indelible mark on her life and continues to shape her character. For four years following her father's death the search for her own identity became a constant motif. As she wrote in her journal, "I still search for direction in my life." She also found a recursive aspect to bereavement as she passed through developmental markers (for example, graduation from college, marriage, finding direction as a young adult) and wished her father were alive to share the moments. Four years after her father's death and a year before she herself married, she took part in a wedding and wrote in her journal, "Dad, I think about things like who would give me away....The wedding made me think of you a lot. But I feel strong and I'll be OK. Love, Rhonda" (Balk and Vesta, 1998, 34).

Developmental Phases of Adolescence

Adolescents in post-industrial countries develop in three phases: early, middle, and later adolescence (Balk, 1995a). Successful transition from early through later adolescence is marked by an increased sense of self, acceptance of responsibility, and direction in life. In short, adolescents face crucial developmental tasks:

1. To determine a direction or focus for work as an adult
2. To become an autonomous individual
3. To maintain intimate friendships and relationships

Early adolescence ranges from ages ten to fourteen, and entrance to puberty marks the beginning of this phase of development; however, the age range is inexact, and admittedly not all youth begin puberty between the ages of ten and fourteen. Developmental tasks facing early adolescents involve coming to terms with their changing bodies; learning new social skills with peers, family members, and other persons; mastering more difficult academic material; spending increasing time with peers; and gaining increasing autonomy from parents.

Middle adolescence extends from ages fifteen through seventeen. Middle adolescents are expected to demonstrate increased maturity in decision making. They spend more time away from home and with peers, rely more on persons their own age, and learn more about being friends with persons their own age. A growing proportion of middle adolescents work twenty or more hours a week in addition to going to school. For many youth, questions about personal identity become prominent during middle adolescence and continue into later adolescence.

Later adolescence rounds out the adolescent years, and extends from ages eighteen through twenty-two. Developmental tasks that mark these years are separating from one's parents, gaining independence, and entering into intimate friendships and relationships. Fulfilling these tasks is made easier if the youth has completed developmental expectations of early and middle adolescence. Older adolescents who manifest "ambivalence toward responsibility, identity, and interpersonal maturity" (Balk, 1995a, 7) are often individuals whose transition into young adulthood will be difficult. During the later adolescent years individuals gain greater facility in thinking about and dealing with the ambiguities and complexities of human existence (Pascarella and Terenzini, 1991; Perry, 1970).

Bereavement Considered as a Life Crisis That Threatens Completion of Developmental Tasks

Distressing situations that threaten a person's social and psychological equilibrium and that defy typical coping strategies are, by definition, life crises. The paradox is that life crises pose both a threat and an opportunity: Coping with a crisis can produce growth and maturity and a sense of confidence about dealing with life; however, a crisis can overwhelm a person, leave the person emotionally and socially devastated, and undermine confidence in dealing with life.

Bereavement presents the prototypical life crisis. For adolescents, this crisis places severe obstacles to fulfilling necessary developmental tasks. If coped with successfully, bereavement can lead to greater maturity and greater appreciation of life and of others. Offer (1969), for instance, reported that adolescents who had coped with a family tragedy such as a father's death were mature beyond their years. However, bereavement during adolescence can leave individuals with diminished self-confidence and groping for purpose well into adulthood.

Coleman (1978) argued that youth typically deal with the normative crises of adolescence by facing one issue at a time, resolving it, and then focusing attention on another issue. The intensity, duration, and all-encompassing nature of grief does not allow normative issues to be placed on hold while the person deals with bereavement. However, there is a danger in focusing solely on grief to the detriment of accomplishing normative life tasks. Rhonda noted in her journal, for instance, that "I never thought I would miss you so intensely that it would almost control me" (Balk and Vesta, 1998, 35).

A review of common manifestations of grief (see Marrone, 1997) will make clear the obstacles to completing the developmental tasks of normative adolescence. Physical manifestations include chills, diarrhea, and fatigue. Behavioral manifestations include startle reactions, sleeping problems, risk taking, and seemingly uncontrollable crying. Cognitive manifestations include memory and concentration problems, intrusive thoughts and images, and distressing dreams. Emotional manifestations include fear, anger, lack of hope, and loss of confidence. Spiritual manifestations take such forms as a crisis in faith, a search for meaning, and doubt about the importance of anything. Outsiders to bereavement seldom realize the intensity and duration of the feelings (Silver and Wortman, 1980). As an example, bereaved college students acknowledge being surprised at how sad they felt, how long these feelings lasted, and how little their unaffected peers appreciated what grief involves (Balk, 1997).

We will look at two models that provide useful perspectives for understanding what is at stake for bereaved adolescents. One of these models emerges from scholarly work done on stress, and the other from research about critical tasks and issues faced as adolescents mature.

A stress model for understanding adolescents faced with bereavement

Scholarship about stress has emphasized a holistic framework for understanding the impact of life crises upon individuals, families, and communities. Some of this scholarship has emphasized the psychological and the social forces producing stress and influencing adaptation (Avison and Gotlib, 1994; Kaplan, 1996).

Moos and his colleagues (Holahan and Moos, 1994; Moos, Fenn, and Billings, 1988; Moos and Schaefer, 1986, 1993) have proposed that coping with any life crisis involves six aspects: background and personal factors, event-related factors, physical and social environmental factors, cognitive appraisal, adaptive tasks, and coping skills (see Moos and Schaefer, 1986).

- Background and personal factors include gender, race, religious belief, age, and previous experience with distressing events. As an example, a teenage girl who has had no experience with making her own decisions will be in a dramatically different position than her more self-assured friend who has coped successfully with earlier challenges.

- Event-related factors are situation specific. Examples would be the extent to which the crisis was anticipated and whether the individual is responsible for the crisis.

- Examples of physical and social environmental factors are the quality and accessibility of family relationships, the availability of mental health professionals, the support of friends, and a sympathetic work or school environment.

- Background and personal factors, event-related factors, and physical and social environmental factors influence cognitive appraisal of a crisis. How the individual sizes up the crisis triggers or deters adaptive tasks and coping skills. As an example, consider the care of a teenage boy who is introspective, ambivalent about his feelings toward his father, and distant from his siblings. His father's diagnosis of cancer has come two years after his mother's death in an automobile accident. He still has unresolved feelings about her death, and the threat to his father (and to his future) becomes all the more pronounced due to lingering grief and feelings of isolation from his family. He will recognize that there is a threat, but will likely not have the familial resources with whom to share ideas and size up the situation.

- The adaptive tasks are 1) to establish the meaning of the event and to comprehend its personal significance, 2) to confront reality and respond to the situational requirements of the event, 3) to sustain interpersonal relationships, 4) to maintain emotional balance, and 5) to preserve a satisfactory self-image and maintain a sense of self-efficacy. There is no order to these tasks.

- Three areas of coping skills enable a person to accomplish the adaptive tasks. The first area involves appraisal-focused coping: logical analysis, mental preparation, cognitive redefinition, and cognitive avoidance or denial. The second area of coping skills involves problem-focused coping: seeking information and support, taking action, and identifying alternatives. The third area of coping skills involves emotion-focused coping: emotional control, emotional release, and emotional acceptance.

A stress-buffering hypothesis (Coyne and Downey, 1991; Kaplan, 1996; Kessler, Price, and Wortman, 1985; Monroe and McQuaid, 1994) suggests that some factors can serve to lessen the effects of distress. Religious beliefs (Pargament, 1997), hope in the future (Frankl, 1962; Lynch, 1965), and social support (Stroebe and Stroebe, 1987, 1993) are three examples of factors that mitigate stress for some persons.

Application of the stress model to adolescent bereavement

The model Moos proposed formed the basis for a social support intervention with bereaved college students (Balk, Lampe, Sharpe, Schwinn, Holen, Cook, and Dubois, 1998; Balk, Tyson-Rawson, and Colletti-Wetzel, 1993). The program comprised eight two-hour sessions providing (a) education about the most current information known about grief and about bereavement resolution, and (b) a safe environment within which participants could share their stories and respond attentively to the stories of their bereaved peers. Experienced group facilitators ran the meetings. The objectives were to provide an intervention that promoted resolution of bereavement and prevented the onset of debilitating consequences. Longitudinal data were collected on all persons who participated in the study.

The project had noticeable effects in reducing distress experienced by bereaved college students in support groups, especially in comparison to two control groups: a control group of bereaved students and a control group of non-bereaved students. The reduction of distress provided evidence for the effects of social support. However, once the support group was over, effects leveled off. This may have been a methodological artifact, an effect of the attrition rate in the control group. But it may indicate, too, the importance of designing follow-up activities that continue to provide social support, such as periodic get-togethers or rituals, much as vaccinations need occasional booster shots.

A developmental model for understanding adolescent grief and loss

Fleming and Adolph (1986; see also Fleming and Balmer, 1996) have linked adolescent bereavement with critical issues and developmental tasks of early, middle, and later adolescence. In their words, "What is needed... *is a model of grieving for adolescents* that reflects the distinct and differing maturational levels of adolescence, one that offers insight into what happens to adolescent development when the conflicts of grieving collide with those of ego development" (Fleming and Adolph, 1986, 102-103).

In Fleming and Adolph's thinking, bereaved adolescents must cope behaviorally, cognitively, and affectively with five core issues:

- Learning that predictability marks some events but not all
- Gaining a sense of mastery and control in their lives
- Forging relationships marked by belonging
- Discovering that fairness and justice mark some outcomes but not all
- Developing a confident self-image

These core issues and the person's behavioral, cognitive, and affective responses vary according to the adolescent's developmental level. Bereaved adolescents may face anew their grief as their development proceeds from one developmental level to the next. Earlier I called this the "recursive aspect" of grief, and we saw this phenomenon in Rhonda's journal entries about attending a wedding years after her father's death.

Examples of Critical Life Tasks Unfolding in the Lives of Bereaved Adolescents

The critical life tasks mentioned by Fleming and Adolph are part of the unfolding life and coping of bereaved adolescents. We will look at examples of these critical life events as found in different studies.

The predictability of events

In a longitudinal study examining the grief experiences of children and adolescents for two years after the death of a parent, data clearly showed that anxiety and fear were markedly greater as compared with non-bereaved peers (Silverman, Nickman, and Worden, 1992; Silverman and Worden, 1992; Worden, 1996; Worden and Silverman, 1993). One of the researchers speculated that such anxiety and fear emerged from "the lack of predictability in their lives caused by the death of a parent" (Worden, 1996, 90).

Tyson-Rawson (1996) studied female college students whose fathers had died. Her participants commented on problems emerging from a loss of predictability. One person reported, for instance, "I realized recently that I'd always thought—even when he was sick—I thought that no matter what I did, no matter how we argued, he'd be there. But I was so wrong. I've had to work to put myself back together—to make sense of it so I can go on" (Tyson-Rawson, 1996, 156).

Mastery/control

A sense of self-efficacy is placed in serious imbalance during a life crisis. Bereaved individuals note a loss of confidence and a notable increase in self-doubt as they struggle with grief. Gaining a sense of mastery and control is one of the crucial tasks of adolescent development and one of the adaptive tasks for coping with life crises.

College students grieving the deaths of family members or friends included the theme of self-efficacy in nearly 40 percent of all their written responses to pictures about which they were asked to write stories (Balk, Lampe, Sharpe, Schwinn, Holen, Cook, and Dubois, 1998). However, non-bereaved students used self-efficacy themes much more often and consistently over time than did bereaved students. Looking at these results, the authors wondered "whether bereaved college students faced with the distress, intensity, and duration of grief find projecting a sense of self-efficacy a more difficult story line than do non-bereaved peers. Perhaps grief poses a particularly difficult challenge to college students' feelings of self-confidence and control" (Balk, Lampe, et al, 1998, 18).

Belonging

Worden (1996) reported bereaved adolescents had greater problems than non-bereaved peers in getting along with others and being accepted. Fleming and Balmer (1996) noted that early adolescents whose siblings had died were quite reluctant to talk about their grief with peers; they surmised that fear of being considered different than others in the peer group led early adolescents to shy away from discussing their grief. In Fleming and Adolph's thinking, older adolescents' greater ego strength would enable them to share grief experiences with peers. Experience on college campuses, however, indicates that few persons are willing to be in the presence of bereaved college students. Unaffected students typically shun bereaved peers, consider the distress manifest in grieving too much to handle, and expect bereavement to be less intense and to end soon. They figuratively, if not literally, leave the room when a griever enters.

Discomfort at being around the bereaved seems much more the norm than openness and compassion to their situations. Oltjenbruns (1996) has noted that non-bereaved individuals frequently dismiss the intensity and the duration of grief for those facing the death of a friend. Ironically, bereavement can lead to losses of friends who are not grieving, who find the person's grief both disquieting and wearisome, and who draw back from the relationship. Thus, grief can jeopardize a sense of belonging by producing what Oltjenbruns called "incremental grief and secondary loss."

The sense of belonging in one's family is pertinent when talking about critical tasks of development and adolescent grief. Even while achieving independence from the family of origin, adolescents care about their families and are distressed when events threaten the stability and even survival of family relationships. Bereavement over a sibling's or parent's death poses a critical threat to a family's stability and ongoing relationships. Evidence indicates that adolescents' emotional responses to sibling grief are associated significantly with family coherency (that is, how close family members feel towards each other and how often they talk about things that really matter). Adolescents from families with greater family coherency (Group 1) are more likely after a sibling's death to feel shocked, numb, lonely, afraid, and concerned that the feelings will never cease; adolescents from families with less family coherency (Group 2) are more likely after a sibling's death to feel guilty and to keep their feelings to themselves. Over time adolescents in Group 1 report a lingering depression about the death but do not report being afraid, lonely, or numb, whereas adolescents in Group 2 report an enduring confusion about the death (Balk, 1981, 1983). A major task facing adolescents is to attain emotional autonomy from parents. This task's difficulty is compounded when familial patterns lead to ambivalent feelings toward parents (Group 2) or when death ruptures familial patterns that have been a source of support while achieving independence (Group 1).

> The role of communication and of interpersonal bonds seems paramount in this regard. A tradition of greater family coherency tends to assist teenagers to work through problems by using the family as a resource; however, these teenagers reported current feelings of depression unlike their counterparts from families with less family coherency. Perhaps depression is the price for close personal sibling relationships severed by death. The lack of family coherency insulated youth from many emotions, but they tended to feel guilty at first and later felt confused; perhaps guilt and confusion are prices paid for distant sibling relationships severed by death (Balk, 1981, 152).

Fairness and justice

The refrain, "It's not fair," is heard commonly on the lips of bereaved adolescents. Reflection on their experiences, tempered by coping with their bereavement, leads to revised assessments about fairness and justice in life. Take, for instance, the words of a college student whose father and brother had died in rapid succession: "I thought that it was extremely unfair that I had to go through two [deaths] and especially in such a short period of time. But then, after I readjusted my thinking I realized that sometimes things just happen and whether or not there's a reason for them you have to go on and suffer them" (Tyson-Rawson, 1996, 161).

In a different vein a middle adolescent talked about what his sibling's death had taught him: "It taught me—I don't want to say it this way but this is sort of what I mean—it taught me to expect bad things, so that I could protect myself from when they happen. It made me realize the things that could happen, that do happen to people. It happened to me, you know" (Balk, 1981, 317).

Self-image

The *Offer Self-Image Questionnaire for Adolescents* (Offer, Ostrov, and Howard, 1977) measures self-concept based on several dimensions such as impulse control, ego strength, and moral values. Responses to this questionnaire by bereaved adolescents whose siblings had died did not differ from the responses of non-bereaved adolescents except in one dimension: "Participants' mean score and standard deviation on the moral values scale indicated better adjustment than Offer's norm groups had achieved" (Balk, 1981, 151); they "demonstrated a sense of concern and responsibility for others," and "said they valued persons more and valued more the very fact of being alive" (Balk, 1981, 127).

Self-concept scores measured by the Offer instrument were shown to differentiate adolescents' grief reactions (Balk, 1990):

- Adolescents with high self-concept scores were less likely than other bereaved adolescents to report feeling confused, lonely, afraid, or depressed several months and years after the death.

- Adolescents with average self-concept scores were much more likely than other bereaved adolescents to report feeling angry, lonely, and depressed about the death several months and years after it happened.

• Adolescents with low self-concept scores were much more likely than other bereaved adolescents to report that their current feelings about the death resembled how they remembered feeling in the first few weeks after the death happened.

Hogan and her colleagues (Hogan and DeSantis, 1992, 1996; Hogan and Greenfield, 1991) provide evidence of the influence of self-concept on feelings of grief following a sibling's death. They reported an inverse relationship between self-concept and intensity of grief over time: the higher the bereaved adolescent's self-concept, the lower the intensity of grief as time passed. They concluded that "dysfunctional patterns of self-concept were associated with adolescents who continued to experience intense grief for eighteen months or more since the death of a brother or sister" (Hogan and DeSantis, 1996, 179).

Discussion

Understanding grief and loss in the lives of adolescents requires appreciation for two separate areas of scholarly inquiry: scholarship about adolescent development and scholarship about grief. Gains have occurred in both areas, and now bereavement researchers place their studies in the context of developmental concerns. Less and less do we see published works referring to adolescents as children; people realize that adolescence forms a distinct part of the life cycle, and is not merely a way station on the way to adulthood.

Since the early 1980s adolescent bereavement has gained increasing attention. What is needed is more attention to variation and similarity in adolescent bereavement experiences linked to levels of adolescent development. Fleming and Adolph (1986) provide a promising model to guide such inquiry.

Other areas needing attention are longitudinal studies, use of non-bereaved control groups, and careful study of interventions to assist bereaved adolescents. Longitudinal studies can overcome the reliance on cross-sectional and retrospective data, and can trace the trajectory of adolescent bereavement in later life. Well-designed longitudinal studies, with representative samples, will help us gain greater understanding about the unique ways that early, middle, and older adolescents grieve and the ways that their grief affects and is affected by developmental issues. The work of Worden and his colleagues (Silverman, Nickman, and Worden, 1992; Silverman and Worden, 1992; Worden and Silverman, 1993; Worden, 1996) is a premier example of a carefully designed longitudinal study using control groups.

Also needed are studies examining the effects of interventions to assist bereaved adolescents. A potpourri of approaches suggest themselves, ranging from education in schools about death and grief, to interventions following traumatic events such as occurred at Columbine High School. An introduction to the range of interventions is provided in the *Handbook of Adolescent Death and Bereavement* (Corr and Balk, 1996).

More than anything, we could provide help by teaching non-bereaved peers how to listen attentively and how to remain courageous in the face of another adolescent's pain. Rather than waiting to assist bereaved adolescents, a stronger preventative approach is to help more adolescents become skilled at being supportive of friends and acquaintances in distress. Training programs geared toward the developmental differences presented by early, middle, and later adolescents would go a long way toward helping.

Suggested Resources

A comprehensive list of various resources, including organizations, is found in *Dying: Facing the Facts* (Wass and Neimeyer, 1995). An excellent list of selected literature for adolescents on death and grief is found in *Death and Dying, Life and Living* (Corr, Nabe, and Corr, 1997), as well as in the Bibliography section at the end of this book. Among the many Internet sources that address issues of adolescent grief and loss, consider www.rivendell.org and www.grief.org.au. The International Work Group on Death, Dying, and Bereavement recently published a paper addressing the myths, realities, and challenges of adolescents facing issues of death (Work Group, 1999). Other resources include Appendix B in Corr, Nabe, and Corr (1997), a list of selected literature for adolescents; the website for the Dougy Center (www.dougy.org), and the Internet search tool Simplesearch. Entering the phrase "teenage grief" when using Simplesearch will produce many resources specifically for adolescents.

David E. Balk, Professor and Department Head of Family Relations and Child Development in the College of Human Environmental Sciences at Oklahoma State University, is the author of several manuscripts and textbooks on adolescent bereavement. Balk is a member of the International Work Group on Death, Dying, and Bereavement, the Book Review Editor for the journal Death Studies, *and guest editor of three special issues devoted to bereavement.*

V · O · I · C · E · S

No One at School
Knew Tammi

Sarah Janczuk

I heard the news at 3:30 a.m. on Sunday, January 18, 1998, after a night out with friends at school. I got a message on my answering machine from a friend, frantically asking me to call him as soon as I got in, no matter what time it was, as he had something important to tell me. I woke him up, and he groggily told me the news—Tammi had been driving home to Michigan State University from our hometown and was in a collision with a truck. No one knew the exact details of what had happened, but one thing was clear. Tammi had died in the accident.

I remember my first thought and statement on the phone was, "I don't know what to do." I kept repeating that statement over and over again through my tears. I had never faced anything like this and had no idea how to handle it emotionally. It was as if I couldn't put my mind completely around the idea that Tammi was dead. That night, I stayed at a friend's house, knowing that I could not stay in my apartment alone. I got about two hours of restless sleep, and was up at 7:00 a.m., unable to pretend to sleep any longer. It just all seemed so surreal. But as the day wore on and I spoke to more and more people from home, the reality of it hit me full force. I was in a daze all day, as if I was in a bubble through which I could hear and see what was going on around me but could not actively participate in anything.

It was a struggle. I felt alone, confused, sad, and helpless. I talked to friends at school who offered their support in many ways, and I was truly grateful for that, but I felt that something was missing. I finally figured out what it was—no one at school knew Tammi. No one knew my friends from home, no one knew our stories and our memories, and no one knew what we all meant to one another and how hard it was to lose a part of us. No one could truly understand what I was going through except my friends from home. I knew in my heart that the only way I could deal with this was to be surrounded by those people I trusted the most, who were going through the same thing I was. My friends at school were extremely supportive, and I would not have made it through that first day without them, but I knew I needed something more.

I buried myself in logistics the day after I heard the news, and tried to figure out how I was getting home for the funeral; all the planning seemed to take my mind off what I was facing. I was able to book a flight home for the wake and funeral, and left on Monday. The three days I was there were the most intense I had ever experienced. It was a mixture of tears, laughter, sorrow, disbelief, comfort, and strength. Friends leaned on one another and came together as I had never seen before—I think we all realized the strength we needed was going to come from one another. Tammi was part of our group of friends; she was closer to some than others, but she was part of all of us. We all kept reiterating a feeling of disbelief that this could happen to one of our friends; it was completely unexpected and knocked the wind out of everyone.

In returning to school, it seemed as if everything had been put on hold for three days; my life was not the same for quite a while. I walked through a haze the first few days I was back; I had to cope with the overwhelming emotions I was still feeling about what had happened and at the same time take care of daily responsibilities which did not stop while I was gone. The thought that kept repeating in my head regarding Tammi's death was about how young she was. She had everything in front of her, and everything to live for; trying to figure out why this happened and why she was taken at such a young age was the most difficult struggle in the weeks following the funeral, and even to this day. Talking about what happened, seeking comfort in those who were having similar feelings as me, and talking about Tammi were what helped me through my disbelief and my struggle to figure out a reason behind it all. I still have not figured out why this happened, but I do know I learned a lot about myself and about true friends in those days, lessons that could not have come any other way.

I think what helped me when I returned to school was having those friends willing to listen to my stories and to share in my memories. My biggest comfort, when not with friends from home, was being able to talk about all of us, what we had all meant to one another throughout junior high and high school, and to tell stories about times I spent with Tammi. Those friends who were willing to listen and provide needed comfort were invaluable to me; I know I was not strong enough to make it through this difficult time without them. There were a few unexpected reminders of what happened in the months following the accident. I received an e-mail with the exact details of the accident about two months later, and on the eleven-month anniversary, I found a prayer card in the back pocket of a pair of pants I had not worn since the funeral. Throughout all of this, I leaned on friends— friends from home and friends from school who offered unconditional support and comforting words, and sometimes just a simple hug that said everything.

Sarah Janczuk grew up in Rochester Hills, MI and graduated from The George Washington University in 1998 with a BA in Human Services. She currently works at The George Washington University and is pursuing a Masters in School Counseling.

4

Culture and Class:
The Different Worlds of
Children and Adolescents

By Margarita M. Suarez and Susan J. McFeaters

Why Culture? Or, When Being Good Is Not Enough

A review of the grief process will show many universals: the need for rituals to say goodbye; feelings such as anger, guilt, and sadness; the need for support both at the time of death and afterwards. Amidst all of these universals, the question arises, "Why deal with different cultures? If I am a loving, caring individual who understands the grief process, why do I have to consider cultural differences?" The following example demonstrates the need to adapt our own cultural sensibilities in order to help others.

Margarita

When I was stationed in Vietnam as a United States Army nurse, I had the privilege of working with Vietnamese children in the children's wing of the Army hospital. There, Vietnamese parents could bring their children when the local hospital could not take care of them. One day we admitted a little girl, about nine years old, with burns covering 60 percent of her body. According to the story, she was burned when placing some explosives in the road where American soldiers were supposed to go by. (Please do not blame her. One of the prices of war is that even children are involved.)

One evening we heard an "alert," warning us to move to a shelter. We started to relocate the kids to the shelter, but of course we could not move the girl who was so badly burned. She had too many tubes hooked up to her body. After all the children and Vietnamese nurses left, I decided to stay with the girl. We would take the risk together; I would be there with her in the event of a direct hit.

When I entered her room I saw panic in her eyes, and at first I could not understand why. Then I realized that I had not previously been in her room by myself; there had always been a Vietnamese nurse to explain things. Because I was required to wear the Army uniform—the green fatigues—from her point of view I was an American soldier. She had learned to fear, maybe even hate, my uniform. To make matters worse, all the other kids and Vietnamese nurses had left to what I'm sure she knew was a safer place. I did not know any Vietnamese and could not even pronounce her name. I did not know how to talk with her.

Once I realized all of this I felt what I now call the "arrogance of being good," or the "ignorance of good people." Before, I felt that my knowledge of how to deal with burned patients was enough, and it never occurred to me to spend time trying to find out how she felt about being in an American hospital. After all, we were offering her the best kind of medical care she could receive.

Often when I relate this story, others let me know that I was not that bad. However, being "bad" is not the issue. I have already forgiven myself for making the girl afraid, and one of the ways I have done this is to pass on the lessons of my experience.

The point we want to make here is that "being good" or knowing the universals is not enough. Many of us, when dealing with other cultures, may be unaware of the "uniforms" we wear that represent the power relationships between us and the people we are trying to help. Where one person has the uniform of power, the other may feel vulnerable.

Many have already pointed out the need for diversity and cultural sensitivity. One excellent example in the area of grief work is Camp Matumaini, a weekend bereavement intervention for low-income African-American families coping with HIV/AIDS-related deaths in the Baltimore metropolitan area. The camp is named *Matumaini* after the Swahili word for "hope."

Susan

At Camp Matumaini, the administration and staff are committed to providing a safe, non-oppressive environment where families can participate in a weekend intervention and know that they are being respected for their own cultural and spiritual values. In many ways the camp continues to change as needed. For example, the use of pumpkin carving in the fall was eliminated as a family activity to show respect for the religious beliefs of some of the participants. The camp came up with a creative activity in which all could participate: "toolbox planters." Each family constructed a flower-box planter in the shape of a toolbox.

Being open to others' belief systems and working together to find alternatives builds the bridges we need when working across cultural differences.

Some may ask what exactly is meant by "cultural diversity" or "cultural differences." For the purposes of this chapter, we want to define cultural differences metaphorically, as the *filters we use in understanding and dealing with the world*, particularly dealing with grief.

Filters: How We See and Experience the World

One could say that we are all born with our own video camera. Through this camera we look at and experience the world, and soon enough we start to add our own filters. The lens with which we begin is already limited, and we acquire many filters which further limit our scope as we attempt to interpret the world. Some filters come from our families or cultures, and others, called "tradition" and "belief," may come from centuries ago, passed down through the generations.

When relating to children and adolescents, we deal not only with different cultural filters, but also with a set of filters that may be unfamiliar to us by dint of our age. A five-year-old has accumulated only five years' worth of filters, while an adult may have a 30-, 40-, or 50-year reserve of filters. Add to this the filters of family and culture, and one discovers a complex web of parameters within which every child, adolescent, and parent must be helped. Breaking the family rules at the time of a funeral, for example, may bring a high price, such as isolation for the rule breaker. There is thus a balance of personal needs and culture to which we as counselors need to pay attention. Most importantly, we must do this with an acute awareness of our own filters. This perpetual dance of aware-ness has a complex choreography: how we (the counselors) see the grief process, how the children express their needs, how counselors and children understand one another, how children perceive themselves and their peers, how they experience death, and what rituals or tools they are able to use.

It is important primarily for us as helpers to learn to see more than one possibility for "good grief," and then work with others so that they too can see more than one answer. If we have only one solution, we are stuck. If we see only two solutions, we may be in conflict, for they are likely to be opposite extremes. But when we come up with three or more possible solutions, then we have productive possibilities.

When everyone (the helper and those being helped) agrees, and all in the family agree, there is no conflict, and things may go smoothly. When there are differences, however, conflict may interfere with the process. In these situations it is crucial to come up with alternatives that respect the boundaries of cultural filters.

Margarita

I remember a family with three children. The mother died in the hospital, where the children were not allowed to see her. I came to the funeral with the children, where they saw their mother's body in the open casket. The two older children seemed satisfied with just touch-ing their mother and giving her a kiss, but the youngest one wanted to do more. He was about three years old, and he wanted to see if he could wake her up. I let him try, and he did it as little ones do. First he tried to open her eyelids, and then he touched her face. Finally he called her name. After several attempts he turned to me and said, "I cannot wake her up." He wanted to try again, and I let him try one more time, because through my own Latina cultural filters, there was nothing wrong or disrespectful in touching a dead body. The boy's family, however, was getting restless and embarrassed.

It could all have been done differently, in a way that supported the little boy and also respected the family's ideas about the "appropriate" way to deal with the mother's body. All involved could have spent more time before the service finding out what the children needed, what their father needed, and how best to incorporate these needs into the family's European-American culture and ritual. One way could have been to take the children earlier to the church or funeral home and have time for them to do what they needed. The children would have had their needs met with the additional support of adults present, instead of the negative reactions the young boy received in the church.

Cultivating awareness of possibilities requires understanding our own perception of events. We propose three steps for understanding perception. First, a person must review the scope of his or her lenses. This involves developing flexibility in order to see three or more solutions. Second, a person needs to take stock of the filters that influence how he or she perceives events. Values and belief systems, feelings, and past experiences are all important filters to examine. The third and final step is the addition of new filters. New filters develop from understanding the complexity of people's identities (e.g., I am a nurse, mother, woman; there is also a part of me that remains a mystery) and understanding the complexity of events: "An event is the outcome of many variables and not a simple cause and effect outcome" (Loeschen, 1994). In the area of death, there is always a part we may never understand. The answers we find today will not necessarily serve us in the future.

Some of the tools we will use here come from those used at Camp Matumaini. The tools help facilitate self-awareness, at the same time enabling counselors to see how to use them with others. The first tool is a sentence-completion activity. At Camp Matumaini this is done in groups, but it can also be done individually.

Susan

Sentence completion allows for awareness in a non-threatening way, since the beginning of the sentence gives permission for what is coming next. In this way it normalizes the feeling or answer that may come after the start of the sentence. Within a group the sentence-completion activities create group cohesion and the development of support among participants. The bonding that can be established comes from participants' own self-awareness and reflections as well as listening to others with similar experiences. In the groups, facilitators participate in the sentence completion to model sharing and to eliminate the risk of being first. Of course this requires sensitivity to the group process as well as to the age of the participants.

One way to tie all of this together (reviewing my camera, lenses, and filters) in coping with grief is to think of a loss we have experienced and complete the following sentences:

- The name of the person who died is…
- The one thing I remember the most about him/her is…
- One hope I have is…
- One fear I have is…
- Right now I am feeling…

Susan

In the children's group at the start of the camp, an eight-year-old girl responded to the sentence completion this way: "My name is Lakeesha. The name of the person who died is my mom. The one thing I remember about my mom is her smile." In the adolescent group, James answered, "Right now I'm feelin' alright. I came to camp because my mom made me come." He said smiling, "No I'm just kiddin'." Some of the other teens laughed. "No, I came here with my mom because my dad died of AIDS. His name was Kenneth, I didn't really know him that well. One hope I have is…" he paused, "One hope I have is for my mom to stop buggin' me 'bout school. And I can't say I have a fear 'bout bein' here."

Margarita

While working on this chapter I talked with Brandon, a thirteen-year-old third-generation Cuban-American, and gave him several sentences to complete regarding the funerals of his grandmother in 1996 and his grandfather in 1998. Brandon answered that one of the hardest things was seeing the dead bodies. After more thinking, he said, "Having other family members there to talk to was a big help, especially at Grandpa's funeral, since that was the first one. Like I said before, seeing my dad cry for the first time really affected me. Both experiences were also a learning and growing process for me."

These three examples show the spontaneity and age-appropriate responses to the sentence completions. They also show the cultural differences among the three individuals. Socio-cultural differences surface in part through the language of James and Brandon. James, although trying to sound 'cool,' is expressing the pain of not having known his father. His mild joking and casual tone reflect not only his age but also a male tendency to distance himself from emotional expression. Brandon reacts most powerfully to seeing his father cry for the first time. After taking the time to think things over, his language takes on a pensive timbre.

Working with each individual involves understanding the filters that precipitate their responses. Who *we* are (personal qualities + gender + mystery component), who *they* are, and the complexity of the events in question all figure importantly. Explaining events as an outcome of many variables rather than as a linear relationship allows for a wider perspective with more possibilities (Loeschen, 1994). When working with grief it is crucial to see that grief is not a linear process and that not everyone goes through it the same way (Davidson and Doka, 1999).

Power of Self-knowledge and Understanding

In a recent Avanta, The Virginia Satir Network workshop on diversity, one of the most difficult aspects of self-awareness for some was privilege. In one exercise participants stood side by side and were asked to take a step forward or backward as questions were asked that had to do with issues of racism, e.g., "Take a step forward if your parents have college degrees," "Take a step back if you have been denied a job because of your race." Later, in the evaluation, one participant shared, "The exercise was most effective and challenging and eye-opening. I grew more and more uncomfortable the more steps forward I took... and looked back and saw friends I love deeply receding in the distance."

It is important to see the distance and to be aware of the feelings it engenders, the uncomfortable feeling that leads to awareness about ourselves. Part of "getting it" is seeing our own areas of privilege and then learning to work within (and perhaps to close) that distance. We "good" people may have a hard time with this dissonance, and at times we may want to believe it is not there. Some of the distance may be closed, but some of it may always remain. And privilege, of course, is not solely racially based, but also economically based.

Margarita

In 1960 I left Cuba, and in July 1999 I returned to visit for the first time. I went with "old filters" about Cuba. Even if I had seen pictures and videotapes, I would not have been prepared for the many signs of poverty I encountered. As we (there were three of us) rode around in our rented car, most of the population had to wait for hours to get a ride in a bus full of people, or in a truck or an old car. We had more space in our mid-size 1999 air-conditioned Peugeot than anyone else I saw for the duration of my stay.

One of the most difficult moments was passing a funeral procession. The only car in the procession was an old truck carrying the casket. Everyone else was walking or on old bicycles. I do not wish to suggest that the funeral attendees felt badly. (I did not stop to ask.) I, however, did feel badly, especially in light of my own experience. At my dad's funeral, just three years ago, I remember riding in a limousine followed by some fifty cars. Now I was passing this procession of what were, in a sense, "my people" in a tourist rental car. What I felt was the pain of recognizing my own privilege and the distance between myself and other Cubans. I was now the one in front of the line.

Self-reflection and Feedback

We update our filters of self-knowledge and understanding through both self-reflection and feedback. It is important to take time to ask ourselves, "How do I see myself? What kind of feedback have I received in the area of understanding and respecting other cultures?"

There are many tools in the area of defining the self. The one we want to use here is a simple one. First, write your name and a nickname you have now or have had in the past. Then write five to ten adjectives or terms that describe who you are, paying attention to what you "edit," or leave out. Also, pay attention to the overall meaning of your description: Is it positive, negative, neutral, or some of each? These questions are part of reflection, a way to be aware of our own filters. When working with others, we can use our descriptions as a way of listening to one another.

The next step is to integrate all the parts you have identified about yourself and work with each of them. What will you keep? What will you add? The more we can accept and work with our own inner diversity, the better prepared we are to deal with differences in and among others. After reflection and integration comes looking for feedback, a task which may not be easy.

Good feedback regarding cultural understanding and sensitivity to others may be hard to find, and still harder to accept. There are numerous ways to go about getting feedback, one of which is to take inventory of our own (inter-)cultural or racial experiences (see Ford, 1994, 28). Another way is to find someone you trust who is knowledgeable in the area and ask that person for feedback. An ally or mentor with whom you can walk into the arena of cultural competence is often a good source of feedback. Families and co-workers can also provide valuable feedback. Ask them how well they feel you are able to listen, because it is in listening that we learn most about others. But be aware that, unless you are genuinely open to both praise and constructive criticism, this may create some conflict in your workplace or family. Perhaps a less threatening way of getting feedback would be in a group, where the goals are to develop listening skills, understand diversity, and move into action (Ford, 1994). All of the above suggestions require honesty and a will to seek those who, gently, will tell us the truth.

When working with children and adolescents, even stronger listening skills are required than when working with adults. Some children may not have the language to express their feelings, while others may never get to the bottom line of their stories. Still others may answer most questions with "I don't know." To help, then, with the process of intervention and support for children and teens, we want to share some practical tools.

Steps for Working With Others

We received permission from Sharon Loeschen (The Magic of Satir, 1994) to adapt the phases of her book into steps for working with others in the area of grief, particularly in understanding diversity. To begin with, there are four critical steps that lead up to intervention. As we have already mentioned, listening is essential to understanding others. However, for others to feel safe exploring and relating their feelings, we need to create a safety net. The components that go into that safety net are as follows:

- Making contact
- Validating

- Facilitating awareness
- Promoting acceptance (of self and others)

Only after these steps can the actual intervention begin. We will explain these steps and give examples of how they are accomplished.

Making contact

For our purposes, "making contact" means establishing rapport, making a personal connection. The most obvious way to begin making contact is, of course, learning the person's name and how she would like to be addressed. Another important part of making contact is some gesture that communicates respect. This is how a connection gets established.

Validating

"Validating" requires us as counselors to affirm the value of children and adolescents by acknowledging the importance of their experience as they see it and share it with us. The value of their experience is made up of feelings, points of view, and their own place in the grief process. Three ways to practice validation are "appreciating, reassuring, and affirming" (Loeschen, 1994, 15).

Facilitating awareness

By "awareness" we mean awareness for all, the counselor as well as children and teens and their families. Awareness is that "Ah ha!" that comes from the inside out. For the counselor, it may be reflected in the words "I get it; I hear you." For the person being counseled, the feeling may be a realization that "I am the one that came up with this idea; I am the one who understands me."

Promoting acceptance

"Acceptance" here signifies ownership of our filters without having judged them good or bad. In a sense, acceptance is being able to admit that we see and experience the world (particularly grief) through a unique set of filters, just as others do the same with their own filters. *I am me, and this is what I am feeling and thinking at this moment.* Similarly, *You are you, and what you are feeling and thinking may be different, but nonetheless legitimate* (Satir, 1975). Acceptance does not mean that we are not open to change or to other ideas. Rather, it means a healthy ownership of and respect for our filters, just as we respect and hope that others will own their filters. We normalize our feelings by acknowledging that they are common reactions; we personalize them when we accept responsibility for our own feelings, rather than projecting that responsibility onto something else; we bridge our feelings when we make connections between ourselves and others with similar feelings (Loeschen, 1994, 51).

Practical Tools

Some of the tools described here are group activities that can be adapted to a one-to-one situation. Some tools may also accomplish more than one step.

The greeting: Whose place is this, anyway?

At times the counselor's office or the hospice is a place of power. That is, those who work there have the power, and the children, teens, and families are the outsiders. We all may have ways of making others feel at home in our space. The tone of this first meeting at Camp Matumaini is instructive:

Susan

> Families arrived in vans. Some of the adults said they were tired as they stepped off the vans. The staff members escorted the families to the cottage on the other side of the road, where they would be housed for the weekend. Several staff made sure that each room was equipped with enough sheets, pillows, and blankets. Then the families were escorted to the dining hall. The first dinner was somewhat subdued, as families and staff sat together talking politely, getting to know each other.

What we hope to convey by citing the above paragraph is the attitude of service that helped the families to feel comfortable: the sharing of food, space, and time, and allowing the meeting to be "subdued."

Sentence completions

As stated before, sentence-completion exercises allow for a great deal of sharing in a safe way. When done in a group, these exercises have the added advantage of establishing a bond within the group. It is also a way to cultivate awareness of one's own filters while practicing listening to others. The counselor's or facilitator's sensitive sharing in the activity not only allows for modeling, but also establishes an equal footing for the counselor and the rest of the group. That said, it is crucial for the counselor not to burden the group with information that may make them uncomfortable. Sentence completions done in a safe environment help with connecting, validating, bringing awareness, and promoting acceptance.

Sculpting

One of the most powerful tools for building awareness is "sculpting," or making a picture. This allows for moving away from talking and using other ways to explain what one is feeling or seeing. It also allows for seeing how others see the same event. The counselor, then, becomes the facilitator, not the producer. The "producer" and "director" are the children, teens, and parents.

Margarita

I was working with a family whose baby had died. In addition to the parents, there were three siblings, the youngest of whom was four. The meeting took place several months after the baby's death. In an effort to find out where the family members stood with respect to their filters, I used a sculpting exercise. I explained, "Each of you is going to get a chance to make two pictures. You will place all the members of your family as if we were going to take a picture. Everyone will take turns, and no one's picture will be wrong. We will use this little pillow to represent the baby that died. Now the first picture is of how you see your family now. The second picture is of how you would like your family to be."

To my surprise, the four-year-old wanted to go first. He sat his parents side by side, although the father was turned a little bit, looking away. He placed the older siblings by the door fighting with each other. He took the pillow and placed it on one parent's lap. Then he placed himself on the floor in front of his parents, but not touching them. There was some protest from the parents that this was not the way it was, but I reassured them that this was just the boy's picture, taken through his filters. Then I asked him to create the picture of how he would like it to be. He kept the older siblings by the door but not fighting. He left his parents as they were. Then he removed the pillow and placed it on the desk, saying "The baby is in heaven." Then he sat himself between and closer to his parents. All the other members did their own pictures, which had many differences and some similarities.

The Web activity

Susan

On the first night of Camp Matumaini, group participants are asked to sit on the floor and are introduced to "the web activity." A facilitator begins by saying something like, "We all share something in common this weekend: someone special to us has died. Right now we are going to talk about those special people. I have this ball of yarn, and I am going to hold onto one end of it while I tell you about my loss. Then I will throw the ball of yarn to someone across from me. It will then be that person's turn to talk. After each person talks, he or she will throw the ball of yarn to someone else." After the web has been woven and all group members have spoken, each holding onto the yarn, they are asked to pull the yarn tight. This forms a design. Members are asked to describe what they see and feel. Many say the design feels like a safety net or a spider's web. Others indicate that they feel connected to the group through the yarn.

Name collages

One of the most difficult issues for all of us to deal with is the "guilt of the survivor." Children and teens who hear about the greatness of someone who has died may think, "Maybe it would have been better if I were the one who died." Counselors, too, may have those feelings as we work over and over again with people who have experienced great losses. At Camp Matumaini, parents are asked to write their surviving child's or adolescent's name on a piece of paper and identify the positive attributes and talents that they recognize in the child. The resulting collage of words can be shared later on with the child. This exercise is adaptable to many situations, but it is especially germane to coping with grief over someone who has died. It brings much-needed attention and reassurance to the survivor.

Once a safe relationship has been established with connections, validation, awareness, and acceptance, the counselor can move into the "doing," or helping phase. These first steps must not be abandoned, however, as the counselor must continue to look for differences, and for what really fits or can be healing to this child or teen within his or her needs and cultural parameters.

The doing

Every person experiencing grief needs some ritual or way to say goodbye. To find what fits for each individual, the counselor needs to listen very carefully. A deceptively simple way to begin is by asking what the individual wants to do. Once the person begins to articulate what he wants, the counselor can draw out more information by asking, "Tell me more about it. What would it look like to you?" These questions are more respectful and more productive than "Why?" which often precipitates a defensive reaction.

Tell me what you want

Margarita

> I was working with a family whose father had left. Later, the father died, and the son (age ten), who had never met his father, was not able to attend the funeral. I asked him what he wanted to do. Some of what he asked really surprised me. He wanted, of course, to visit the cemetery and the grave. He asked me to bring a piece of wood and good markers and a camera. The trip to the cemetery was a team job with two counselors, the boy, and his mother. Once we were at the cemetery he took the piece of wood and wrote "To Samuel Sr. from Samuel Jr. I love you." He placed the piece of wood on the ground by the grave and, placing one hand over it, asked for his picture to be taken. There he was standing tall by his dad. Later as we were leaving, he showed me a penny and asked, "Miss Margarita, is this a lucky penny?" I answered, "Of course, if you want it to be, it is a lucky penny." He went back to the grave and, throwing the penny onto it, said "Here Dad, this is for good luck."

Memorial banners

Susan

> On Saturday night at Camp Matumaini, there is a family activity called "the memorial banner." Materials are provided so each family can make their own banner. The family writes the name of the person who died, along with messages to and qualities of that person. What is important is to have each member of the family participate in whatever way fits for him or her. The staff helps the families and also praises and encourages their work. They validate feelings and assist

some families in problem solving. At times, some of the children and adolescents may not have strong memories of the deceased loved one. Staff will often ask an adult family member to tell children a story about the loved one to help them participate in this project. In one case, a twelve-year-old expressed his feeling that this activity was "dumb." He knew little about his dad, who had died. His mother shared with him, "Your dad was a carpenter, and he was really good at it." After more stories from mom and encouragement from the staff, he decided to outline and cut a hammer from a brown piece of felt to add to the family banner.

We have adapted the memorial banner to several different groups. In many settings we have brought stickers for participants to use. We found that this allows those who feel they are not artistic to make banners without worrying about being "good enough."

Sunday morning reflections

At Camp Matumaini, Sunday morning reflection builds on the memorial banner activity. Families take turns talking about their banners, usually with a mixture of laughter, joy, and sadness. All are given the freedom to participate in a way that fits for them. This is an activity that can also be used at a funeral or memorial service. People may, in lieu of banners, share stories about the person who has died or create a poster with pictures from their loved one's birth or other special occasions.

Like the memorial banner, the reflection or celebration activity can be adapted to different groups. This can be done in the counselor's office or in a one-to-one intervention. Both activities, although classified as "doing," are also ways of connecting, validating, facilitating awareness, and promoting acceptance. All of this can take place if the counselor or facilitator is in a position to listen, encourage, and share without passing judgment.

Conclusion

When working with young people coping with grief, especially in multicultural settings, a detailed examination of the self is important for both the counselor and the child or adolescent. Developing an awareness of one's identity and knowledge, as well as the filters associated with these, is a crucial first step toward becoming who we want to become (e.g., a more effective counselor; a more fulfilled individual). After self-awareness come self-acceptance and feedback from others as to how well we understand and work amidst difference.

In developing our philosophy of the grief process, our greatest strength as counselors is listening. Through listening we are able to work with others to find different options for coping with grief. This flexibility provides an extremely valuable backdrop for working within the needs and cultural parameters of others. Working with children and adolescents involves the preliminary steps of connecting, validating, promoting awareness, and cultivating acceptance, all of which must be done prior to intervening in order for the interventions to be effective. Finally, change is effected for the child or adolescent when the counselor is able to help build a safety net. By making tools available to others, the counselor provides choices for self-expression and growth, thus bridging differences and facilitating healing.

In everything we do, the importance of allies and support networks cannot be overemphasized. Accepting our limitations and availing ourselves of others' services can make our work even stronger.

Margarita M. Suarez, MA, RN, started her work in the area of grief as a US Army nurse in Vietnam. Her graduate research at the University of Washington School of Nursing was on childrens' understanding of death. Ms. Suarez is currently the Executive Director of Avanta, The Virginia Satir Network.

Susan J. McFeaters, LCSW-C, is currently a doctoral candidate at the University of Maryland, Baltimore, where she is researching AIDS-related loss in low income, urban African-American families as well as the complex psychological issues that surround families affected by HIV/AIDS. Her most recent work has been in the area of pediatric AIDS.

V · O · I · C · E · S

Where's Your Father?

Anonymous

When my father got arrested, I was at his apartment and the police broke into the door. They took me and my father down to the precinct and they took my father and locked him up and called my mother so she could come pick me up. When my mother came to pick me up, I was very scared. I was crying because my father had been arrested and I was there to see it.

A couple of weeks after that, they sent him to a prison in another state and he was supposed to spend ten years there. But during his fifth year he was acting good, so the Warden was going to only make him serve the five years and give him two years probation. Some of the other prisoners found out about this and they got very jealous that my father was going to get out. That same night he got killed. I was on the phone with him. It was about midnight. The guard said that right after he got off the phone with me, he was walking back to his cell when three men came from behind him, one stabbed him in his back, and the others beat him up.

The next day, when I went to go visit him, they said that his name wasn't on file—that he wasn't checked in that morning and they couldn't find him. We stayed and waited at the jail for about two hours for them to find where he was. When they finally found out where he was, they didn't come out and tell us. They sent the priest. He came out in a black jacket and black robe and my mother saw the priest with a guard and the guard came over and got my mother and he took my mother over to talk to the priest. As soon as he took off his jacket and she saw the black robe, she knew something had happened to my father so she started crying. Then my sisters came and they told them and they started crying. All of us were crying. We had to wait for the bus to go home and they had us wait at the jail until the bus came. That day, I wasn't feeling very well. I remember feeling like I was going to throw up after I heard that my father was killed. At first they told us that they didn't know who killed him, and then they told us that it was three men and they finally found out who they were. One of my father's friends knew who did it, but he was too scared to tell the guards. But when he realized how this was really hurting everybody, he finally told the guards and they put them in solitary confinement.

When we got home, everyone was just crying. It was the day my father had gotten killed and we couldn't believe it. A month later, we finally had his funeral and buried him. At the funeral, my father's cousin walked in and he looks exactly like my father. It was spooky. They even used to dress alike, and had the same hairstyle, so he looked so much like my dad. When I saw him, I ran to him to talk to him because I was so scared. Till this day, it is hard to believe that my father is dead. I feel sort of like he and my mom are just separated and I can't visit him.

My teacher, she doesn't understand anything. She's not my teacher anymore, but she still doesn't understand and I don't think she ever will. My father got killed a week after my birthday. It was so sad and when I went back to school, my teacher was acting like it doesn't hurt when your family member gets killed. My teacher would say stuff about my father, and then I would talk back to her, curse her out and stuff.

The next year, I had her again, and she was talking so much stuff about my dad that it got to the point that I wanted to kill her. I wrote a letter saying that I was going to kill her. She got scared and told the principal. The principal came to the classroom and asked who wrote the letter. I said that I did it. The principal told me that I had better be glad that he hadn't called the police because if he had I would be in jail for a long time. I told him that I didn't care because she talks so much stuff about my father and

I don't care where I go. My big brother told me that my father wouldn't want me to go to jail so I got back in shape. I went back to school and apologized to the teacher. She would say that my father never wanted to be with me. She said that he was stupid, and that she was glad that my father was dead. It made me so angry. She made me stay back for what I did.

It had gotten so bad that I threatened to kill myself and my teacher got scared and told the school counselor and they sent me to a psychiatric facility for one week. It was like a jail. They had a hole—if you acted up too much, they would put you in the hole. It's like a room with brick walls and a glass that they can see you through but you can't see them. It has a bed, a mattress on the floor. It's just like a jail cell. You can't do anything and you miss out on stuff. I was so glad I only had to stay there for a week. The last day I was there, they took us on a fun field trip and I finally cooled off. I was so mad that I had to be there, but I finally cooled off on the last day.

I went back home and it was like people were just watching me all the time because they thought I was going to kill myself. I couldn't really stay home by myself because my mother was scared that I was going to kill myself, which I wasn't going to because I knew if I did, I wouldn't go to Heaven. In the Bible, if you kill yourself, you won't go to Heaven, you'll go to Hell. So I didn't kill myself. I wanted to kill myself so I could be with my father.

I changed schools, but so did she, and believe it or not, she was my teacher again. We were in the same style again. She talked about my father and I would curse her out. She would talk about me, I would curse her out. She would talk about my mother and sisters, and I would curse her out. I got to a point that I wanted to beat the holy mess out of her. But since I was going to counseling that year, I knew that wasn't the right thing to do. I knew I would get in big trouble and I think I would have ended up killing her.

And it continued; she would talk about my father and I would curse her out. Then my counselor told me to ignore her, and so I did. When she would say stuff, I would ignore her and go about my business. Now if people talk about my father, I just ignore them because I know that they don't know any better. And I know my father is richer than them and though my father is not better than them, he's in a better place than them, so I don't have anything to worry about. They can talk about him all they want because it's not hurting me, or my father, or anyone else in my family. So I don't have anything to worry about.

I know that he didn't deserve what they did to him and I said that the guys who killed my father better hope that they never get out of jail because something will happen to them. Since I have been going to counseling, I don't feel like I want to kill them anymore, I just feel like it wasn't right for them to do what they did. I know my father is in a better place now.

When my dad and I used to talk he would tell me about all the things we would do together when he got out of jail. He would buy me things, like model airplanes and model cars, go-cart cars, and a little jet airplane with remote control. When he was in jail, I was feeling like, "Why did he do what he did to go to jail?" I was mad because he was in jail and we couldn't spend time together. I didn't really blame him because what he was doing was addictive because he was making fast money. It was really addictive what he was doing. I forgave my father, but then that bad thing happened. They killed him.

The kids at school didn't know that my father was in jail. I didn't tell them. They just thought that I just didn't spend much time with him and when they finally found out, they would say stuff about him. I had two good friends and they were good about it, but the rest of the kids were so mean. They would tease me about the fact that he was killed. They would ask, "Where's your father?" I couldn't say anything back. They would talk about my father and about the things that might have happened to him in jail, and stuff like that. I wouldn't say anything back because if I did, I knew that I would probably really have to hurt them, so everything I would do, I would do by myself. It was really lonely.

I started collecting cars. My father loved cars and so do I. He taught me how to fix cars and even how to drive a car. He used to let me drive his car with him. It was great. He would put me on his lap and let me steer the car in the parking lot. He taught me everything about cars. So I collected cars, but my little sisters would always get into them and ruin them. That used to make me so mad because the cars were really important to me. It was something special that my dad and I shared. I kept buying new cars and they kept losing and ruining them, so I gave up. I didn't have a safe place to put them. If I could, I would buy all the cars in the world and collect them as a way of honoring and remembering him.

When he was in jail, it felt awful. I had no father figure. I was lonely. Seeing my dad in jail, I knew that I wasn't going to end up like that. I knew that I was going to do better. I know now what I am going to do. I am going to be an antique car collector and dealer. I just love cars. I want to follow in my father's footsteps in his love of cars, but not the other stuff.

I have hope now. I have hope from counseling. My counselor helps me figure out what the right things are. I listen to what she says because I know she is right. I trust her because I know she loves me and she wants the best for me. I don't get into a lot of trouble anymore like I used to. I know that it's wrong to kill my teacher and I know it's right to ignore her. For other kids in my situation, I would tell them, if someone talks about your parent who is dead, know that they don't know what they're talking about. They are just trying to be mean.

When I feel sad and mad that my dad isn't here anymore, I just look up in the sky, picture him in the sky, talk to him, and picture him talking back to me. Like if I'm about to get into a fight or do something I know I shouldn't, I look up in the sky and ask for the answer, and he'll give it to me. My dad's telling me to do the right thing—go to school, get an education so I can get a good job and get paid and help out my mother at home. My mother says that I'm like my dad. I look like him, make jokes like him, have a great sense of humor, and love cars like him. How I wish he was still here.

The author is 13 years old. He likes computers, cars, and riding his bike.

5

The Role of the School

Stan Johns

Today's youth face a potential multitude of critical loss situations. It can be safely assumed that by the time a student is leaving adolescence, some form of loss has affected his or her life. There are, of course, the obvious, highly visible, and sometimes newsworthy scenarios of critical loss such as the death of a parent, sibling, friend, teacher or other individual of a close relationship. However, there are also many more subtle forms of separation and loss in a young person's life that can go unnoticed and yet have a long-lasting and major psychological effect upon the individual. Perhaps the most prevalent form of subtle loss in a child's life comes in the form of disruption of the family unit though divorce. The divorce rate in United States continues to occur, on average, at about 50 percent according to 1997 final statistics from the Centers for Disease Control and Prevention (www.cdc.gov). There may be other losses as well, such as family or friend relocation, death of a pet or death of a distant relative, physical or sexual abuse, change of school, or any other event that affects the attachment bond of a child.

The School in a Child's Life

Children spend much of their time attending school and being involved in school-related activities. School is the hub of a child's life. School is where friends congregate and social life flourishes. It is not unusual for parents to expand their social circles as a result of children forming new friendships with classmates and subsequently wanting to socialize outside the school setting.

The school offers a sense of community for the first time in a child's life. Academic tasks and social interactions are successful because of cooperation. School fosters self-esteem, builds character, and provides an environment of security where students can make choices with the support of the adults around them. A continuum of socialization and learning where experimenting leads to success and self pride are all part of the importance of school life. The school often acts in place of parents, with the best interest of children in mind.

It is the overall sense of community and partnership that becomes a major foundation of support for youngsters when they face a critical loss. As children have come to spend more and more time in school over the past several years and as the structure of the family has changed, it has become incumbent upon the school to serve as a strand of stability for children.

Since the school is a vitally important part of life from age five upward to eighteen, it becomes evident that the school must be prepared, willing, and able to respond to critical loss situations that involve the lives of students. Generally speaking, schools across the nation have responded. The first type of response is to a sudden tragic loss and the second is the response to the more subtle set of circumstances that are internalized by a child as a loss.

When the school receives word of a traumatic crisis, details may not be readily available. For example, in the event of a suicide, initial information may only serve to inform the school that a student has been involved in an incident involving a firearm. As parents and significant relatives of the student are notified, information to the school will become more detailed regarding circumstances and fatality. Because of information coming in sporadically, the school administrators must be proactive. It becomes critical that the chief school administrator take charge of the situation by first verifying information regarding the tragedy. This is not a time for speculation. One must deal with the facts at hand. With as much data as can possibly be gathered, the event must be defined so everyone involved has a clear outline of the situation.

First, the safety and well being of students and staff must be ensured. Safety may encompass both the physical as well as the emotional realm. As soon as it becomes clear that there is no immediate danger to other students or to faculty, general communication regarding the tragedy can begin.

Information dissemination must be done as quickly as possible. Central office administration personnel should receive all information that comes to the school and should have all the facts so that they can serve to control rumors. It is recommended that media releases be monitored though this channel. The school secretary must be provided with current information, as this person will be taking a majority of telephone calls and many of the face-to-face questions.

Since school staff will need time to react and begin processing their feelings and emotions, schools should have a telephone calling system for purposes of communicating crisis information, just as they communicate other information such as school closures.

Regardless of how initial communication is accomplished, it is essential to have school staff gather prior to the next direct contact with students. Faculty should be given a fact sheet to help them deal with the issues that will probably arise in the classroom. Faculty should also be prepared to provide the names of students for whom they have concerns and report students who are not in class in the event counseling is needed. It is extremely important to know the whereabouts of all students during a time of crisis. This is especially true in situations involving suicide.

Once information is shared and the school day begins, the classroom teachers play a key role as to how the day will go. They become the front line for communication, handling emotions and reactions, and setting the tone for making it through the day. Perhaps the most difficult task of the day stems from the necessity to communicate information surrounding the tragedy to those students who have yet to hear the news. This should be done in a straightforward manner and, as stated, with as much accuracy as possible.

Since it is recommended that students hear initial information from someone who is familiar, mass communication in the form of a school assembly is not a good idea. Allowing information to circulate unchecked is even a worse idea.

The key to working through this first day is to make the day as normal as possible with regard to routines and familiar schedules. Structure, order and stability are critical. But we need to recognize that this is not a normal day. Since regular classes should be held, it is critical to discuss the tragedy. If conditional rules need to be put into effect, the reasons for these rules should be explained in terms of what is best for the students and the school.

Most importantly, students will need a time and a forum in which to talk about their emotions, concerns and feelings. When students feel the need to discuss the situation, it is imperative that faculty allow open communication and take care to ensure accuracy of information. Rumors and judgmental comments should be countered. Teachers should show sympathy and concern for family and friends.

Students may need to spend time in the processing phase of coping with traumatic loss with peers rather than with parents or other adults. This is especially true if the deceased person was known in the school setting. When this is the case, there is usually a small group of students who have been particularly impacted by the event, and this group may need special times set aside for mutual support. It may be a good idea to set aside a consistent time over a long period, such as meeting with the counselor, sharing lunch or just getting together to help these students work though their grief.

It is a good and necessary practice to have a pre-designated room where students can go for emotional support and relief from the classroom when a crisis situation is new. This is often referred to as a quiet room. In the event that school is not is session, this can be the regular classroom. During the school year, this will be the counselor's room, an empty classroom, or other area where students can feel the privacy to explore their feelings. The adult who serves as the facilitator in this room must demonstrate an attitude of sympathy and understanding.

It is vitally important for students who come to the quiet room for reflection to have their feelings and emotions validated, but it is never advisable for an adult to tell children that they know how they are feeling. We can never know how someone is feeling during a time of critical loss. Individuals staffing the quiet room should simply be good and kind listeners.

Depending on the circumstances of the tragedy, the quiet room can be supervised by members of the teaching staff, support staff, or individuals from outside the school setting such as parent volunteers or members of the clergy. These individuals, unless previously trained, should be briefed regarding the exact information surrounding the crisis event. They should also be given specific guidelines on how to handle questions from students as well as how to respond to the emotional reactions that will be encountered. It has been my personal observation that students feel most comfortable when the adult in charge of the quiet room is someone they know and can trust with the strong emotions they are experiencing. Likewise, it is best if the quiet room is set up in an area with which the students are familiar. A smaller space should be made available for the occasional student who may need ongoing emotional support.

The quiet room should have materials available for students to write letters, compose messages of sympathy, or draw pictures that will be sent to the immediate family. Students can then show their feelings of sadness and sympathy. This will also help children to begin to process their own sense of loss. Such cards and letters are very much appreciated by a grieving family.

Generally, students tend to want to remain among their peers and friends during a time of critical loss. They find comfort and support in the familiarity of friends and surroundings that are known to them. The quiet room concept is meant to serve as a safety net for those students who need some time alone for personal and private reflection and to cope with a set of emotions that may not have been felt before.

At the close of the school day a staff meeting should be held for a time of debriefing and to make plans for the next day. This is also a good time for adults to hear updated information and to lend emotional support to one another. A discussion regarding funeral services, memorial activities, and plans for meeting with family members may also be addressed in this meeting.

Follow-up care should continue in order to nurture and lend emotional support to those students who are affected by the critical loss. Generally speaking, this need may exist for several months. Administration would be well advised to establish a network of communication for students to use over any extended break from school. Students should have a designated person they can call if they feel the need to talk about the critical loss. This may be a homeroom teacher, school counselor, or other significant adult. Faculty should discuss the progress of students on a regular basis. A close monitoring of the diverse grieving patterns students will experience should be a primary focus with a continuing offer of support.

If the tragedy involves a student or staff member, a discussion regarding taking care of personal items should be conducted. This may not involve the full staff, but should include persons who were close to the deceased. Knowledge of the group personality of students is essential, as one group of students may find comfort in keeping some items close where another group might wonder why personal items are still present.

In the event that a loss happens during the summer months when school is not officially open, it is recommended that the building be made available to students and staff. Again, the school is the natural gathering place for students. The procedures for when school is in session should be followed as closely as possible.

Memorializing a loss is critical. The memorial must be perceived as significant and should happen soon after the incident. It is also advisable to have student representation in the planning of the memorial activity. Small groups of staff and students may work together in the planning phase so that all students can have a sense of participation. That participation will make for a meaningful memorial.

Funeral services, too, can provide a meaningful memorial. Depending on the circumstances, students might be given release time in order to attend. Faculty should attend at their own discretion, but certain individuals such as the homeroom teacher and the building administrator should make every effort to be present. Their presence will affirm the school's interest and caring.

Even in the school setting, students will grieve. As individuals are different, so is their grief. Therefore, there is no single method or strategy for supporting students though their grief. Each child will require individualized attention at times.

Anger, due to traumatic loss, is an issue that is frequently dealt with in the school setting. Children can feel very uncomfortable and confused emotionally. A child might ask, "How can I be angry at the person I am supposed to feel sorry or care for?" Our conscience tells us we should not be angry at a suffering or deceased person, and yet this is the emotion that is felt, which may be very confounding for the child or adolescent mind.

Just as adults vent anger in many ways, so do children. Some will have a cathartic reaction and let go of this feeling while others will brood, misbehave, or even be a discipline problem until a resolution is reached. It is important that negative behavior in school be understood with empathy, but not excused. This relates back to the idea that the constant, stable school environment is necessary to keep things in order as much as possible. If children display inappropriate behavior when coping with loss, they should be provided a place to go if the behavior affects the learning or normal school setting for others. A "think time" consequence may be appropriate. Care should be taken to make the consequence manifest a tone of helpfulness and support as opposed to punishment. The school counselor or mental health therapist, if available, should play a major role in guiding students though this period. Feelings of anger may continue for several weeks or even months. The school should prepare to support students for an extended period of time.

Grieving may affect cognitive processing. It is vital to recognize that a student's ability to learn can be greatly affected by traumatic loss. Teachers may not always recognize this. Many times I have seen a teacher become frustrated with a grieving child when he or she cannot recall today what was taught yesterday. This manifestation of grief can continue for several months after the critical loss. Educators may need to employ several strategies to adjust expectations for students in order to help them function with as much academic progress as possible and to cope with their feelings of being unsuccessful.

The School and Other Losses

Thus far critical loss has been discussed. However, issues surrounding the other losses in a child's life should not be overlooked or underestimated. Events such as disruption of the family unit, death of a pet, death of a distant relative, breakup of a relationship, or any significant change can be a loss. Events such as these need to be dealt with in a nurturing manner. Children may display all of the characteristics of grief, and classroom learning and school behavior will likely be impaired.

Children often experience grief when family friends or distant relatives die. Although the child may not have been particularly close to the friend or relative, they still feel a sense of loss. They may remember the person as being nice to them or feel a kinship through adults who were close to this person. It is not unusual for children to idealize a person in death. And though they may not really have known the person well, they may still perceive the loss to be great. Children also feel a sense of loss when significant adults around them are experiencing loss. The important aspect to remember is that as children perceive, it is true for them. So if they perceive a loss, in a large sense, it *is* a loss.

The same holds true when a child loses a pet. This is a serious and emotional event for anyone who loves their pet. Children, however, are often responsible for much of the care and well being of the pet. Children may confide and share secrets with pets that they would tell no one else. Pets offer the gift of unconditional love. When a pet dies, a child may feel a great deal of direct responsibility for the loss. The death of a pet is often his first experience with death and dying. This is a huge emotional burden for a child. Therefore, empathy should drive an adult's interactions with the child, and offering sympathy and understanding is vitally important. It is also a good idea for the pet to be memorialized in some manner. This can happen by displaying pictures, writing about positive qualities, sharing conversation, or any activity in which the child may want to participate.

It is a wise practice for teachers to conduct many of the same activities during these times of loss as would take place around other losses. Making cards, drawing pictures and writing letters in support of the affected person are reassuring strategies that lend sympathy and understanding.

Often, moments of sincere thoughtfulness given from the adult to the child are most helpful. Regardless of the magnitude of critical loss, there will be times when feelings of grief will overwhelm individual students. This happens with suddenness and may be triggered by anything—from hearing a name to having a memory flash.

In my observations of students over the years, I have come to refer to this emotional cloud of grief as the "homesick feeling" syndrome. Nearly everyone has suffered the lonely, longing feeling of being homesick. This is an intense downward emotional spiral that makes a person feel like a large black cloud is hanging overhead and all that can be seen is bleak and gray. This is a moment when a child will rely on a key school staff member for strength and understanding. Again, the arm around the shoulder, the words, "I am sorry and I am here for you," are the best remedy. Kindness and compassion must drive actions.

In reflecting on loss and the school, I often tell people that when I chose to enter the education profession, they never told me I would have to face the day when a child would die. I wasn't taught how to conduct myself in such situations. I was never told that I would be called upon to talk about a deceased child at a funeral service. I was never told about the ultimate pain I would see in the faces of parents when they have lost a child, nor the lost look of confusion in the face of a child when a parent has died.

Through my experiences, I have learned a great deal about loss and grieving. I have learned that critical loss has many faces. Children must be given the latitude to process all their experiences. I have learned that remembering what is lost is vitally important.

One of the most important things I have done, as a school principal, was to have a short remembrance activity for a group of students who were leaving elementary school for middle school. This group had lost a classmate every other year since second grade. Coupling the milestone of leaving elementary school and going to middle school with a time to remember their classmates helped them close a chapter of their lives in a psychologically healthy manner. It was good for them to hear the names of their classmates spoken aloud and to see the plaques that will be placed in memory of the deceased children. It was important for them to understand that these children will always be friends and classmates, and it was good for them to be told that their feelings were natural. Remembering a lost friend fosters a healthy sense of spiritual well-being.

It is also very important and helpful for the school staff to remain open in communication with the parents of a deceased student. Parents need and want to remain involved in the lives of their child's friends. Parental support of activities such as athletics, school plays, social activities, and graduations needs to continue as a means of healing and coping with the loss. Parents who have lost a child fear that the deceased child will be forgotten. Active communication from the school helps alleviate this fear.

The school becomes the setting within which children need to have the freedom to experience and harmonize their emotions. The school provides counseling, support, and understanding. The school may also serve as a mechanism to coordinate social services for students and their families. For today's schools, supporting children and families through critical loss situations is not an option, but part of everyday school life. I applaud today's professional educators for the care they give our children.

Stan Johns, MA, has been a practicing school administrator in Oregon for twenty years. He has worked with children and families dealing with separation and loss issues as a volunteer with the local Services for Children and Families Office and in his role as a school principal.

V · O · I · C · E · S

Counterpoint: A Dialogue

Throughout this book, contributors wisely stress that schools can be valued resources in assisting children and adolescents adapt to loss. Schools do play a critical role in the lives of children and adolescents. Beyond the academic role, schools are a developmental arena, a place where students grow socially and psychologically as well as cognitively. It is often the center of students' lives, a place where students meet and interact with one another, even a place where families come together.

Yet in this dialogue, two adolescent boys, Keith and Matt, remind us of the limits of the schools' ability to help. Both are well-adjusted adolescents, clearly connected to a range of supportive adults and involved in their schools. Yet they demonstrate the traditional reluctance of adolescents to reach out to the adults in their schools.

Their reasons are varied. Like many middle and high school students, their relationships with teachers are fragmented. Unlike elementary school students, they see their teachers for only limited times each day. They barely know their guidance counselors and administrators. They are sensitive to the fact that these teachers also have an evaluative role to play in their lives. They struggle with varied codes, in their case the code of "family business" that constrains them from sharing with outsiders. They are confident, perhaps overly so, in their own ability to handle difficult situations.

Since Keith and Matt identify a range of adults that they can and would turn to in trouble, their reluctance to seek school support is less worrisome. Yet one can wonder if more alienated youth would be more open to seek support from their school staff. That is, of course, unlikely. The point of this piece is not to discourage schools in assisting grieving students. Rather, it is to remind them of the considerable barriers they may need to overcome as they try to reach out to grieving students.

Ken: Why don't you begin by describing the social structure of your high school. What are the cliques?

Matt: What?

Ken: What are the different groups at your school?

Keith: Oh, there really aren't any.

Matt: Yes, there are. There are preppies, trackers, skaters...

Keith: Yeah, but it's not like people fight each other...

Matt: No, like everyone gets along. It's just who you hang with...

Keith: Where you sit at the cafeteria, and I mean for the most part, you can sit sort of anywhere.

Matt: Yeah, remember Sol, last year he sat at a table with his old girlfriend 'cause that's the only person he knew.

Keith: And they didn't even like him. (laughing)

Matt: Some of them didn't.

Ken: Who do you stay with?

Keith: Skaters.

Ken: Are they sort of rebels?

Keith: No, just kids who like to skate.

Ken: Now, suppose you had a problem, let's say someone special died. Could you talk about it with your friends?

Keith: I don't know.

Matt: Maybe at the beginning, I don't think after awhile. They just want to hang, they don't want to hear about it.

Ken: Would you talk with your teachers? For example, if you had a loss or were worried about a family member's illness?

Keith: No!

Ken: Any reasons?

Keith: They really don't know you. Plus, you wonder if they might use it against you. Say something like, "Don't think you can get away with something just 'cause someone died."

Matt: I really don't know them either—and they really don't know you.

Keith: Plus, my mom always says, "This is family business, keep it in the family."

Matt: Yeah, my mother always says, "This does not leave this house."

Ken: Well, suppose a parent was ill and you were really worried about it. Your grades started to go down and your teacher asked if anything was wrong. What would you say?

Keith: "I am just having trouble with the work. I don't understand it."

Matt: I would say, "I'm having personal problems."

Ken: Suppose they asked if you wanted to talk about them?

Matt: I would say, "No, none of your business."

Ken: Would you talk to your guidance counselor?

Keith: If I wanted to change my program. I really don't know my guidance counselor. My guidance counselor has half of the alphabet for freshman and juniors.

Ken: Would you trust your guidance counselor?

Keith: Yeah, to change my program.

Ken: What about a principal or dean?

Keith: Never.

Ken: Are there adults you would trust?

Keith: Sure, I would talk to my mom, maybe my godfather or grandmother.

Matt: I would talk to my sister or my parents.

Ken: Suppose it was a situation that did not involve family. Suppose a friend says, "I'm thinking of committing suicide." Would you tell anyone then?

Keith: I would try to talk him out of it.

Matt: I might tell his parents.

Ken: Suppose his parents were part of the problem?

Matt: I would say to them, "You better lay off your son, he has problems."

Ken: Suppose someone brought a gun to school. Let's say you saw it in a locker.

Matt: I would say, "You better get that out of here or I'll tell someone."

Ken: Who would you tell?

Matt: I don't know if I would. I would just say that.

Ken: Suppose you knew that he had a fight with someone the day before?

Matt: I would tell the other kid, "You better stay away."

Ken: Suppose you knew kids were planning to come in and shoot up the school?

Keith: I would stay away. I would warn my friends.

Matt: I would tell on them.

Ken: Who would you tell?

Matt: (After a very long pause) I guess I wouldn't tell anyone.

Keith: I'd tell my mom.

Ken: Anything else you would like to add? Thanks for your help.

Matt Atkins is a fourteen-year-old high school freshman. An average student, he plays Junior Varsity Basketball.

Keith Whitehead is fourteen years old and in the ninth grade. He likes aggressive rollerblading, hip-hop music, and snowboarding.

Part II

Clinical Approaches with Children and Adolescents

One of the major goals of this book is to be a clinical resource, with strategies and interventions that counselors, parents, and teachers can use as they work with grieving children and adolescents. The central theme of this section is that, while children and adolescents share similar needs with grieving adults, the strategies and methods used to meet these needs are likely to be different. Other themes emerge as well.

Children and Adolescents Share a Need for Support

Smith's *Voices* piece reminds us how much children need the support of others. In Smith's case, the support of her mother, a priest, and a social worker were critical. For Blake, the support of his guardians and counselor helped him cope with the loss of his mother. But while support was forthcoming, even in their cases support systems were weakened. Some friends were uncomfortable dealing with the loss. Others may not have known how to be helpful. And when children or adolescents experience a loss, it is often shared by the family system. Normal sources of support in their intimate network may be limited as members seek to protect one another by not sharing grief, or have limited energy to deal with the grief of other family or friends.

One of the most critical interventive strategies is to help create a supportive network for the grieving child or adolescent. Sometimes friends and family, the child's natural support system, can be empowered to deal with the grieving child or adolescent, a point explored in Grollman's chapter. Stevenson considers the role of death education in strengthening support. But sometimes neither school nor family can meet the needs of the grieving child or adolescent. Here, counseling and support groups can provide vital assistance in empowering, creating, and offering the necessary support.

Children and Adolescents Share a Need for Validation

All of the chapters and *Voices* emphasize the need for validation. Validation, a common need of all grievers, means that grieving individuals value reassurance that the ways they are responding to loss are normal and natural. As individuals adapt to loss, they may struggle with uncomfortable feelings and fears, confusing thoughts, and serious spiritual questions. They may experience grief in frightening physical ways. They may be confused by their own behaviors.

This is particularly true for children and adolescents. This loss may very well be their first experience with grief. Their world may seem chaotic and unsupportive. They may feel isolated and alone. They need reassurance that the ways they are experiencing grief are not unusual. They need to have a safe place to think out loud, to express their feelings and fears, to feel that they are listened to and valued.

Different Strategies May Be Useful in Dealing with Grieving Children and Adolescents

The chapters in this section stress another critical point: The most useful interventions are those that are the most natural—those that draw upon the child's or adolescent's peers, play, creativity, or spirituality. Simply talking with an adult is perhaps *not* the most effective way for children to adapt to loss. A number of strategies for intervention are offered in this section. Ward-Wimmer and Napoli, as well as Fry, review the different approaches that they use in their work, some of which are further explored in subsequent chapters. Boyd Webb discusses the value of play therapy. Schuurman offers an exploration of the value of groups as well as discusses the different strategies groups might use. Readers are reminded of Corr's valued bibliography, which lists not only varied resources but also offers principles for their use. Byrne passionately advocates the development of grief centers that can utilize these approaches. And Doka discusses the valued role of ritual as a way to help children and adolescents deal with the transcendental dimensions of loss.

The chapters here remind us that multiple strategies—art, music, play, dance, books, storytelling, activity, the use of video and audio technology—can all be put to service to assist grieving children and adolescents. They can be used in varied settings—counseling offices, centers, schools or even camps designed for grieving youth. They can be usefully employed with individuals or groups. But one other point should be made: They need to be used intentionally. In my classes, I discuss the need for *interventive intentionality*. That term means that counselors are clear about what they hope to accomplish in their use of a strategy and then tailor that strategy to the needs and interests of clients. Some youth may feel self-conscious about their art, music or storytelling, and some other approach may be the best way to appeal to their creativity. As each child or adolescent is different, interventive strategies should be designed with that individual's preference in mind. In group settings, a variety of approaches are useful as they are more likely to draw on the varied strengths of individual members.

Do Not Wait

Another theme is implied in this section as well. Adults can be proactive in their approach to grieving children and adolescents. Myra MacPherson (1999), in the wonderful book *She Came to Live Out Loud*, recounts the story of Anna, a young mother dying of cancer. One of the most powerful sections of the book explores the ways Anna and her husband Jan, with the help of a counselor, prepared their children for the inevitable loss even as they grieved the losses that occurred within the experience of illness. Stevenson takes this idea a step further. One of the valued roles of death education, he asserts, is that it prepares children and adolescents for the losses they will inevitably face. It rescues them from the false reassurance of "the kingdom where nobody dies."

6

To Everything There Is A Season
Empowering Families and Natural Support Systems

Earl A. Grollman

Glenn, an eighth-grader, was diagnosed with leukemia. The principal decided to share this information with his classmates. They needed to know why Glenn wore a baseball hat to cover his bald head and why his attendance at school was sporadic. Later the principal remarked: "Once they understood the situation, the kids were wonderfully understanding. When Glenn was hospitalized there was a rush of cards and visits from many friends. Conversations were the normal chatter—what was happening in the Boy Scouts, who had troubles in school, and the latest baseball scores."

Glenn died. Immediately afterward, the principal met with each class. He told them the sad news and that they had a right to grieve in a way that was appropriate. He alerted the faculty to be available to the students "since death would be a very important topic on their minds."

Forty percent of the students elected to go to the funeral. Many wrote personal letters to Glenn's family and interspersed their remarks with anecdotal material. In the ensuing days, teachers held small discussion groups for those pupils who wished to express their feelings both about Glenn and about the subject of death in general. Some talked about the injustice of Glenn's dying and how long he had suffered, and their own fears about death.

After the funeral, the principal, the school nurse, the physical therapist, and some of Glenn's classmates visited his family. Glenn was dead, but they desperately needed community support. "Our conversations were never long but we hoped our visits would help the family feel that the school cared about them and that Glenn was not forgotten."

What a meaningful contribution the staff made in helping Glenn, his family, the students, and the community! They understood that school is like a second family for children and adolescents. They spend much of their day surrounded by classmates, teachers, and friends. Young people are drawn together in times of crisis in search of understanding, consolation, and strength. That is why educators must be aware of their needs, their fantasies, and their images of death. They need to acknowledge their fears as real—they are! The death of a classmate especially has a ripple effect when peers quickly become aware of their own mortality. How then to create teachable moments and support children and adolescents in what is perhaps the most profound and far-reaching trauma of their lives?

Yet there are parents and even teachers who might say: "Children are too young to understand death. Why burden them with things they cannot possibly grasp?" Children growing up today are all too aware of the reality of death, usually more than adults realize. Even at very young ages, they are confronted with the inevitable moment when life no longer exists: A pet is "put to sleep," a grandparent dies, Bambi's mother is killed, a murder is reported on the evening news. Children need guidance to make sense of these events.

Traumatized by death, many adults avoid the topic, but avoidance does not make the painful reality go away. By offering children only silence and secrecy, adults deny them the opportunity to go through the grieving process with the support of teachers and family members. When children and adolescents are invited to become part of the mourning process in an accepting and supportive environment, they feel it is safe to ask questions and share feelings of sadness, anger, guilt, or protest. Only the frank acknowledgment of painful separation, not the denial of tragedy, will lead to good mental health.

Educators might heed the sage advice of the writer of Ecclesiastes (Chapter 3):
"To everything there is a season
and a time to every purpose under the heaven
A time to be born, and a time to die;
A time to plant, and a time to pluck up
That which is planted;
A time to weep, and a time to laugh;
A time to mourn, and a time to dance;
A time to cast away stones, and a time to gather stones together."

With any death that affects anyone in the school community, there is . . .

. . . a time to confront one's own feelings

I will never forget being called to Oklahoma City after the calamitous bombing on April 19, 1995. As the plane left the Boston airport, I was filled with personal feelings of horror, shock, frustration, and anxiety. I tried every relaxation technique I had learned to be better prepared to confront the appalling catastrophe. I knew that how I would react to the event might evoke similar responses from the survivors. Were I to communicate a sense of powerlessness, helplessness, and hopelessness, my counselees would mirror my own panic.

Emotional conflicts erupt during heightened moments of tragedy. "I'm a pastor and I can't possibly explain how a loving God would allow such suffering." "I'm a therapist and yet I never considered that he would take his life." "I'm a teacher and I still have unresolved grief because of a death in my own family." Just remember the admonition of the psychologist Carl Rogers: "One anxious person in the room is enough."

Talking about death is a complex and disturbing responsibility, and in the end what adults feel will largely determine what they teach.

. . . a time to plan

Don't wait for a crisis. This is the season for calmer heads to focus upon proactive procedures with written policies to determine the best possible controlled and organized structures for the future. Discuss such questions as:

What are the roles of the principal, faculty, counselors, and students, as well as outside resources such as clergy, social service agencies, funeral directors, and police?

What is the best way to announce the death?

What pertinent information about the death should be disclosed?

What is the best way to prepare for children's and adolescents' reactions?

How available are school-based counselors and where are they located?

How to reach out to students most affected by the loss?

Who should/can attend the funeral?

What community services are available?

What about media contact? Memorialization?

Follow-up procedures with a planned operational framework will be of invaluable assistance in facilitating the grieving process for the entire school community.

A staff meeting might be arranged to provide formulated procedures as well as an opportunity for educators to ventilate their own concerns and feelings. A prepared, simple, official statement of the death announcement will give the same accurate information to all personnel, including cafeteria workers, secretaries, janitors, etc., who are also affected by the loss. Delay in informing the group may mean that both adults and children might first hear the news told by the wrong people in the wrong way.

After the death of one of its members, the entire community bears responsibility for healing and helping. A crisis response team should consist not only of educators but parents, students, and leaders of key agencies. They should identify the possible needs of the school with recommended resources for mutual support. No one should stand alone with the crucial burden of postvention.

Prevention is even preferable to postvention. This is the season to take the word death off the taboo subject list in the classroom. The eminent critic, Clifton Fadiman, lamented the fact that teachers often avoid discussing the death of the main character in such classics as *Little Men* in English class. The question is not whether children and adolescents should receive death education. Death and violence are omnipresent, with school shootings, brutal wars, and world conflicts televised nationally. The question is whether the education they are receiving in school is timely, helpful, and reliable.

Talking about natural processes is a good way to introduce the concept of death. Change and growth occur each day—from larva to butterfly, from tadpole to frog. New leaves replace the old ones that die. A living tree produces seeds so that life may continue. One can point out the diverse forms, shapes, and colors of nature, such as bugs, slugs, and butterflies. Once they moved; after death they are quiet and still. Alternatively, an immediate experience, such as the death of a pet or witnessing death on television, may be a springboard to a discussion about how animals live and die and the sadness that it brings. Teachers should emphasize that, while separation is sad and painful, it is an essential part of life and nature. "There is a time for every living thing to grow and to flourish and then to die" (Eccles. 3:1).

What is encouraging are the many death education courses now being offered in the United States and Canada. Dr. Robert G. Stevenson, a pioneer in this field for more than two decades, finds these courses to be both intellectually and emotionally powerful. He writes: "The need for preventative education in the area of loss is clear today. The time to begin was yesterday."

. . . *a time to talk*

Good communication is the first step in helping children and adolescents confront loss. There is no single "right" way to tell children about death. Discussions must correspond to the young people's own emotional involvement as well as their developmental age. It is important to remember that even children of the same age may differ widely in their comprehension and behavior.

Don't be afraid to admit that you don't have all the answers; no adults do. (Children have probably reached this conclusion a long time ago.) It is far healthier to seek understanding together than for teachers to protect their authority with glib half-truths or evasions. Don't be didactic; leave the door open with such comments as, "Lots of people think about death in different ways, but no one has the final answers. Tell me what you think."

Provide structure by citing some of the processes of grief so they may be alert to their own possible reactions. Be clear and direct. Give honest explanations without unnecessary details of how the person died. What is said is significant, but how it is said is almost equally important. Talk slowly to help them understand the impact of the crushing blow. Pause from time to time to allow them to absorb the shock. The tone of voice— warm, sympathetic, kind—will encourage ongoing discussions.

To elicit concerns and feelings and facilitate verbal expressions, inquire what they heard, thought, and felt. "Where were you when it happened?" "What were you doing?" "Who was with you?" "What were your initial thoughts?" "What might change your life?" "What makes you feel better?" "What could I or someone else do to help you through this ordeal?" By ascertaining their needs, you help to relieve their tensions and create for them a sense of control over their lives. Questions should be open-ended and never answered by a "yes" or "no" response. Let them know that in times of trouble, silence is not golden. Keeping feelings bottled up inside does not lighten emotional burdens. The only cure for grief is to grieve. Talking helps to release the anguish building inside them.

Be prepared for their searching questions about that rite of separation, the funeral. They should be told that the service/burial is a significant occasion to say goodbye to the one who died. Explain the details of the funeral simply, directly, and honestly, giving answers to build on later, not ones that will have to be unlearned.

. . . a time to listen

While insight is a gift, educators must first be in a position to receive it. They may be so concerned about what to say that they frame answers without hearing what is said. As important as sage advice is, the ability to be quiet and listen not only to what is said but how it is said is important.

There are two kinds of listeners: passive and active. Passive listeners hear only some words and only occasionally look at the person speaking. More often they look at their watches. They convey the message that they are not totally interested and respectful of the speaker. Active listeners quickly establish eye contact. Their verbal and nonverbal clues demonstrate that they are carefully following the conversation and care about what is being said. Passive listeners seem to say: "I understand your feelings." Active listeners seem to say: "I want to understand your feelings."

Initially there may be little response from the children and adolescents. Do not mistake silence for uncaring or unfeeling emotions. They may be numb, their emotional systems shut down in order to avoid suffering overload. Be patient and calm. Tolerate this necessary stillness. Perhaps give reassurance: "It must be hard for you." "There is no hurry." "Take your time." Only when the mind is ready does speech appear. Listening reflectively gives the young people more time and space to eventually explore their inner feelings. An old maxim reads: "We have two ears and one mouth so we can listen more than we speak."

Grieving children need to be heard. Especially in their play, the language of childhood, they are able to deal with their feelings in an often disguised and displaced manner. These nonverbal messages might be the most important clues to their real inner emotions. In this safe place, play becomes an escape from their discomfort as they attempt to gain mastery over their confusing and bewildering sensations about death. Active discernment and listening become essential in understanding their frightening feelings.

. . . a time to cry

Crying is a natural emotion, a vital part of grieving. A newborn enters life crying for more oxygen. In early life tears are an infant's means of expressing needs, pain, and discomfort. Even after children are able to verbalize their desires, they continue to weep in order to release painful emotions. Crying helps to assuage heartache and express hidden depths of despair.

Unfortunately there are some male students who may think that tears are for "sissies" and are caused by weakness, cowardice, or self-pity. The truth is that people of all genders and ages often feel better after a good cry that eases anguish and emotional strain. A hopeful sight is the televised pictures of teenage boys, including athletes, crying unashamedly after a school shooting.

Each young person will react differently to loss. Some will cry freely. Some may shed a few tears. Some may not weep at all. Teachers need to grant license and permission to allow to students to express feelings that are appropriate to their needs.

... *a time to laugh*

The late president John F. Kennedy said: "There are three things that are real. God, human tragedy, and laughter. Since we cannot understand completely the first two, we must do with the third—laughter."

Human tragedy may be so overwhelming that bereaved young people must reduce it before they can put it into words. That is why serious things are often said in jest. They release nervous tension with a joke, and laugh to keep from crying.

Children and adolescents should understand that they can smile, laugh, and still care deeply about the death. Norman Cousins, in his book *Anatomy of an Illness*, said that ten minutes of laughing allowed him to sleep without pain for two hours. Humor is gaining a reputation as the all-natural, do-it-yourself wonder drug. It works without bad side effects. Children might be told: "Cry when you must; laugh when you can."

... *a time to reach out to parents and siblings of the deceased*

When a student dies, a designated member of the school such as the principal should contact the family immediately—preferably with a face-to-face meeting. Together with warm personal condolences would be a discussion of the family's wishes in such matters as the disposition of locker contents and their thoughts about planned memorial activities. It might be beneficial to suggest community services that could assist them in their bereavement process.

Siblings may dread returning to class after the death of a brother or sister. They are frightened: "How will friends and teachers react?" "What if someone makes an incredibly stupid remark?" "How can they concentrate and study and continue to live as if nothing had happened?" "What if they cry?" Special intervention by a counselor or member of the crisis team may help them to pass more gently through their grief and make their return to school a little more comfortable and reassuring. They might benefit from follow-up meetings to determine their post-trauma adjustments.

... a time to address parental concerns

Parents are the first and foremost educators of their children. They should be notified of significant happenings in the school environment. It would explain why a seven-year-old girl was in a panic when her father was late in picking her up after school. One of her classmate's parents had recently died and she was fearful that a dreadful accident had befallen her father.

For sudden, traumatic school losses such as murder or suicide, parents might be invited to attend a special meeting. A prepared statement describing the circumstances of death might immediately dispel rumors and hearsay. Such discussions might include possible reactions of children, with the understanding that there is no prescribed manner to grieve; the school's operational framework for coping with loss; availability and location of school counselors; community resources; attendance at the funeral; and procedures for treatment referral if they think that their child may be vulnerable and at high risk. A planned, coordinated, and comprehensive approach to crisis management is of invaluable assistance to parents, teachers, and students.

... a time for farewells

The funeral is a rite of separation. The service actualizes the parting experience, transforming the process of denial to an acceptance of reality. An important opportunity is provided for the expression of feelings and for saying goodbye to the one who will no longer be part of their familiar environment.

The school's protocol, parental permission, and the wishes of the bereaved family will determine whether students may leave class to attend the funeral. If at an unfamiliar church, synagogue, or mosque, a member of that particular faith might explain in advance the unique customs and ceremonies so that the students better understand the order and procedure of the forthcoming spiritual experience.

Young people often come in groups to the wake, the *Shiva*, the funeral for added support. Facing the loss together is a significant step in their healing and recovery. It also strengthens the bereaved family in the knowledge that their loved one had touched the lives of so many.

This was eloquently demonstrated at the beginning of this chapter in the story of the eighth grader, Glenn, and the helpful support systems of students, family, and school personnel.

. . . a time for support groups

In many schools and communities there are support groups for bereaved children and adolescents. They are no longer isolated in their grief but can interact with those who may have had similar experiences and will understand and help them.

Young people explain how support groups are so healing for them:

I don't feel embarrassed to cry here.

I can let go of my anger and pain without someone telling me that I shouldn't feel that way.

I can smile, I even laugh, without feeling guilty.

I don't feel like I'm so alone anymore. People can reach out to me. And I can reach out to them.

I've learned to be more patient and more of a friend to myself.

I know that others have been through this, and they've survived. I think I can, too.

Together they form friendships and learn how better to cope as they begin to rebuild their lives.

The common ground of group support with peers who are similarly bereaved has been started internally in many schools. There are other community resources such as hospices, hospitals, churches, synagogues, and funeral homes. For referral you might contact your local mental health agency. The French author Antoine de St. Exupery (1948) expressed the feelings implicit in such an approach: "I am of the group, and the group is of me."

. . . a time for professional help

Children and adolescents face multiple losses in their lives. These may include the deaths of family members and friends; yet as Rainer Maria Rilke, the German poet laureate, observed, there are other small deaths in a person's life. As young people grow, there might be the death of childhood in the struggle for roots and wings. There are the other possible losses, such as abuse, relocation, dysfunctional families, divorce and separation, broken personal relationships, physical or mental disability, as well as unaccomplished goals and dreams. It is so difficult to separate painful casualties when experiencing more than one "small" death at a time. When their basic sense of trust is challenged and the world seems insecure and unsafe, they may require additional support and guidance.

The question is not how the child is acting, reacting, or overreacting, but for how long. After an initial period of mourning, children are often able to work themselves back to some degree of productive and near-normal living. After several months have elapsed, danger signals may be present if children continue to:

- Confront other major stresses in their lives
- Think or talk about suicide (They need help immediately.)
- Feel stuck in sorrow without significant emotional movement or progress
- Rely on drugs or alcohol
- Avoid social activities and rarely want to be with others
- Are always tired
- Feel like they're always racing and can never relax
- Are indifferent to school and the activities that were once important to them
- Take risks—as in tempting fate
- Experience physical pain or can't sleep
- Feel anger that is constantly erupting
- Can't overcome feelings of powerlessness and sadness
- Don't have anyone safe to talk to
- Feel no purpose in being with anyone or doing anything
- Decline in grades and school performance.

Consider a one-to-one meeting with a professional (school counselor, psychologist, psychiatrist, social worker, nurse, member of the clergy, mental health professional, or grief therapist) for understanding and support. Children must understand that seeking professional help does not mean that they are mentally ill. Rather it is a sign of courage and willingness to go on with life. A listening ear can help them to express their feelings and better cope with the loss.

. . . a time to remember

An important policy might be established for all memoralizations. Controversies may erupt when the flag is lowered for one student who died of cancer and not for another who took his life (for fear of glamorizing suicide and creating copycat deaths).

Memory books with classmates' reflections, poems, and art afford bereaved families comfort and consolation. A bookshelf with volumes on grief and loss will commemorate the memory of the deceased as well as help the living. Scholarships assist future generations. Just a word of caution about memorial tree plantings: What distress when the trees die or have to be relocated because of school renovation! It is strongly recommended that a uniform policy about memorialization be established, regardless of circumstances of death.

Educators can do so much in empowering families and peer groups to support grieving children and adolescents. An added bonus, besides the gratification of helping the young cope with loss, is the challenge for teachers to discover meaningful explanations and to comfort themselves even in the midst of lingering doubts and suffering. The real challenge is not only how to explain death to children but how to make peace with oneself.

Earl A. Grollman, DHL, DD, is a rabbi, a pioneer in the field of death and dying, and the author of 26 books on crisis intervention. He speaks frequently at conferences and symposia and is often called to trauma scenes as a counselor to victim families and to caregivers.

7

Counseling Approaches with Children and Adolescents

By Dottie Ward-Wimmer and Carol Napoli

This chapter is really about attitude: our attitudes as we witness, comfort, educate, and normalize the process of healing from loss. It is about the sensitivities and understandings one can acquire when working in the presence of a grieving child. It is about what the children have taught us and will continue to teach us as we walk beside them in their journeys through grief. Our knowledge comes from their unique stories, their love, their anger, their courage, and the breadth and depth of their feelings.

This chapter attempts to reach out into the "how to be" with children who grieve. Although the death of a loved one is primarily addressed here, any loss—moving to a new home, divorce, or even the goldfish dying—requires our full attention and the same respect and honor bestowed upon the bereaved child.

The Child's Meaning of Loss

When all else looks helpless, consider the spirit of the child as having the potential to heal. We cannot fully enter into relationship with children if we do not embrace their spirits. We must be willing to experience the world through their eyes.

Kneel down and walk around the room. What do you see? Can you look in the mirror? How does it feel to be that size? Now close your eyes. What does the world smell like? How does it feel? Explore the space with your hands. Isn't that what a child does? He reaches for whatever he is "looking" at. Listen carefully to all of the sounds in the room.

Children are magical, curious sponges. They are constantly receiving life in all of its dimensions. It's important to remember that when we think about grieving youngsters and how they experience loss. A child whose mother has been hospitalized for a long time becomes accustomed to the sights, sounds, and smells of the hospital. A wheelchair becomes what a tricycle might have been if mom had been able to be at home.

When Mommy was alive she was three-dimensional. Her hair had a certain smell and so did her apron. The way her voice sounded told more than her words and the child knew the way her breath tickled when she whispered in his ear. She had a "flavor" when he kissed her cheek and he was especially happy when she gave him the spoon from the cake batter to lick.

So you see, grief isn't just about sadness, or anger, or the list of other emotions. It is also about the very visceral experience of hunger for the taste of her cheek, the echo of the silence in that space no longer filled with her voice, and the searing numbness of his arms that can no longer wrap around her.

The Counselor

Children's counselors are not all-knowing psychics. The best ones are compassionate listeners with the courage to hang in there and stay out of the way as the child makes her way through. Their skills lie in keeping the youngster safe and in having the patience to allow her to find the insights, answers, and promise.

As counselors, we must appreciate the fact that much of a child's work is done in the metaphor. Play, art, music, and other projective modalities are best because they facilitate the expression of feelings that simply cannot be captured in words. They provide a place to see, experience, accept, reject, and try on feelings, all in the child's native tongue (i.e., pre-verbal). It is often quite different from working with adults (although adults really enjoy and benefit from these techniques). Sometimes, interpretation is necessary. But every good therapist knows that, as Freud once said, "Sometimes a cigar is just a cigar."

And good therapists love. They know how to maintain appropriate boundaries and, at the very same time, hold the child's heart with reverence. In the purest way, they simply love. It's essential, for this isn't about what's in the child's head, it's about healing the soul. It's about exorcising the deepest pains and letting the child know all the feelings are normal and she didn't do anything wrong.

Counseling children who have sustained a loss is not traditional psychotherapy. It is a combination of comforting, educating, exploring, and inviting expression. Good therapists must be skilled clinicians, surrogate parents, spiritual nurturers, and pompom-waving cheerleaders.

Approaching Grieving Children

We always start gently and respectfully to find out what happened. Facts can be gathered from adults. Understanding the child's primary support system is essential, as is knowing how those support systems will be affected by the loss. In assessing a child's grieving process, one must be cognizant of the impact of parental grief upon the child. A grieving parent may not be able to support the grieving child, so we always recommend that parents get support for themselves first. The work of William Worden has clearly shown that children do better when the caregiver is also receiving support.

When back-up supports are needed, you may have to be creative in identifying them. In addition to friends and relatives, find out if the school principal's secretary, the library aide, a Girl Scout leader, or Sunday school teacher is well known to the child, and use whomever the child and family trusts.

Practical implications must also be understood. There are two aspects of practical implications to address. The first is how the loss impacts on the child's life circumstance. Will the child now be going home to an empty house after school? Will the family need to move? How will the lifestyle socially and economically change? Who is available to bring the child to you? The second is what we as caregivers must think about in planning how to support the child: cost and access issues as well as the best culturally, spiritually, and socially acceptable resources.

Once we have gathered some basic information, we assess the child's perspective. Projective techniques work best. Directly talking about feelings, especially in the beginning, may be way down on the list of what the child wants to do. While we may need to unwind complicating perceptions and feelings, grief, in itself, is not something we can "fix." Instead, we are asked to walk with the child and witness the healing at his own pace.

A simple drawing of what happened is rich with the child's view. Secondary losses unfold in sand trays, drawings, or puppet shows about how life is different now. Children's play is their work. We must honor its importance. Teens, too, often find it easier to use art, games, music, and drama to explore feelings. Be willing to try new things and configure your approaches to each child or group based on personality. Reading books or writing stories together may be perfect for one and not another. Remember, even a sure-fire technique simply won't be right for everyone.

Consideration of the child's age is necessary to better understand the child's ability to grieve, but we must be careful not to overlook the "street smart" youth. He may appear knowledgeable and possess well-honed survival skills, but he is often emotionally still a frightened child in profound pain. These youngsters often need extra time to establish a trusting relationship, but are then able to do their mourning.

It is important to determine what the primary issue really is as children often regrieve the event(s) as new coping and cognitive abilities emerge (Kubler-Ross, 1969). As children's developmental capacities and coping repertoires increase, they are able to revisit life events and often rework or regrieve a loss. For example, it has been our experience that a preschool age child whose parent dies will often present as a preadolescent with depression or school difficulties triggered by a significant life event such as graduation or a prom. Such significant events cause the growing child to rethink and re-experience the loss within the new context created by changing circumstances and his maturing ability to comprehend and appreciate more fully the ramifications of his loss. One preteen was brought in because of temper tantrums. What emerged was her anger at her mom for having died several years earlier, leaving her with a dad who now couldn't help her cope with puberty. She was given some support in working through her feelings, Dad was taught some practical tips on train-ing bras and other important facts of life, and both learned some more effective ways to communicate within their reality.

We must also assess if trauma is involved because that must be attended to before the grief work. Trauma work consists of wrapping our arms around concrete images. Drawing scenes and recalling events as soon after as possible enable the child to then look at the associated feelings. Attempting to explore the emotions around an event that is murky and overwhelming only intensifies the helplessness and thus recreates traumatic impact. The writings of Dr. Robert Pynoos and Dr. Lenore Terr are essential reading for anyone working with traumatized children.

And finally, we must remember that no matter how good our intentions or how skilled our interventions, a child who has been traumatized by a loss, or victimized by other uncontrollable forces, may not welcome us. He, depending on the nature of the loss, may anticipate it happening again with us. This is so important to understand when entering into a relationship with a grieving child. How do we honor the unfolding and closing of the relationship? Boundaries must be clear, preparations for breaks in the schedule (vacations, etc.) must be thoughtful, and lots of time should be left for closure.

Grief work takes time. The more opportunity for reflecting, experiencing, processing, and actually making closure, the more likely it is that the child will avoid complications. Anticipatory grief, i.e. beginning the process before the actual loss, can facilitate an uncomplicated journey. It allows for clearing up negative feelings and for saying and doing the things that need to be said and done. It can be a valuable way for avoiding the post-loss "if onlys," and it may make possible a clearer journey through grief. But there are no short cuts. We must be willing to offer whatever time it takes. In those instances where sufficient time will not be available, don't try to rush it. You serve the children much better by educating them. In whatever time you have, give them the tools they will need and permission to grieve when they are ready.

The Unique Essence of the Grieving Child

To understand a child's experience of grief, you must be willing to walk into a free fall, for that is where much of it happens. A child whose mom or dad was killed in an accident may be drawn to objects in the playroom such as ambulances, doctors, gravestones, or puppets that speak his pain. A child too young to comprehend the loss of a mom as being " forever" may replay "mommy dead" over and over. Teenagers will sit mute for an entire session or talk about music or football—anything but the loss. Each, in his own way, leads us into his inner world and we must follow respectfully.

The behavior of grieving youngsters is a large part of their language of grief. We often get calls from parents saying their child has been sent home or suspended from school for aggressive behavior. The child is stunned. He doesn't know why he lashed out. He may not be able to articulate the origin of the outburst, and sometimes words alone simply aren't enough. Consider the child who insists on sleeping in her parent's bedroom now that Mom or Dad, a sibling, or a friend is no longer there. The unspoken words may be: "Now I'm afraid I'm going to lose you." "Who will take care of me?" or "The world no longer feels safe." Or consider the child who is told only that, "Daddy will be living in a new house" because the parents think it will upset him if they use the word "divorce."

Teenagers, appropriately both egocentric and ambivalent as they move toward individuation, are profoundly affected by real and perceived role changes as well as by peer reactions. They often need a great deal of permission to experience and express the depth of their feelings. It's not easy for the 6'4" football player to acknowledge that he misses his mom so much that he often sneaks into her room just to sit in her closet because the scent makes him feel like she's still there. For teens, peer group experiences are often invaluable.

We must be mindful that their grief work is intermittent. Imagine being in their pain and having only limited coping skills. Children have not yet learned how to stay in the presence of pain because they have limited ways of dealing with it. So grief is usually expressed in brief episodes of overt sadness layered between apparently happy, normal behavior. Children are often seen crying one moment at a funeral and at the next moment are playing happily. Adults, observing this behavior, assume that children don't understand. The fact is, however, that the children on some level understand quite well but can only tolerate feeling the experience for brief periods of time. The same behavior is seen in therapy settings. Usually, only about one-third of the session, if that, is spent consciously focusing on grief. Children need and deserve our gentle guidance and encouragement as they grow and learn how to cope.

And where do they turn for comfort? Usually a child, when hurt, will turn to her parent. Imagine being in this kind of pain and being alone. Imagine being in this kind of pain and having your surviving parent emotionally unavailable because of his own grief.

Also unique to childhood loss is the very real possibility of the loss of one's right to be born into a safe world, a world that makes sense. Consider the child who dives under his bed at night at the sound of gunshots. Imagine the child who visits a prison to see his father who is no longer there to protect him. Imagine the child whose immigrant mother dies, leaving him as the only English-speaking person in the family to care for younger children and act as interpreter, without any real skills in survival in this foreign culture. Imagine a ten-year-old, now the only male in the family, trying to fill the hole his father has left.

It is important to bring to light the very questions that lie in the heart and mind of children suffering a loss. There are five questions that we hear over and over. They are the essence of the child's grief work as he unties the knots of confusion and disorientation.

What is dead? To a child, especially under the age of five, this is an ongoing question. It is reworked as the child develops cognitively and emotionally. The answers must be clear and accurate, even when the questions seem unreasonable. What would you say to the teenager who, while struggling to wrap his mind around the shooting death of his best friend, says, "What will happen to his body in the ground? Will his eyeballs pop or do they melt?" Questions like these should be answered with facts: "The body decomposes—it gradually breaks down and literally becomes like the earth again. The eyeballs probably leak their fluid as they too change." Factual statements can be followed with reflections such as, "It's so hard for you to really believe he's not alive anymore." It is important to stay where the grieving person is and not to try to rush the process.

Did I cause it? The egocentricity of children places them in the center of the universe, omnipotent and responsible for good and bad. Did my brother die because I wouldn't share my toys? Did my father die because I was angry that he wouldn't let me buy the same bicycle as my friends? Children who lose someone from homicide actually fantasize about how they could have stopped the bullet and saved their loved one. Allowing the expression of these painful distortions and working to reframe them in reality are an important part of our role in aiding the healing process.

Who will take care of me? Children become very clingy following a loss. They need to be close. They need consistency. They need real answers and tremendous reassurance that they will be cared for. A young girl whose mom died of lung cancer cried out when she saw her dad light a cigarette. A child whose dad was quite overweight and died of a heart attack will watch everything that goes into her mother's mouth at meal times. Caregivers and counselors need to work together to give the child a clear awareness of what the future holds—without making promises.

Am I going to die too? Children may physically express their fears after a death and experience the pain a parent may have had in the course of a terminal illness. A child who loses someone to suicide may fear his own lack of control and being pulled into the abyss. A youngster whose loved one dies from an illness often wonders if she can catch it and die too. Because children may not overtly express this fear, it may be useful to say something like, "Some children worry that they can catch the same illness your loved one died from. I want you to know that we can't catch it, and since we're both healthy we'll probably live for a long time." Be careful to appreciate the fear first with statements such as, "Sometimes it is scary when someone we love dies;" then you can move toward allaying these fears. It is sometimes helpful to have the child brought to an understanding pediatrician for a routine check up to assure him he is fine. Note: If the child does have the same disease as the dying mom, we can point out the differences (such as T-cell counts, in the case of HIV), but we must be willing to embrace fear and hope together with the child.

Who am I now that I have lost this important person? A child who lost his dad when he was four is now eight and wants to give up team sports. Everyone else has a dad on the sidelines. So who is he now? Adopted children have especially complex journeys through this question when their adoptive parent dies. Activities that focus on how the child is like mom or dad vs. how the child is just like himself are important as he works to figure it out. The goal of these activities—which include drawing, looking at photos, or using the dollhouse to show how the house would be set up—is to allow the child to appreciate her own unique qualities. Work with the understanding of "who I am," moving toward "who I will be." Future orientation walks hand-in-glove with hope.

Questions are important, yet all too often in our culture, children must grieve in a social and cognitive vacuum, as they may lack the grief-related vocabulary and social skills needed to fully participate in or benefit from mourning (Ward-Wimmer, 1993). Therefore, the child's journey includes the need for a great deal of learning, for he must give names to the feelings and find appropriate ways to express them. While children are exposed to death frequently in the media, there is almost no attention paid to bereavement other than occasional pictures of survivors in immediate shock or crying at a funeral. Where do they learn that grief is a process that goes on and that the feelings may be intense? It is often our job to teach them and their caregivers.

In addition, children may find themselves needing to learn more about the world around them. For instance, what does *cremation* mean, or *insurance, stillborn, contagious,* or *hereditary*? Fear and general uneasiness are bred in the isolation of the funeral industry from mainstream education. Rarely, if ever, are funeral directors listed in chapters on community helpers, nor are they usually represented on career day. Youngsters are taught how to write formal letters and thank-you notes, but how many English teachers include sympathy notes in their curriculum? Grief and its rituals, impact and language are all too often taboo, thus inaccessible at the time the child needs most to understand and use them.

Factors Which Influence Mourning

It is always helpful to know as much as you can about the child and his world, the loss itself, and the circumstances surrounding it, for they influence how the mourning will be experienced.

The role the deceased person played in the child's life must be appreciated if we are to understand the child's reaction. For example, the death of a close relative, friend, or primary caregiver may elicit a more traumatic reaction from the child than that of a distant cousin with whom the child did not share a relationship. However, it is essential to avoid judgment. The distant cousin who offered unconditional love at the annual family reunion may be, in fact, a more significant loss than the emotionally absent parent. Saying to a child, "Tell me about him or her," and then listening carefully to the content as well as watching the child's affect will provide useful material with which to assess the relationship and its potential impact. Parents and caregivers cannot assume that a child will react to a loss because they themselves feel a sense of grief, and they must be ready to accept intense reactions to a loss that seems insignificant to them. It is the child's perception of the loss that triggers the response, and the accompanying grief must be honored.

The nature and circumstances surrounding a death also greatly influence the child's grief response. A sudden death from an accident, suicide, homicide, heart attack, or stroke leaves a child in a state of confusion, disorientation, and shock. Sudden loss, especially if violent in nature, is laden with guilt, rage, and recrimination all compacted into one sudden blow. It's the difference between turning around twenty times slowly, noticing your surroundings, perhaps touching something for balance now and then, and being whirled around wildly twenty times and then let go with no supports or balance points in sight. In each case you have revolved twenty times, but going through the process too quickly leaves you dizzy, nauseated, off balance, and probably feeling out of control and very angry with what happened. Both experiences describe grief yet they are experienced quite differently.

Consider, too, the reaction of a child to an unexpected or traumatic loss that has happened to a schoolmate whom the child did not know. While the child may not, in fact, have personally known the victim, the fear that it might also happen to him can be intense. We must also be careful to assess impact even when the death was due to a chronic illness. If the child was not included in the awareness of the loved one's illness or invited in some way into the process of anticipatory grieving, the death may be a sudden and overwhelming event for that youngster.

The child's developmental level and cognitive capacity influence her perception of the event(s) (Furman, 1978; Wilder, 1980). In general the pre-language child experiences separation as abandonment: You leave, the baby cries. The child age three to seven (approximately) is a literal thinker and views death as an extension of this life elsewhere: Grandma goes to heaven just as though she is going to Pittsburgh. The eight-to-twelve-year-old is able to understand death in its fullness and is most often concerned with the impact of the loss on himself: Who will take care of me? Will we have to move? Experience has taught us, too, that children often experience significant confusion during grief because:

1. They are often younger emotionally than intellectually and therefore find it difficult to experience and process emotionally what they know cognitively to be true.

2. As many religions prepare children for a profession of faith (confirmation, witness, bar/bat mitzvah), they become caught in the tension between what they are "supposed to believe" and their anger and confusion toward a god who they feel let their loved one die.

In addition, we must be mindful of how culture and ethnic identity impact on how the child experiences a loss. It is essential to understand methods for coping with loss and expressing feelings which are acceptable within his particular community and family. Is loud crying appropriate, indeed, might it even be expected? Or is the opposite, i.e. stoic acceptance, the norm? You need to find out what is true for the child in front of you. All African-Americans do not grieve the same, nor do all Italians, etc. Talk to the adults in the family. Often, the best thing to do is simply ask, "How do you and your family express grief?" "What does your faith belief teach (or what is your own belief) about death?"

Other important influences are the opportunities provided for the child to process the grief, including the clarity of information given and the degree of experiential participation in rituals, both formal and informal. We are far better able to cope with a situation that is clearly understood. All too often youngsters are given inadequate information and "protected" from funerals. Yet children are often far better than adults at facing even the most gruesome realities. It may be that their natural curiosity just gets the better of them or, perhaps, they are simply so connected in love to the person that the "externals" aren't as big an issue, unless they are kept secret; then they become very powerful. Rituals are essential to children's (and often adults') healing. They serve to bring into reality that which is unbelievable and to provide a way for the mourner to embrace closure by saying verbally or symbolically that which needs to be said. When children are denied ritual, they are denied a very important step in the process of saying goodbye.

Parents experience many of the same emotions as the child after a death. A parent may often feel depressed and emotionally drained, with little energy to face the difficult tasks of family life after a death. They may feel helpless in the face of the child's pain, and their grief influences the child in several ways (Figley, Bride, and Mazza, 1997):

1. Parents are likely to be preoccupied for periods of time, which would make them less nurturing and responsive at a time when a child most needs nurturing and recognition. The child's sense of a secure attachment figure is threatened, and the child may feel more sad and lonely. The child's behavior will speak to this problem through anger, depression, disruptive behavior, or regression (e.g. bedwetting).

2. Bereaved parents are likely to be emotionally labile and inconsistent in both their behavior and their discipline. This causes the child to feel that her world is not as safe and predictable as it was before.

3. The parents may appear more vulnerable and weak at times, causing the child to worry about the parent's well being. This perception magnifies the child's fear that his remaining parent may die as well. Children may feel guilty about placing demands on a parent who already appears overextended.

4. Parents may avoid talking about the person who has died. This may increase the child's feelings of sadness and longing for the deceased. Children naturally reminisce about a person they miss but often refrain from doing so to protect the grieving parent.

Conclusion

Counseling grieving children means being willing to not have the answers most of the time. It means using theory as a framework and your heart as the guide. We provide a safe place for them to do this work and help them make sense of their confusion. They share with us their wisdom and their joy.

We close with a story that portrays exquisitely the spirit of a child who entered into the grief process. It speaks eloquently of a child's potential for healing. It shows what can happen when a youngster is provided with a safe place to grieve.

Emma was eight years old when her mom died. She had been part of her mother's care and was with her when she died. Emma attended a grief group for one whole year. She rarely missed. She came in ready to work and had many stories to share. For her, the group was a place where she could honor her mother's life, build memories that are now solidly ingrained, and even admit to the things she didn't like.

Emma knew that she would be leaving the group, as she and her father were moving away. On the last day we invited the children to make a symbol in clay of a gift their deceased parent had given to them. They were also invited to make a gift they might like to give to that parent or loved one. Emma worked hard to create her image, using many different colors of clay. When she was satisfied with the results, she then made the gift to give her mother. She could not wait to share when she had finished. The first gift she made was from her mother. It was a clay heart of several layers. "This is what my mother gave to me. She gave me her heart. She gave me her love." Emma spoke with such certainty.

Her second gift was what she had given to her mother. Emma had fashioned from clay an intricate mandella-like design that sent spokes of colors in all directions from a center spoke. It had life, it had color, and it spoke of Emma's grief work. She proudly showed it to the group, holding it up in her hand for all to see. "This is my gift to my mom. It is the gift of life. I have given to her the gift of life." And indeed she had done just that in her magnificent labor of love. Emma had cared for her mom in life and found a way to give life to her memory as she participated in, and allowed us to witness, her own healing.

Dottie Ward-Wimmer, RN, MA, is a Professional Counselor and Registered Play Therapist-Supervisor. She is the Director of the Children's Program at the William Wendt Center for Loss and Healing in Washington, DC and is on the faculty of the Chesapeake Institute for Play Therapy.

Carol Napoli, RN, MA, is a Professional Counselor and Play Therapist. She is a former hospice nurse and now serves as the Activities Coordinator for the Children's Program at the William Wendt Center for Loss and Healing in Washington, DC.

V · O · I · C · E · S

How I Coped with Loss

Brett Hardy Blake

When most eighth graders think of loss, they think of losing their CDs or their favorite shirt. I think of my mother and one of my friends.

My mother died of breast cancer and my friend died of cystic fibrosis. They were very different experiences, but many of the feelings were the same. At first, I was shocked. As I grasped what had happened, I became sad. Once I was more comfortable with my grief, I was able to be a little angry with the person who died, for leaving me. I found out this is a very common reaction. I often felt scared that what happened to them would happen to me, and that's a very common reaction, too.

Though my reactions were similar, the losses were very different. My mother was in many ways my best friend. We did almost everything together. She was sick on and off for seven years; she died when I was ten. In that respect, my loss was very different from the loss of someone in a car crash. I had a chance to say goodbye to my mother. However, I was forced to take care of her, physically and emotionally, as best I could. I was very scared. I had trouble sleeping, my grades dropped, I would be sitting in class and just start crying.

After my mother died I moved and left my home, my school and my friends. These are all things that I am still working through. I started a new school in fifth grade. In my sixth grade year I met Jonathan Rhodes. Jonathan always had lung problems, but they were not very serious. We became good friends. At the end of sixth grade, he was absent a couple of days a week, and was in and out of the hospital. In March of seventh grade we found out he was dead. None of us had expected it.

I felt awful! I had not visited him in the hospital enough, and I was too caught up in my own life to worry about him. I felt horrible. I also felt sad, mad, scared and shocked. Our class organized a memorial service; everyone participated and made a wonderful service. It made me feel a little better about neglecting our friendship, and it helped me to pay homage to Jonathan. His parents really appreciated it, too.

My experiences were very difficult, but they allowed me to be more compassionate and appreciate life more. There is nothing good about losing someone you love, but that doesn't mean that something good can't come out of it. When you lose somebody special, it is extremely important to talk about it with somebody. It may not always be the right time to talk, and your family and friends should respect that. But you must talk about it when you're ready. If you never express your feelings, they will build up, and eventually explode.

Brett Hardy Blake is fourteen years old. He is a freshman in high school. He runs cross-country, plays basketball, and writes.

8

Part Of Me Died Too
Creative Strategies for Grieving Children and Adolescents

By Virginia Lynn Fry

Sarah rested her small, sad face in her hands as she stared at the cookies and milk that sat untouched in front of her. "What's the matter, Sarah? Don't you want to eat?" asked her kind neighbor, who had volunteered to watch the six year old while the rest of her family went to the hospital. But Sarah only sighed and poked at the cookies with an uninterested finger. Her neighbor sighed too. Then she brightened with a sudden thought. "Would you like to play with some clay instead?" she asked. Sarah looked up and nodded quickly.

Soon Sarah was busy shaping the colorful clay into thick ovals. "May I please have a knife?" she asked her neighbor. Surprised, the woman handed her a small butter knife and watched as Sarah carefully cut off the bottom third of each oval. Then she stood each one up, pushing the flat ends into the table, placing them all in a row. Silently, she scrutinized her work, then asked, "Do you have a tooth pick?" With her new tool, Sarah carefully etched letters into the soft clay. Her neighbor watched with fascination that slowly turned to shock, as she recognized the names of Sarah's sister, Catherine, and their parents emerging on the clay shapes, turning them into tombstones.

"There! That's everyone! Even one for me—so we can all stay together as a family!" Sarah looked enormously pleased with her personal cemetery, and she smiled for the first time that day. Her stunned neighbor could only smile back and say, "My!" She wondered what Sarah's family would say when they saw this on their kitchen table, and she wondered if she should hide the *cemetery before they got home. She knew that Sarah had not been told that her twelve-year-old sister was dying of leukemia. And now she saw that Sarah knew it anyway. She worried whether she had done the right thing by encouraging this play. But one look at Sarah's relaxed face, eating cookies, told her this was all right. In fact, the change in Sarah's demeanor was amazing, and her neighbor wondered what had happened. Why was Sarah so happy while she felt so much sadness, as they both stared at the row of colorful tiny tombstones?*

Why Do the Arts and Creativity Help Grieving Children?

In my work as a hospice artist and counselor for the past twenty years, I have learned a lot from children like Sarah, and the caring, concerned, and confused adults who try to help them. Despite often-repeated phrases like, "She's too young too understand," or "He doesn't know what is happening," children actually do know and understand in their own ways, as Sarah showed us. It is in the *showing*, rather than the *telling*, that children can explore their understanding of life, death, dying, grieving, and surviving. But because children, even very young ones, can be so articulate, we forget that talking may not be their primary mode of expression, especially when they are young. Even teenagers often find it safer and more true to their feelings to express them in paint, poetry, clay, theater, crafts, and created rituals, rather than trying to tell someone explicitly how they feel. After all, are there really any words adequate to express how it feels to have your big sister dying in front of your eyes? But a row of little clay tombstones, one for each member of the family—not just the dying sister—set up on the kitchen table for all to see, expresses perfectly the reality and fears and hopes of this little girl.

It's not that all this death made Sarah happy. It was the sheer joy of *expressing* it, of literally getting it out of her body, that brought enormous relief and pleasure to Sarah. I once overheard my young children's uncle explain this to them: "Now remember, whenever anything leaves your body, it feels good!" The children's whoops of joy at the recognition of one of their basic truths were the opposite of my own automatic adult reactions to this dubious bit of wisdom. But upon further consideration, and the children's graphic examples, I had to admit that he was right. And when it is feelings and thoughts that are leaving the body, instead of bodily fluids, the results are the same—it feels good! It's the sheer relief of expression that lifts one's spirits, even though the subject may be as unknown and frightening as death.

Creative artists of all media have known this for hundreds, perhaps thousands, of years. It's the shedding of light and air on our darkest fears, closeted away in secrecy inside of us, sometimes so hidden that even we don't know what it is that is terrifying us—this is creative expression. But in our society of specialists, we've gotten in the bad habit of thinking that this province of creative expression belongs to artists alone. So often I have heard my dying patients, who are dying of boredom as well as disease, say to me, "But I'm not an artist! I'm not creative!" And yet the sheer act of being alive and being human is to be creative. It is only the artists and children that I don't have to persuade of this truth. They know it in their bodies.

When Sarah transformed her secret fear that her sister would die into the first clay tombstone, she recognized the truth hidden inside of her: "My sister is going to die." The relief of finally having it out in the open and clearly expressed eased the sadness Sarah had been feeling. Physically manipulating such a huge unknown reality as death, as she worked the clay, may have brought her a sense of power as well as relief. It surely gave her some control over something that frightened her. And the resulting little colored clay cemetery is unforgettable. It is this ability of art to serve as a witness to our pain, to show the depths and profundity of our lives, that gives it as much of its therapeutic power as ridding the body of uncomfortable feelings or illuminating our darkest fears. Creating her private and personal cemetery also enabled Sarah to transform difficult feelings into knowledge and wisdom. She made something she could learn to live with, the reality that someday everyone in her family would die. Sarah created a very neat solution to the enormous problem of how her family could still be a family after her sister died. It is in death that she could hope that her family would be reunited. Sarah got it right.

Sharing Bad News with Children

But did Sarah think that her whole family would die when her sister died? This was quite an unsettling thought for her neighbor and would be for most of us. Sarah had not been told that her sister was dying, so she had no opportunity to clear up any misconceptions she might have or to air her fears and questions. Like most kids, she was very sensitive to the level of anxiety in her parents, to the increasing frequency of phone calls, and to Catherine's worsening condition, which she could observe. Like most kids, Sarah knew the truth before she was told. But she still needed the opportunity to talk about this important eventuality with a trusted adult who could give her the facts and help her sort out the questions.

Children generally cope better with witnessing the dying process when they have concrete information about the disease and treatment in the beginning, and when they are invited to ask questions as things change. Being allowed to help with physical tasks of caregiving serves to calm their fears and give them a sense of empowerment and belonging in a situation that might otherwise exclude them. The old style of protecting children with silence and evasion has proved to be damaging, leaving them isolated and alone with their fears.

What and how you tell children about illness and death depends on their developmental age and the impact of the disease on their daily lives. It is very useful to explain the illness by simply drawing the body and identifying the affected areas. Naming the organs and the related systems can be done in simple terms with a drawing or a model of the body. Be honest about the possibility that the illness could cause death, then describe the treatments that will be used to try to heal the child's loved one. You can explain therapies in terms of efforts to help the person by poisoning the dangerous cancer cells with chemotherapy or invisible rays of radiation. Surgically cutting out the sick parts of the body, or using medicine to strengthen the body's ability to fight the disease with its own immune system, can also be explained.

It is also necessary to describe more passive efforts to heal the person, like changes in diet, increases in vitamins and herbals, massages, acupuncture, counseling, and lots of love from the family. These are all part of treatment and may be the more tangible and therefore important ones to the child. There are supportive things that children can help with, such as bringing cool cloths to soothe irradiated skin and preparing hot packs to ease aches and pains. They can rub lotion into sore hands and feet, make drawings to decorate a sick room, and give lots of hugs and kisses—these all make for "good medicine." Doing concrete tasks increases feelings of control and confidence and reduces fears in a situation that is frightening for adults as well as children.

We also need to carefully explain what changes will take place in the daily routine of the household, such as who will take the children to soccer practice, help with homework, or prepare meals. Children also need to plan and practice what to say when people ask how their loved one is doing or how they are coping, so they don't feel overwhelmed by phone calls and questions from concerned friends.

Sarah's tombstones demonstrated that she needed an adult to help to explore her thoughts about the timing of the deaths of the rest of the family. The time factor can be very confusing for children. Children's concepts of time are key to their understanding of illness, prognosis, treatment, and death. Typically an infant lives in the moment, while a two- to four-year-old can conceive of the whole day. A kindergartner may be able to conceptualize a school week, but still be very confused about time. My six-year-old son asked repeatedly, "Is today the tomorrow that was yesterday? Or is yesterday the tomorrow that you get today?" Most third graders can do a week in advance in their minds, and sixth graders can conceptualize longer periods.

But the concept of forever—an infinite amount of time—escapes most children until their teens. My four-year-old daughter questioned me six months after her grandfather died. "Is it forever yet? You said he'd be dead forever. Is it forever yet? I want him back!" I realized that she knew "forever" was a time word, and six months sure feels like forever to a four year old. So it was natural for her to expect him back soon. It was shocking for an "expert" on children and death to realize that I had used the wrong words with my own child! But children have a way of humbling their parents. I apologized for the confusion and explained to her that I should have said, "Not ever. He's dead and not ever coming back." Then I held her as she cried with this new realization of the enormity and finality of death.

Warning is another key ingredient to successful coping with the death of a loved one for both children and adults. When deciding to tell a child that death is approaching a loved one, consider how much time the child can conceptualize. Use seasonal changes and family holidays such as birthdays to anchor expectations. Give the child something creative to do while you have this discussion, so the child's body and imagination can help him or her to process what is being said. You can watch the evolution of a drawing or of clay shapes and learn a lot about the level of agitation, distress, fear, or calm inside the child. Begin this conversation by asking questions, not making statements. Then confirm observations and fears if they are true and clear up misconceptions. The conversation might go like this.

Have you noticed any changes in Catherine lately? You are right, she does sleep a lot of the time and her voice is very weak and she can't eat much now. Yes, her feet are swelling and getting bigger, but they won't blow up like balloons. Her skin is thicker than balloon skin. But we can put pillows under her feet to help drain the water in them back into her body.

Can you tell if she is getting sicker and sicker or better and better? Yes, she is getting sicker and sicker. Do you know what happens to animals or people when they get sicker and sicker? Yes, they die, you are right. Do you know what death is? Death is stopping. Everything in the body stops. Stop breathing, stop eating, stop moving, stop sleeping.... Everything stops. I'm sorry to tell you that this is going to happen to Catherine. I don't know exactly when she will die. She will probably be with us next week for your birthday. But I don't think she has the strength left to live until Christmas. I think she will die before then. But you can help her feel better during this time by giving her your love in any way you want to, with lots of gentle hugs and prayers. Maybe you can read her stories or sing some songs. We'll do this together with lots of love for everyone. You are the best little sister—and Catherine and I love you very much!

As hard as this conversation is to have with a child, it is a serious mistake to avoid it and leave the child alone in the dark with only his fears and no help with coping. Such abandonment can have a devastating impact on the child's mental and physical health. Doing something creative together as you talk, even if it is just mindlessly squishing clay or doodling on paper, will take the edge off the tension and provide a focus and a way to process. The drawing or clay piece that the child makes as you talk will help her to remember this important conversation, and all the facts and reassurances that you gave. The child will remember especially the loving open hearts you both showed by trusting yourselves to talk about death in a safe way. You could end an important talk like this by making something together to give to your loved one.

The process of being creative in exploring dying, death, and its many meanings is natural for children. But it takes quiet time, a safe space, adequate materials, and a supportive environment—people that understand, or at least accept, the therapeutic value of creative expression. The process demands what my son calls, "Being quiet inside my mind." It facilitates deep breathing, focused thoughts, and concentration. It requires a willingness to let go of foregone conclusions and to just see what happens. All these things are part of every meditation practice. And like meditation, the creative process enables us to tolerate intense feelings without having to run away from them or numb them with dangerous behaviors. Being creative can have a restorative effect on children's and adults' sense of well-being, especially during a difficult time. It can provide the calm eye in the hurricane of life.

Tasks and Conditions that Enable Children to Grieve

How can a family be a family without the missing person? This is the problem of all bereaved families, which Sarah was trying to solve with her cemetery. Exploring this question and many others is what the mourning process is about. Grief in children encompasses a wide variety of feelings and expressions that may be puzzling to adults, and it may seem like a child is not grieving at all. But children are "do-ers," and their ways of mourning will be through activities.

Sandra Fox, of Boston Children's Hospital, describes tasks for children to obtain "good grief," and includes four steps. First, the child must gain an understanding of the event as a loss. Then the child must go through the feelings of grief about the loss. The third task is to commemorate what has been lost. And finally, the child must receive permission to go on with his or her life. Children will naturally fall into these tasks of exploring what's missing and what happened by drawing maps, pictures of the family, and making lists of questions they have about the loss. Feelings seem to pour out of young children as they pound clay, though it may be harder for an older child to let go. Repeatedly throwing big lumps of pottery clay against a plastic tarp on the floor can release the toughest of teens. Making objects for the coffin, building shrines, and decorating candles to honor the missing loved one are all favorite activities of grieving children and adolescents. Learning to celebrate and have fun again is about going on with life and being a kid.

But sometimes this natural process is blocked and grief goes underground inside the child, handicapping emotional development. In my experience, it seems there are conditions that are necessary in order for a child to grieve successfully. The meaning of any death will change over the years as a child develops and grows in his or her cognitive ability to understand the complexity of life and death. That makes grief a recurring theme in children's development. In each new developmental stage, the meaning of the death must be explored once again. For six-year-old Sarah, the death of her older sister will bring her first clear understanding that everything that lives must die. It means becoming an only child, supporting grieving parents, experiencing loneliness, and perhaps regressing to find comfort in the ways she did when she was a toddler. She will probably want to be rocked like a baby, sleep with her parents for a while, and be afraid to be alone.

When Sarah is eight or nine she may become fascinated with the physical details of death and explore these with "morbid curiosity," as do most children of this age. But when Sarah is twelve, the meaning of Catherine's death will shift again. Reaching the age that Catherine was when she died will increase Sarah's anxiety and thoughts about death. By twelve, she will understand that death is universal and irreversible, and Sarah will realize that she could die young, too. And she may feel a strange mixture of guilt and relief when she survives her twelfth year and turns thirteen.

When Sarah is old enough to date and think about romance, she will miss her sister in new ways. On her wedding day, Sarah may find herself surprisingly grief-stricken again and long for her sister as her bridesmaid. Thus, the meaning of death and the ability to explore these meanings continues to change for a child, adolescent, and adult with each developmental stage. Parents are often mystified and upset by this recurrence of grief, which can be very painful for them. They may discourage their child from bringing up such a difficult subject again after so many years have passed. Parents need to know that this is natural and necessary for the child's growth and well-being. Looking at photos, writing a letter to the missing one, and telling of the changes in one's life since the death can revisit the grief. Asking for help or advice from a dead loved one can be reassuring, even if one only hears one's own voice and inner wisdom answering.

A child needs to feel safe in order to experience the difficult feelings of grief. If a child suffers other losses as a result of a death, such as a sudden move, foster care, impoverishment, or parental depression, that child will not feel safe enough to grieve. Children can swallow, ignore, suppress, or inappropriately act out feelings of grief, which may leave them frozen at this task and unable to develop in a healthy way.

A sixteen-year-old girl whose mother had died, leaving her in charge of a chaotic and destitute family, said this to me: "In order for me to be able to grieve, I've got to be willing to fall down a deep, dark, bottomless well, and I don't know if I could ever get out again. There's no way I'm going to let myself do that. It's not safe. Who's gonna take care of the family if I can't get out of the well?" She was so right! Grief support for her meant first finding a place where she could shower everyday, clean clothes, money for food and school supplies, and help for her brother. One day she told me, "I'm ready to go down that dark well now. But I don't want you going with me. I need to know you're standing at the top of the well, holding tight to the rope that we're going to tie around me, so I can come back up when I'm ready." She had great wisdom to recognize when she was safe enough to grieve, and when she wasn't.

Children are very sensitive to subtle taboos in a family. They know when it is not acceptable to speak of the dying, death, or grief. Adults may not intend to give this message to their children, but parents' tears can be so alarming that kids will avoid the painful subject. They need to be told clearly that it is all right to talk about the missing one and their changing feelings about the death and to ask questions as they grow and can understand more. Children need to know that their feelings of grief are acceptable.

In a culture that seems to only take time to honor and grieve the deaths of astronauts, presidents, and princesses, children can get the idea that their losses are not important. As one outraged ten-year-old boy said to me, "I've done more for Christa McAuliffe than I have for my own dad who died! I've written her family a letter, raised money for her monument, planted flowers at the statue, drew a picture and wrote an essay! But who's more important—a dead astronaut or my father?" His words rang true and his anger was justified. Adults in a child's school, neighborhood, and spiritual community need to create a culture that values every child's loss and grief.

Healing seems to require a transformation of the raw feelings of grief into something else—something that is easier to live with, that shows us that it is possible to find gifts in the death of our loved one. These are creative transformations that change grieving children and adults from wounded creatures to wise and compassionate people. Some of our best music, poetry, paintings, and monuments have sprung from this deep well of grief, to soar in our hearts and endure through the years, giving us the courage to survive and help others. Children need opportunities to transform their grief through creative endeavors and discover new strengths and abilities in themselves.

The conditions that are necessary for children to do the tasks of grieving and thus heal as they grow can be summarized in these questions:

What does this death mean to me now? What has been lost?

What will happen to me? Am I safe enough to grieve?

Can I talk about it? Are my feelings acceptable?

Is my loss important in this world? How can I know?

How can I change these feelings into healing?

Using the creative arts to explore these questions can provide developmentally appropriate activities that change in medium and complexity as children grow. Paper, clay, music, dance, and craft projects of all kinds provide a safe haven of creative expression. If the feelings are too difficult to put into words, the medium can serve as a safe witness to the pain of grief, a record of the relationship and of the moment in time. Creating such a witness allows the feelings to change and seems to release the grieving child to grow and to go on with life. Creative expression can manifest deep pain that might otherwise remain hidden, and provides recognition of what has been lost and insight into positive changes that may occur.

Creative Survival Strategies for Children and Adults

When I meet a grieving family for the first time, I offer them a colorful variety of small pieces of clay arranged neatly on a plate. It's easier to talk when you have something in your hands. Everyone seems to agree and enjoys playing with the clay. As I listen to the story of their loss, I ask a lot of questions about the details. Somehow it is reassuring to be able to answer concrete questions when there is so much about death that we can't answer. I also show them how to make worry beads and explain that in many cultures around the world people carry beads or stones in their pockets, to rub during times of stress. Sometimes prayers are said silently as the beads are rubbed, like the Catholic rosary or Islamic prayer beads. We usually end up making enough beads or rubbing stones for everyone in the family. We bake them in the oven, and string them on dental floss during that first session. I leave knowing these suffering people literally have something to hang onto—something of their own creation that is beautiful and soothing to hold. Children excel at this creativity and gain confidence and trust. Adults as well learn through their bodies that something good can come from all this pain.

The second visit with children is often spent decorating wooden or cardboard boxes and making them into Memory Treasure Boxes. Pasting fabric, sequins, jewels, and adding fabric paints to spell out words transforms recycled containers into beautiful boxes filled with objects that represent memories of the missing loved one. Each one is different, just as each family member's grief is unique, and the project presents a good opportunity to talk about sibling rivalry in grief. There is something magical about a treasure box. They can be used to contain our pain, to gather up the odd pieces and keep it safe in one place. They help us to literally "put a lid on it" when we don't want to be distracted by grief.

A third visit to a grieving family often coincides with a birthday or holiday, which intensifies the grief. Then we concentrate on exactly who this person was by making a Name Poem with drawings. You write the name of the dead or dying loved one down the side of a piece of paper, vertically. After each letter, you write a word or phrase that describes the person. Twelve-year-old David described his mother, Harriet, like this:

> **H**aving good hope made her last much much longer,
> **A**nd
> **R**eally believing made
> **R**eligious faith stronger.
> **I** wish she'd be here, but
> Th**E**n again, I realize she's happier
> **T**here, with no cancer, which I despise.

He added a drawing of her grave to the bottom of the poem, which he had recently visited and found to be peaceful and reassuring.

Sometimes a fourth session is all I get with a grief group in a school or with a family. At this time we usually explore any regrets the adults and children might have about the death or dead person. We talk while decorating candles with bits of soft colored wax. Then we light the candles in memory of the missing one. In the soft candlelight, each person privately writes down whatever he wants to let go of, while listening to quiet Native American flute music. Then we go outside and burn the papers in a cauldron or iron pot. As we stand in a circle around the flames, sometimes we sing or simply hold onto each other and sway.

Purging by fire is an ancient tradition in many cultures. Cleansing our souls by writing and giving up regrets by burning them in this simple ceremony is like unloading our emotional backpacks that are so heavy with unresolved losses. When the ashes cool it is important to put them into a garden to fertilize something that is living to complete the metaphor. As my Tibetan friends say, "All is manure." Children appreciate learning that even the most terrible feelings can be transformed into something that gives heat, light, and helps the flowers grow.

Other techniques can include using paper and markers or crayons to draw out a favorite memory of the person who has died. Preserving memories in this way helps to heal the panic that children sometimes feel when they fear they will forget or lose the images of their loved one. The ability to draw is located in the same area of the brain where memories are stored, which makes it an excellent medium to use for exploring the past.

With adolescents, I often use the Native American concept of grieving as a "soul-retrieval journey." I invite the adolescent to draw a map of his or her life, beginning in the present moment and going back in time, drawing all of the places in which an unresolved loss was experienced. Many Native Americans believe that you lose a piece of yourself with each unresolved loss, and that you must retrace your steps and "retrieve a piece of your soul" at each place of pain. This map drawing allows the youth to recognize all of the losses that are part of the current grief, and anything that needs to be done to heal each. Relief usually accompanies this recognition, as well as the hope that pain can be healed and the excitement that comes with seeing life as a "soul journey."

As wonderful and healing as creative strategies for grieving can be, none of them will take away grief. Nor should they. Sometimes the pain is all we have left of someone we love. Taking that away would rob us of something precious, if painful. The purpose of using creative arts with grieving children is to provide them with a means of expressing their grief. Using their senses and bodies to manipulate a medium while focusing on death builds a tolerance for the intense and difficult feelings. Creativity transforms acute grief into bittersweet sorrow, which is easier to live with and will always have a special place in our hearts. As I write this, the charcoal portrait I drew of my brother, David, smiles down on me. I drew it three years after his death and cried bitterly, uncontrollably, with every stroke. Miraculously, it didn't smudge and it looks just like him. It even feels like him. And now, twenty years later, it gives me great pleasure to be with him in this way, and I thank him for his inspiration as I shed just a few tears.

Virginia Lynn Fry, MA, is an artist, counselor, author, and educator who has worked in hospice care for twenty years. She is the Director of the Hospice Council of Vermont, Bereavement Coordinator for Central Vermont Home Health & Hospice, and adjunct faculty member of the University of Vermont, Johnson State College, and Community College of Vermont.

9

Play Therapy To Help Bereaved Children

Nancy Boyd Webb

Death is a difficult concept to grasp. Upon hearing news of a death, adults often respond by saying, "I just can't believe it." Later, when the actuality of the death sinks in, the adults may move from disbelief to a state of temporary paralysis in which they find themselves unable to carry on their usual activities or to express their sorrow in words. If adults find death so daunting, it is not surprising that children have even greater difficulty comprehending and coping with the reality and the emotional impact related to the end of a life. How can we possibly expect bereaved children to be able to express their feelings verbally when they usually have had little or no previous experience with death, and they simply do not have the vocabulary to describe their complex emotions?

The literature on children's bereavement increasingly recognizes that children's bereavement differs from that of adults. Children's grief responses depend strongly on age and developmental level, which, in turn, affect their ability to comprehend irreversibility and other characteristics associated with death. Experts agree that a child's understanding of death develops gradually, and studies indicate that most children by the ages of seven to nine have achieved partial or complete mature understanding (Speece and Brent, 1996). For example, a preschooler who was told that her father had died and gone to heaven expected him to return "when he is finished being dead." Her nine-year-old brother, whose understanding was more mature, became irritated and angry with his little sister's repeated statements that "Daddy's coming back soon." Because the older child understood that dead people don't come back, he was pained by his sister's frequent references to their father's return, which only served to remind him of his loss. Both of these children benefited from individual play therapy sessions that permitted each of them to express their grief through the symbolic displacement of play. The boy drew pictures of volcanoes erupting, and the girl played with a doll house and female dolls, having them announce, "We can't find the daddy" (Webb, 2000).

What Is Play Therapy and How Does It Help?
Definition of play therapy

Play therapy is a helping interaction between a trained adult and a child that seeks to relieve the child's emotional distress through the symbolic communication of play. The assumption upon which play therapy rests is that the child expresses and works through emotional conflicts within the metaphor of play, providing that the child knows the reason for coming to therapy and the role of the therapist (Webb, 1999).

Children express and process their varied feelings of grief through the outlet of play, even when they cannot discuss their internal world. Children typically "play out" their feelings, rather than talking about them. Play therapy is therefore the method of choice for helping bereaved children express their feelings, since it does not depend on words. Grief counselors and other adults who understand the symbolic nature of children's play communications are better equipped to respond appropriately to bereaved children, using children's "language of play."

Orienting the child to the play therapy process

Ideally, the therapist tells the child in the first session that he or she is someone who helps children and families with their troubles and worries and then (in bereavement situations) further acknowledges that somebody special has died and that this may cause some troubles and worries. Another important component of orienting the child to the play therapy process is to say to the child that "sometimes we talk, and sometimes we play." This implicitly gives the child the choice and the control about how to convey his troubles and worries.

Play therapy is different from "just playing," due to the therapist's ability to communicate with the child through the play process. An example that illustrates the difference between "just playing" a game and playing "therapeutically" involved an eight-year-old girl who repeatedly played the board game "Operation" during the terminal phase of her mother's progressive decline from cancer. The play therapist understood that the child was attempting, through this game, to gain some comprehension and sense of mastery related to her mother's medical condition and repeated surgeries. As she played the game with the girl the therapist helped validate the child's feelings through comments such as: "Oh! this poor man; he's had to have so many operations, and he doesn't seem to be getting any better; the doctors keep trying to help him, but he's just getting weaker and weaker! This is so upsetting and sad; it's not fair! It's so hard on his family!" Obviously, the therapist was addressing the child's own experience, but she did not say to the child, "This is like what happened to your mother." Such a statement might make the child very upset and anxious, and she might not want to continue playing. It is important to stay within the metaphor of play.

How Play Therapy Helps

Children in play therapy use dolls, drawings, games, and other toys as shields that protect them from admitting that frightening things have happened and may still be happening to them. An implicit assumption of play therapy is that "an entire treatment through play may be engineered without stepping far beyond the metaphor of the 'game'" (Terr, 1989, 14). While it is true that some children will themselves make the connecting leap between the play scenario and their own lives, this initiative should come from the child, not the therapist. In most instances the child prefers to maintain a comfort zone of distance between the play content and her own circumstances, and the therapist should respect this need. The play "disguise" permits the child to express anger, jealousy, and fear through the mouths of the puppets or dolls, instead of requiring admission that these feelings belong to the child's own experience.

Sometimes children can talk about the deceased person and their feelings directly, and in these instances the therapist listens supportively. Other times children may initially express their feelings, but then they become uncomfortable and "retreat" into the world of play. When children are able to talk, the play therapist encourages this, but also accepts their need to gain sporadic relief through the less emotionally demanding outlet of play. In my first session with children, as previously recommended, I state clearly that "sometimes we talk, and sometimes we play," giving them permission to move within the two modalities.

In summary, the rationale for use of play therapy with bereaved children is based on the following factors:

1. Children have limited verbal ability for describing their feelings.

2. Children have limited emotional capacity to tolerate stress and the pain of loss (they have a short sadness span).

3. Children communicate their feelings, wishes, fears, and attempted resolutions to their problems through play.

The goals of play therapy with bereaved children

The goals of play therapy with bereaved children involve: 1) helping to facilitate the child's mourning process, and 2) helping to clarify any cognitive confusion the child may have about the death.

Do All Bereaved Children Need Therapy?

Many bereaved children go through their grief process without the assistance of mental health professionals. Others benefit from the compassionate counseling of teachers, religious leaders, nurses, and scout leaders who may or may not have had training in grief counseling. Because of the growing public awareness regarding the impact of traumatic and violent death on children, referrals to specialists are becoming more common following such deaths. But how can a parent, teacher, or other layperson determine the need to refer a bereaved child in less obvious circumstances?

There are many interacting factors that affect the reactions of a particular child to a specific death situation. An earlier publication (Webb, 1993, 30-41) presented a chart and some accompanying forms to assist in weighing the influence of various conditions on an individual child. The Tripartite Assessment of the Bereaved Child outlines three groups of factors that interact and influence a child's response:

1. Factors pertaining to the child's personal background and experience

2. Factors related to the particulars of the death and the nature of the child's involvement

3. Characteristics of the family/culture and community and
the nature of their response to the child

The numerous items contained in each of these three broad categories will not be repeated here. Instead, specific circumstances are identified that often create concerns because of the nature of the death or the child's particular bereavement response.

Referral of the child

Referral of the child for an assessment and possible play therapy treatment should be considered when:

- A family member commits suicide
- The child develops severe nightmares or sleep disorders
- The child develops difficulty with her schoolwork
- The child develops various psychosomatic complaints
- The child's eating patterns become altered
- The child's behavior becomes regressed.

Some of these behaviors can occur in "normal" bereavement, but when several occur together, or when their intensity interferes with the child's usual activities, it is appropriate to seek the opinion of a specialist who is familiar with normal and disabling bereavement in children. Rando (1988/1991) points out that when there is a question, it is better to err on the side of obtaining a professional opinion.

Therefore the answer to the question about whether all bereaved children need therapy is no, but evaluation for therapy definitely should be considered in certain circumstances. I use the term *disabling grief* (Webb, 1993) to refer to grief responses that justify the need for therapy. These include those already listed and, in addition, situations in which the child remains "in shock" after most grievers have resumed their usual activities, and when the child shows drastically different interpersonal reactions with family and peers than prior to the death. There is no one protocol that describes "normal" grief. Professional judgment must be used to evaluate the degree and extent to which a child's reactions are interfering with his usual activities. It is not the behavior in itself that raises the red flag, but the combination of behaviors and circumstances and the "degree of intrusiveness into the child's life created by the grieving that must be evaluated" (Webb, 1993, 21). The following section presents case examples that illustrate children's different bereavement responses and the role of play therapy in assisting the child's grief resolution.

Example Of "Normal" Bereavement: Todd, Age Nine

This is an example (Webb, 1993) of a boy whose grief reactions could be considered within the "normal" range following the progressive illness and death of his 79-year-old grandmother from cancer. This boy was already engaged in play therapy related to his Attention Deficit Disorder at the time his grandmother's medical condition worsened and she became terminal. This illustrates a frequent occurrence in child therapy—the incidence of a death during the process of the child's treatment for other problems. In this case, the focus of the original referral was on the reaction of the family to the grandmother's impending death, and there had been some work with the parents on family stresses and their typical responses. However, several months later, at the point of Grammy's actual decline and subsequent death, the work with Todd had shifted from family issues to the boy's academic and social problems. The case illustrates bereavement counseling with the parents to prepare the children prior to an anticipated death, and later play therapy with a boy and his father following the grandmother's death.

Anticipatory bereavement counseling

The circumstances of the case permitted me in my role as a child and family therapist to advise the parents to prepare the children gradually for their grandmother's future death. In a separate session with the parents, I advised them to begin to comment to Todd and his two sisters, ages five and 11, that despite all the doctors' best efforts Grammy was not getting better. I suggested that the parents further tell the children that Grammy might not continue to be able to speak to them because she was getting sicker and sicker and therefore they should tell her whatever they wanted to now, while she could still hear them.

The parents prepared their children accordingly, and Todd rode his bike over to his grandparents' house and had a quiet time with his bedridden grandmother. He told his mother that he whispered in Grammy's ear that he loved her, and that he knew she heard him because she nodded her head and smiled.

Ten days later Grammy died, and Todd was distraught. He screamed and cried and only the rabbi could comfort him. After the rabbi's intervention, Todd told his parents that he wanted to go to his friend's house for a sleepover, as previously planned for that evening. Furthermore, he wanted to go with his class on a planned trip to see "The Nutcracker" two days later, which was the day of the funeral. The parents agreed to Todd's requests, fearing that he would become uncontrollable if they did not. Consequently, the boy did not attend his grandmother's funeral or burial.

Family session following the death

Within a week after the death, I had a family session in which I suggested that the parents bring family photographs as a basis for talking about their memories of Grammy. This was a productive session, which graphically pointed out the sibling rivalry between Todd and his older sister (which interestingly paralleled the relationship between Todd's father and his older sister).

Play therapy session

Several weeks after the family session, in a play therapy session with Todd and his father, we played Gardner's (1988) Storytelling Card Game. Todd selected the one background card that portrayed a cemetery scene. He could have chosen one of three other cards that depicted neighborhood and home settings. The game requires the player to put family figures into the background setting and then make up a story about what is happening. Todd's story clearly reflected his understanding of what had occurred at his grandmother's burial, even though he hadn't been there. "Somebody has just died, and the family is here to throw dirt on the casket. The rabbi says prayers. The family all say things about the person. They feel very sad, and some of them are crying." At the end of his story, when I asked Todd, "What happens next?" he said, "They go home, because they are still a family."

This story, created within the context of play therapy, clearly conveyed Todd's understanding about the details of his grandmother's burial, and also about his conviction that his family would survive, despite their loss. The stimulus and structure of the board game enabled Todd to express his convictions in a manner he probably could not have conveyed in response to a question about what happened at the burial. It was especially reassuring to Todd's father, who was present in this session, to hear his son's story.

In summary, I believe this case describes a situation of "normal" grief, in which this child could have managed without mental health assistance. At the time of the death I was working with Todd on issues related to school, friends, and his relationship with his older sister.

With regard to this boy's bereavement response, the counseling by the rabbi on the evening of the grandmother's death seemed sufficient to have relieved Todd and freed him to want to carry out his previous plans. This is an example of a child's *short sadness span*; Todd cried and had a tantrum when he learned about his grandmother's death, but he quickly moved beyond this. My previous efforts in encouraging the parents to prepare the children for the predictable death may have also contributed to helping this boy anticipate the future likelihood of the death and to say his "good-bye" accordingly.

Example of "Complicated Grief": The Martini Sisters, Ages Eight and Ten

This case (Webb, 1993) depicts the increased complexity of grief resolution when two or more loss situations occur at the same time. Different authors have used the term *complicated bereavement* to refer to difficulties in expressing grief due to one or more of the following situations:

- The nature of the death (sudden, traumatic, stigmatized)
- Multiple losses
- Ambivalent relationship with the deceased
- Confusing or ambiguous responses of other mourners
- Distorted, compromised, or absent mourning process (adapted from Goldman, 1996 and Rando, 1993).

In the case of the Martini sisters, ages eight and ten, their parents were initiating a divorce at the same time ten-year-old Linda's godfather was hospitalized with pancreatic cancer. Because of the close relationship between the two families, and the motivation of the Martini family to provide maximum support to the family of the dying man, the plans for the marital separation became temporarily delayed. Everyone rallied together to make hospital visits, to provide babysitting for the godfather's children, and to offer moral support to his wife. Whereas the original referral from the mother had requested counseling and therapy for the girls because of the impending separation and divorce, it immediately became apparent that because the condition of the godfather was terminal, the girls would be losing two important male figures in their life.

Initially, my plan was to have joint biweekly sibling sessions with the girls and to provide counseling to the parents in alternate sessions. The focus was to provide support to the girls at a time of disequilibrium and crisis in their lives, to prepare the girls for their godfather's death, and to assist with the bereavement associated with both losses.

It soon became clear that the girls were embroiled in a hostile, intense relationship that made sibling sessions nonproductive. The anger they were both feeling connected to their anticipated losses was directed at one another, since the circumstances prevented direct expression towards either their father or their godfather. Both men would be abandoning them in separate ways—their father would be leaving home, and their godfather would be dying. We know that anger is an expected component of grief following both divorce and death. Raphael (1993) has stated that responses to divorce resemble those of bereavement, but in divorce, "the bereaved must mourn someone who has not died" (p.228). At one point in my office when the girls acknowledged the fact that they fought a lot, both verbally and physically, Linda said, "I guess we should get a divorce!" I acknowledged that they each had a right to feel very upset and angry about all the very serious changes in their lives, over which they had no control. I commented that they needed to find ways to release their anger without hurting anyone or getting into trouble. I also mentioned that playing can sometimes help. These statements made a direct connection to their own lives, without condoning or encouraging the expression of anger towards people.

Play therapy sessions

In individual play therapy sessions, each girl benefited from the opportunity to express some of her anger symbolically, through expressive art. Although these girls were old enough and able to express themselves verbally, their verbal and physical expressions toward one another were excessive and unjustified, and resulted in their receiving disapproval and restrictions from their parents. They needed an outlet where they could vent their anger safely in play, where they could receive therapeutic understanding about the validity of their feelings, and where they would not suffer penalties for the appropriate expression of their anger. At the time of the sessions reported below, the godfather had died, and the girls' father had moved out of the home (while maintaining regular visitation with them).

Amanda, age eight

Amanda's preferred play therapy modality was clay. I had offered it to her knowing that it is a productive method for discharging anger. The clay can be shaped, pounded, poked, and destroyed, thereby providing a very useful outlet for angry feelings. Amanda's clay productions began cautiously as creations of jars or animals. Her anger came out in the manner in which she worked the clay, rolling, poking, and ripping it according to her mood. Whereas the final object might be a vase, the child's physical involvement with the clay during its creation permitted considerable expression of aggression, including destruction of a previous construction. Amanda could not verbally stand up to her sister, two years older. Yet through the "clay therapy" she expressed feelings of frustration and anger that seemed related to her lack of control about important aspects of her life. Several years after the termination of treatment Amanda accepted my invitation to appear for a follow-up session, to be videotaped for training purposes (Webb, 1994). The video demonstrated different play therapy techniques, with a number of children of different ages. Amanda's participation included a segment with her working with clay, and talking about her previous conflicted relationship with her sister.

Linda, age ten

Linda was very aggressive, and her anger caused many problems in her family. In play therapy, Linda employed drawings to convey her awareness and fear of her anger, and to demonstrate her need for help in controlling her aggression.

In most sessions I have drawing materials readily available on a table, and I invite children to draw as we talk (although when they begin drawing, I try to keep quiet). Linda was very interested in drawing. Her drawings depicted mostly threatening themes, for example, two sharks swimming toward one another with their sharp teeth bared, and a teddy bear with claws on all his paws and his tongue stuck out. The culmination of these drawings was a fearsome werewolf with sharp, threatening teeth, which Linda had drawn on a paper plate during the twenty-minute wait for her sister (she had already had her session with me). Linda presented me with this werewolf drawing at the conclusion of my session with her sister (Webb, 1993, 111). I commented about how scary and dangerous it looked, and how I hoped it wouldn't hurt anybody. She said it might kill somebody. Linda agreed to my suggestion that I keep the drawing in my office, where it couldn't hurt anybody. Symbolically, I conveyed to her that it is all right for her to express her anger in my office, but that it can get dangerously out of control outside.

In summary, this case illustrates children's use of drawings and modeling material to help them express their anger related to their mourning of the dual losses of their godfather and their father. Over the course of several months of individual play therapy sessions with the girls, their expressions of anger towards one another greatly diminished, and they were gradually able to re-focus their lives on school and recreational activities. They had participated appropriately and meaningfully in their godfather's memorial service, and their lives had settled into a regular routine, with ongoing contacts with the father through visits and telephone calls. While they did "lose" the family of their childhoods, they were beginning to realize that their lives were calmer now that they no longer had to listen to their parents arguing. Play therapy had been effective in providing an acceptable means to control their anger.

Play Therapy with Dramatically Bereaved Children

"Although virtually any death may be perceived by the mourner as personally traumatic because of the internal, subjective feeling involved… circumstances that are objectively traumatic are associated with five factors known to increase complications for mourners" (Rando, 1993, 568-569):

- Suddenness and lack of anticipation
- Violence, mutilation, and destruction
- Preventability and/or randomness
- Multiple deaths
- Personal encounter of the mourner (i.e., personal threat or shocking confrontation).

Of all types of bereavement, traumatic death requires the most specialized management and presents the greatest challenge to the therapist. Because of the interaction between trauma and grief, this type of therapy should be undertaken only by professionals who understand trauma reactions and who have been trained to help individuals to recover following traumatic bereavement.

As a rule, it is imperative to help the child with issues related to the trauma before attempting to assist with the mourning process. Because an integral part of bereavement involves remembering the person who died, this process can be terribly painful when the death was traumatic. Every time the child thinks about the beloved person she also imagines the circumstances of death, and the associated details of fear, pain, or violence/mutilation. These mental images frighten the child and lead her to want to avoid all memories of the dead person. The symptoms of Posttraumatic Stress Disorder include numbing of responses, hyperarousal, avoidance, and altered functioning (American Psychiatric Association, 1994).

Play therapy

A nine-year-old girl (Webb, 1993) whose friend had suffered fatal, mutilating head injuries in a car accident, refused to visit the boy's home and became panic-stricken whenever her mother drove even close to his neighborhood. She was having nightmares, had become withdrawn and irritable, and her school work had deteriorated. The treatment of this child, which predated much of our current knowledge of posttraumatic therapy, included the use of drawings, stories, and board games. Many of her symptoms did abate, but she continued to avoid discussion of her friend, and although she signed a release permitting me to write about her therapy she said that she did not want to read what I wrote. If this child were beginning therapy today, I would direct the child to draw the trauma scene, as she imagined it, and a picture of her friend before and after his death. The principle is that until the traumatized child (or adult) has dealt with the details of the traumatic event, he cannot effectively cope with the tasks of mourning.

An important procedure in play therapy with traumatized children includes the use of some behavioral-cognitive techniques prior to initiating the recall of the traumatic event. The therapist actually teaches the child ways to calm his anxiety and soothe himself, explaining that this will help both now and in the future. Some examples of self-soothing behaviors are singing, engaging in physical activity, and thinking of a quiet, special place that is safe and secret.

As the play reconstruction of the event begins, under the therapist's direction, the child can choose to depart from distressing memories, and "change the channel" to more relaxing, happy thoughts. The therapist moves at the child's pace, encouraging the child to reveal all fears and sensory memories. The ultimate therapeutic aim is for the child to put these frightening memories in the past, and to identify himself as a "survivor." Bevin (1999) presents a good example of play therapy reconstruction with a traumatized nine-year-old boy who almost drowned and then witnessed his mother's rape.

Preventing the vicarious traumatization of the therapist

Working with traumatized individuals is very stressful to the therapist, who may actually suffer the secondary traumatization associated with listening to graphic details of violent deaths. In recent years there has been increased attention to "self-help" techniques for therapists to prevent "compassion fatigue" and burn-out (Ryan, 1999; Pearlman and Saakvitne, 1995). Some suggestions for therapists include having a support group for themselves, arranging a varied caseload that is not excessively weighted with traumatic victims, and employing many of the same self-soothing activities that would be recommended for clients. Therapists also benefit from play/recreation to help them maintain an emotional balance that will ultimately help their clients.

Conclusion

Both the public and professional community may not realize the extent to which death affects children in ways that can interfere with their current and future development. Children do suffer pain after the loss of a loved one, although they may not be able to put their feelings into words. Play therapy offers the ideal method for helping bereaved children since it does not require that they express themselves verbally.

This chapter has been written with the hope that it will sensitize and educate teachers, parents, religious counselors, and others who have contact with children about the tremendous relief that is available through play therapy. The child communicates through play, and play therapists understand how to respond helpfully, using the child's play language. Although all bereaved children may not require this specialized assistance, in situations of complicated and traumatic bereavement, play therapists can provide for the assessment and treatment of the child in a manner that provides the best hope for grief processing and resolution. We must be certain that children receive the help they need to cope with their losses and proceed with their development.

Nancy Boyd Webb, DSW, BCD, RPT-S, is Distinguished Professor of Social Work at Fordham University in New York, where she directs the PostMaster's Certificate Program in Child and Adolescent Therapy. In addition to full-time teaching, Dr. Webb is an author, clinical practitioner, consultant, staff trainer, and conference presenter.

10

Using Ritual with Children and Adolescents

Kenneth J. Doka

Corrine was five years old when her father died. She wanted to go to the funeral, but her family did not allow her. They thought it would upset her.

Paul's parents go to the cemetery a few times a year to visit their daughter's grave. Though Paul and his sister were close, they never invite him to accompany them. "Why trouble him now?" they reason.

When Kenny died, the school considered having a memorial service. Many parents objected. They did not want to remind their children of the loss.

We not only protect children from death, but we also protect them from rituals about death. Such attempts are well intentioned. They seek to avoid upsetting the child or reminding them of the loss.

Yet, from time immemorial, rituals have provided a sense of comfort and support. To deprive children and adolescents of the power that rituals offer inhibits their coping adaptation to loss. Not only do they miss the benefit of the immediate ritual, they fail to learn an effective response that may assist them as they cope with future losses.

This chapter explores the role of ritual as a therapeutic tool for assisting grieving children and adolescents. It begins by defining ritual and describing the reasons why rituals can be helpful. The chapter considers, as well, the role of funeral rituals, suggesting ways that children and adolescents can make meaningful decisions on how they wish to participate, as well as how their participation can enhance the value of the ritual for themselves and other mourners. Finally, rituals beyond the funeral, such as anniversary or holiday memorials or private acts, can be helpful to children and adolescents as they continue to struggle with the loss. Some of these may be family events, others simply private therapeutic acts. But these, too, need to be acknowledged and reviewed as well as ritual as a tool for counselors, families, and support groups.

What Is Ritual?

The term 'ritual' is used in a number of ways. One may say that an early morning walk is a daily ritual. However, the term is best reserved for those special activities that extend meaning to a set of actions. These can be public events, such as funerals where a community comes together to mark a passage from life to death, but they can be private actions as well. For example, toasting a deceased aunt during a holiday dinner invests that drink with a special meaning. It is no longer a simple drink. It is now a memorial. That, then, is what makes an act a ritual—it invests even those most common and everyday events with special, perhaps even sacred, meanings.

Why Are Rituals so Powerful?

Rituals are powerful, Gennep (1960) asserts, because they are liminal. To Gennep, liminal means that rituals lie on the threshold of consciousness, appealing to both our conscious and subconscious. Rando (1984) delineates other valuable aspects of rituals. Among them are that rituals contain events; that is, ritual allows a structure for events such as death or other rites marking a passage. A funeral offers a structured time where individuals can emotionally and physically ventilate. In the chaotic time of a loss, a funeral provides a sense of control, allowing individuals to do something in an otherwise uncontrollable situation. Rituals, too, Rando reminds, generate social support and offer opportunities to find meaning, as spiritual and philosophical understandings are applied to the loss. In summary, ritual provides a meaningful, structured activity that allows individuals space, time and support to recognize, respond to, and absorb a significant change.

These benefits are experienced not only by adults but also by children and adolescents who are able to participate in a meaningful way. In many ways, rituals can be especially powerful for children and adolescents since they give opportunities to confront loss in nonverbal and defined ways. Moreover, participation offers children and adolescents an effective introduction to the value of ritual.

Should Children and Adolescents Go to Funerals?

Funerals are powerful rituals that help us confront loss. They are also meaningful family, religious, and cultural events. Funeral rituals bring families together, offering each other support, and they show the ways that our own cultural backgrounds and religious faiths help us address the crisis of loss.

Since funerals are so critical, once children are developmentally able to understand a funeral and sit through a ceremony, they ought to have a choice about the ways in which they wish to participate in a funeral. In order to make that choice meaningful, children need information, options, and support.

In preparing a child to make a decision on whether or not to attend a funeral, begin by explaining what the funeral is and what is likely to occur. Describe its purpose, the physical setting, the ways in which people are expected to behave, and the range of reactions that the child may observe. Tell the child that people may sob or cry because they miss the person. They may even laugh as they remember funny or happy stories about the person who died. Assure the child that any decision that the child makes is appropriate and will be understood. Patiently answer any questions. Most funeral homes will show the child the facility prior to the funeral.

If the child is really going to decide, he or she will need a viable alternative. If a younger child's only alternative is to stay home in an empty house, it won't be much of a choice. If possible, arrange for the child to stay with a sympathetic and trusted adult.

Remember, too, that funerals are, in many cultures, multifaceted events. For example, many American funerals have a visitation period, a funeral service, an interment at a cemetery, and perhaps a post-funeral meal. One of the options for children and adolescents is to decide which events they would find most meaningful to attend.

Children and adolescents also need support. When parents are directly involved in the funeral they might not be able to provide that support. For example, when John's father died, he was both too busy at the funeral and still in too great a state of shock to look after his own children's emotional needs. It is helpful to have a supportive adult not intimately involved in the funeral who is assigned to be attentive to the child, perhaps even taking the child away if the child needs respite. With older children and adolescents it is also important to allow and encourage peer support.

Funeral rituals are most effective when they are personal and participatory. Here, too, children and adolescents can contribute. Their ideas may be solicited on how the ritual is planned and conducted. To this day, Daryl takes great comfort in the fact that his mother allowed him to select his Dad's casket even though he was only twelve at the time. "It made me feel special. I felt I was doing one last thing for him."

They can participate, too. One of the most meaningful funeral rituals I ever attended was for an adolescent killed in a bicycling accident. Her friends participated fully in the service—singing, reading, and ushering. Not only did that participation help them say good-bye to a friend, it reminded her parents of how much their daughter's friends cared.

Even young children can participate. A woman once shared that one of the special memories of her husband's funeral was watching her somber four-year-old great-grandson hand out flowers at the graveside.

Participation does not have to be public. Adolescents and children can be invited to write letters, draw pictures, or offer objects that can be placed in the casket. They can help in selecting photographs to be displayed at the funeral. They can contribute a videotaped tribute. All these actions, whether private or public, make them participants rather than observers. And all serve to make the ritual meaningful.

Developing Rituals as a Therapeutic Tool

Since rituals are therapeutic, they can be developed and used throughout the grieving process. Sometimes children and adolescents may have the opportunity to plan and to participate in public rituals that mark points in the grieving process. For example, Judaism recognizes many of these points—a month, the one-year anniversary. In Catholicism, individuals may mark anniversaries with a mass. Other spiritual traditions have similar rituals. These rituals are valued since they reinforce the memories and validate grief normally experienced at these times. Again, such benefits are not limited to adults alone.

In addition to ongoing public rituals, both families and caregivers can develop and utilize other rituals to assist grieving children and adolescents. Such rituals can have many roles. Drawing from the work of Gennep (1960), Rando (1993), and Martin and Doka (1999), we can delineate four distinct types of rituals. It is critical in designing rituals to be clear about the message the ritual conveys.

Rituals of continuity emphasize the continuing bond with the deceased. For example, after Sari's grandmother died, Sari and her mother designed a quilt representing their memories of her. While the exercise itself was therapeutic, they show the quilt at times such as birthdays and holidays as a representation of Sari's grandmother's continued presence in their lives. Similarly, every Christmas when Kevin decorates his tree, he somberly places a decoration that is a memorial to his father. Kevin and his mother place another similar decoration on a "Tree of Life" organized by a local hospice and funeral home.

Rituals of transition offer a different message. Here the goal of the ritual is to mark a passage from one phase to another. A funeral is such a ritual. But other rituals may be developed as well. When Joey's parents divorced, he found it helpful to remove a plaque he had given to his father. The plaque, made in technology class, read "Daddy's Garage." In removing it he commented to his mother, "It is no longer Daddy's garage." The action was his way of acknowledging that his father would not be returning. Many support groups use rituals of transition to mark their closing session. A common ritual is to give each child a bag of stones, some polished, others rough. The polished stones represent the progress made in the group, while the rough stones represent grief issues still to be addressed. During the ritual, participants name their stones, marking accomplishments and issues still to be reviewed.

Rituals of reconciliation are designed to finish business. They allow individuals to accept or to extend forgiveness to complete a necessary act. Tanya had highly ambivalent feelings toward her mom, an IV drug user who eventually died of complications related to AIDS. When asked where her mother was, the nine-year-old girl said she was a ghost. Queried, Tanya said that if you were good you became an angel. If you were bad, you went to hell and burned to a skeleton. In between you become a ghost. As she worked through her ambivalence, she announced that her mother could now become an angel. We developed a ritual whereby she gave her mother angel wings. Other rituals of reconciliation can be as simple as writing a note to the deceased.

Rituals of affirmation complement rituals of reconciliation. Instead of repairing or completing a relationship, rituals of affirmation simply offer thanks for a relationship, affirming the individual who died. Though her husband died a decade ago, every year on her son's birthday, Magna lights a candle in his memory, thanking him for the gift of their son.

In developing these rituals, a few principles are key. First, the audience, message, and actions must derive from the story. Rituals cannot be imposed; they need to be invited, fashioned as the individual's story of loss is shared. Second, effective rituals usually involve objects—a candle, letter, or picture for example—that also have symbolic value. Third, rituals have to be planned and processed. A counselor needs to make sure all the implications of the ritual are thought out. And, once the ritual has ended, it is useful to share what has occurred and process thoughts and feelings.

It is important to observe these same principles when working with children and adolescents. Rituals need to be planned with, not imposed upon, children and adolescents. Naturally these rituals will reflect the developmental level of the child or adolescent. It is their meanings and symbols that will be reflected in the ritual.

Conclusion

Even before humans could write, they devised rituals that helped them as they faced the vicissitudes of life. They invested actions with symbolism and meaning as ways to cope with their world. When we fail to use ritual effectively or do not allow children and adolescents the opportunities to participate, we deprive them of the therapeutic power as old and strong as humanity itself.

Kenneth J. Doka, PhD, is a Professor of Gerontology at The College of New Rochelle and the author of numerous books on grief and bereavement. Dr. Doka is both the editor of the journal Omega *and* Journeys, *a newsletter for the bereaved. He is past President of the Association for Death Education and Counseling and served as Chair of the International Work Group on Death, Dying, and Bereavement from 1997-1999. Dr. Doka is an ordained Lutheran clergyman.*

V · O · I · C · E · S

It's Impossible to Tell Someone How to Grieve

Maggie Smith

To me, it's impossible to tell someone how to grieve. You can help someone, but never instruct them. I've been to a few grief camps and groups for the loss of my brother Gary and my grandfather Robert. At both, they showed us movies or diagrams about the grieving process. I never really understood them. To me, everyone grieves in a different way, and you shouldn't analyze that, or tell them how it works.

When I lost my brother, it wasn't a shock to me. He had been ill for a long time. There will always be a void in my soul that no one else can ever fill. It was a hole in my entire family, each of us experiencing different pain. To my parents, it was the loss of a son. To me, it was the loss of a brother and a friend. It was an empty room in the house, an empty room in all of our souls.

Of course, there were things that helped, and things that didn't. Without certain people, I never would have gotten through this as I did. One of them was a social worker. She came into our lives after Gary had already lapsed into a coma, so she knew him through me. She was always there to listen when I needed her. She was an escape for me because she was a happy, fun-loving person, but serious when she needed to be.

The constant support and prayers of our local parish and priest were an extreme help to my whole family. Our priest was always there when my mom needed to talk, or when we needed a prayer in a shaky moment, or just for comic relief! How he found the time as the only priest in the parish, I'll never know. I recall one time, my mother was alone at the hospital when my brother was rushed to an emergency CAT scan. As she was walking down the hall, Father Ron appeared around the corner at the exact moment when she needed him the most. She said afterward that he appeared like an angel. And I truly believe he is.

Certain things were not helpful. I'm never sure whether my friends seeming to ignore the fact that my brother had brain cancer helped or not. We were young then—only ten years old. I think back and say to myself, "What could they have done?" They just let me continue in my own way. I suppose it helped me to maintain a normal life outside the hospital, but I could have talked to them.

Another thing was that people would ask, "How's your brother, Maggie?" But they seemed to forget about me. I was still there! But there were also many people who were concerned about me as well as Gary. People would also say to me, "I know how you feel," or, "I understand." But they didn't! Unless your brother died from brain cancer with you watching in a hospital when you were eleven, you have no clue how I feel. I think people were uncomfortable because they didn't know what to say to a little girl in my place.

Another annoying thing that people did, mainly my friends, was to try to cheer me up when I felt sad, try to make me laugh and forget about it. It was well intentioned, but I wanted to cry. I needed to cry. I couldn't forget. I wanted to talk about it, not to laugh at something.

My advice to anyone talking to a person in mourning is just to be kind, gentle, and a constant support. Offer to talk, but don't pressure them. They will trust you and if they need to talk, they will seek you out. When a brother dies, it's hard to say how it feels. It is a hole in my life, an unfixable void. I miss him a lot, but I must go on with my life. Everyone needs to move on. But whatever you do, you don't have to face it alone.

Maggie Smith is thirteen years old and is in the eighth grade. She loves to play field hockey, and she enjoys reading, writing, and America Online.

11

The Use of Groups with Grieving Children and Adolescents

Donna L. Schuurman

It's been 50 years since Ann Bennett Mix's father died in the military in Italy, a casualty in World War II's waning years. She was three years old when he died, one of over 183,000 children of American servicemen awarded financial benefits following their fathers' deaths in that war. Only now, more than half a century later, are some of the emotional wounds beginning to heal. In 1991, when Mix created the American WWII Orphans Network (AWON), she did so because she "realized how important it was for them to talk to people like themselves...." As new members joined the network, they expressed astonishment "that they aren't alone, that others have experienced the same bewilderment and pain" (Malone, 1998, 65).

Although some progress has been made since Mix's father's death in recognizing that children grieve and that their feelings deserve attention and support, it has only been in the last fifteen years that pioneering voices have been heard and recognized, including the clinicians and researchers Corr and Wass (1984), Fitzgerald (1992), Goldman (1994), Grollman (1995), Silverman (2000), Wolfelt (1996), and Worden (1996), among others.

In 1983, when nurse Beverly Chappell founded The Dougy Center, the first peer support group for children and teens impacted by death, she was told by the head of a local pediatric unit that her plan sounded like "voodoo medicine," and that he didn't want anyone "messing" with his patients' heads. But national and international events occurred which required adults to attend to children and the issue of death. Christa McAuliffe's death in the space shuttle disaster prompted an unwelcome focus on how schoolchildren reacted to a catastrophic death. Many years later, Princess Diana's untimely death shed a brief spotlight on the impact of her loss on her two young sons. A rash of violent deaths impacting children has unfolded in recent years: the murder of sixteen kindergartners and their teacher in Dunblane, Scotland; Oklahoma City's 1995 bombing; and school shootings in Paducah, Kentucky; Springfield, Oregon; Littleton, Colorado; and other communities.

Although still occasionally referred to as the "forgotten grievers," young people's voices are finally beginning to be heard. They cry out, and often act out, to inform the adults around them that they are grieving too. This is not to suggest that all children or adolescents who experience a death need therapy or professional help, though some do.

But they all need support.

For some, the support of family, friends, and extended community may provide the healing validation they need. For others, as noted in an article on children and resilience, "The web of relationships that once naturalistically provided many sources of resilience—the extended family, the church, the synagogue, the neighborhood, the union hall—is eroding" (Butler, 1997, 29). Many young people who have family support still express feelings of estrangement, loneliness, being different from their peers, and other fears and concerns.

Since 1983, The Dougy Center in Portland, Oregon has served more than 12,000 children and teens, and their parents or adult caregivers, following a death. The Center was founded by nurse Beverly Chappell, who was inspired by a young boy named Dougy Turno who was dying from an inoperable brain tumor. As Dougy shared with other critically ill children in his hospital unit, Chappell observed the positive power of children helping other children cope with grief and death. She also noticed that the siblings of dying children, as well as the children of critically ill parents, were often left out of the process following a death. Trained volunteers, supervised by professional staff, facilitate support groups for grieving children and adolescents, with age- and death-specific groupings: for three to five-year-olds, six to twelve-year-olds, ten to fourteen-year-olds, and teens; for those impacted by parent death, sibling death, death by homicide, death by suicide, sudden accidental death, and death following a long-term illness. Over the years, more than 100 programs have evolved based on The Dougy Center model, reaching across the US and into Australia, Canada, England, Germany, Ireland, Jamaica, and Japan.

Additionally, many programs serving grieving children and teens have developed through hospice, hospital, and community mental health centers, as well as independent programs like The Coves in Connecticut and Massachusetts. Whether geared toward providing therapy or peer support, through ongoing or time-limited groups, all serve a common goal: to assist young people in their grieving process following a death. Although the group setting is not appropriate for every grieving child or teen, there are at least five reasons group intervention for this population can be beneficial.

Five Ways Groups Can Help Grieving Children and Teens

The following five ways groups can help grieving children and teens are based on the thoughts and words of young grievers at the Dougy Center. When asked, "How does the group help you?", these are the responses they gave.

1. "Hey, maybe I'm not crazy...."

One of the most commonly expressed fears of children and adolescents at The Dougy Center is the fear that they are "going crazy." Grievers often experience frightening or unwelcome grief symptoms including nightmares, voices, aches and pains in their body, uncontrollable shaking, or waves of heat or cold. As fourteen-year-old Heather shared, "I was experiencing stuff I couldn't control and didn't understand. Weird dreams. Stomach aches. Seeing my father's ghost in my room at night. I thought I was losing it, and I was afraid to tell anyone."

Many normal manifestations of grief feel, look, or seem "crazy" to the young griever. One of the benefits of sharing in a group setting is the de-pathologizing of normal grief reactions. Kids find out, through listening and sharing with others their age, that much of what they fear is common and normal.

2. "I'm not alone."

"I thought I had this big mark on my forehead," bemoaned twelve-year-old Stephen. "It said, 'Look, my mom died and I'm different from you.' I had friends whose parents divorced, but no one who'd had a parent die. It seemed like I was the only one this had ever happened to, and I felt completely alone."

No one, least of all self-conscious and peer-conscious adolescents, wants to feel alone. One of the benefits of participating in a group of peers who have also experienced a death is the knowledge that others have experienced, and survived, the loss of a family member or close friend. Katie, ten, expressed it this way: "I can talk to other kids who had a parent die and it helps me feel like I'm not the only one who had a parent die, and I feel less weird and different."

3. "Someone else cares what I'm going through."

Children need validation for who they are, what they feel, and what they experience. While attempting to make sense of their world following a death, they too frequently do not receive support or validation from the adults around them. Young people at The Dougy Center describe encounter after encounter with well-meaning but ill-informed teachers, coaches, ministers, adult family friends, and youth workers who continue to perpetuate the directive that they need to "put this behind them," "move on," "forget," and "get over it."

A sixteen-year-old described her teacher's reaction when she did not have a writing assignment completed four days after she'd witnessed her brother's death in a drowning accident. "She told me I was using it as an excuse not to do my homework!"

Group support helps children and adolescents know that someone cares and understands. In a society where grieving adults are granted three days of bereavement leave and face the avoidance of colleagues who don't know what to say and therefore say nothing, it is easy for kids to feel they don't have permission to grieve. Many uninformed adults pass on misinformation to children.

4. "My feelings matter."

It's not unusual for grieving children and teens to feel overloaded with emotions, ranging from anger and self-pity to relief and panic. These feelings are experienced in random fashion, leaving the griever confused and feeling out of control. Sometimes adults, disturbed by kids' actions or consumed by wanting to alleviate their pain, actually complicate the healing process by short-circuiting, making light of, or attempting to take away feelings they don't want children to have to experience. "People kept telling me not to be so mad after my dad got killed," said eight-year-old Jeremy. "But it wasn't their dad that was gone. I was mad, and still am. It isn't fair that I don't get to have a dad."

Group settings for youth that include appropriate boundaries and supervision provide an opportunity for *all* feelings to be validated, even ones that don't feel good.

5. "I have ways to express what I feel in ways that help me."

Many young people express verbally or by their actions that they don't know what to do with the feelings raging inside them. These feelings frequently wind up being expressed in unhealthy ways through self-destructive behaviors, or behaviors adults pejoratively call "acting out." Accused of "trying to get attention" through crying, withdrawing, abuse of substances, reckless sexual behavior, lying, stealing, or getting in fights, kids who don't get the attention they need are driven to find increasingly reckless ways of seeking it. What they need is adults who will help them express their feelings, even the tough or uncomfortable ones, in a healthy manner.

For some, talking in a safe setting, being listened to and validated, provides the support they need. Children and adolescents with strong verbal skills often make adults feel better because they can understand more clearly what the young person is experiencing. But many children and teens are not comfortable with putting their experience into words. For them, talk therapy or support that only includes verbal expression may prove frustrating.

Play is children's natural activity, and a primary way they make sense of their emotional life and experiences. Providing a range of mediums for expression—art, music, dress-up clothes, playhouses, puppets, sandtrays, punching bags, toys and games—allows each child or teen to find his or her own methods to express the feelings inside.

Ten Practical Considerations for Starting or Running Successful Groups for Grieving Children and Teens

There are numerous models and methods of working effectively with grieving children and teens through utilizing groups. What follows are some of the practical considerations in determining what model best suits your philosophical framework, available resources, setting, and population. These suggestions are based on observing, listening to, and working with grieving children and teens since 1986 at The Dougy Center.

1. Should we run therapy, educational, or support groups?

The decision about whether to run therapy groups, educational groups, support groups, or some combination of all three depends on a number of factors, including but not limited to the population with which you intend to work, and your philosophical orientation. If your population is youth in a mental health setting, a residential treatment program, or those whose emotional problems are severely inhibiting their ability to function, you may elect to run groups whose function is therapy and education, and which are led by professional counselors or therapists. Bear in mind that youth may be resistant to direction and educational efforts if they do not believe that they are being heard and their feelings valued and validated.

Most of the existing programs for grieving children and youth are support-based and necessitated because we live in a death-denying and death-averse culture where adults often do not feel comfortable dealing with the topic. Our culture does not provide many examples for young people to cope in healthy ways after deaths occur. If and when those safe places and ways are available, special groups may not be needed. But this is more often the exception than the rule.

What type of groups you determine to run is also based on belief systems about what grieving means, and what children and teens need following a death. Some programs elect to eschew the "medical model" that views grieving as an illness to be treated, and strictly provide support. Although therapeutic in nature, support groups tend to utilize trained volunteers supervised by professional therapists or counselors, child development specialists, or psychologists. Some support group models also incorporate an educational component, either for adult caregivers or for children and teens.

2. Should groups be ongoing or time-limited?

Deciding whether to hold ongoing groups or time-limited groups depends on a combination of realities including resources and philosophical beliefs about how children grieve and what they need. Most school-based, hospice- or hospital-based, and many mental health-based programs elect to run time-limited groups, most frequently in the six, eight, or ten-week range. These groups usually are closed groups, with the same participants attending, barring dropouts, for the full number of sessions. Most often, they include specific themes for each week's session, along with activities or curricula. Sometimes time-limited groups are chosen because of resource restraints imposed by an umbrella agency such as a school, hospital, or hospice. Sometimes they are the method of choice because they can reach more children with the available resources than ongoing groups might be able to reach. Some believe that time-limited groups more effectively focus the child's attention on the issues relating to the loss. They are generally more cost-effective than ongoing groups, especially when measured in the current climate of managed care. And for many children and teens, they effectively assist healthy grieving.

Those who elect to run ongoing or open-ended grief support groups tend to do so because of philosophical leanings around allowing children and teens to determine their own timing and agenda for expressing their grief. Because kids tend to be in and out of grief, happily engaged in an activity one minute and upset the next, ongoing groups with no time limitations for participation account for the vast individual differences in timing and expression and allow children to guide their own process. Ongoing groups incorporate new members and say good-bye to those who determine it is their time to close from the group. Members may participate anywhere from two or three sessions to two or three years. At The Dougy Center, the average length of time children and teens participate averages between twelve and fifteen months.

The question is not necessarily which format is better. Either can be effective. Rather, the questions to ask include:

    a. What kind of resources do we have to run the groups, including staff and/or volunteers, funding for supplies, location demands, and other direct and indirect costs?

    b. What do we believe is the most effective way to assist children and teens in groups?

    c. What are we trying to accomplish through these groups?
       What external expectations, if any, are placed on us?
       Using either model, can children return to or repeat groups?

3. Should we run curriculum-driven groups or non-directive groups?

Curriculum-driven groups tend to select topics for each of the allotted sessions, complete with activities to help children or teens focus on issues related to the death they have experienced. These topics may include identifying and coping with feelings, looking at the funeral, hard stuff and happy stuff, etc., and may include creating memory books, drawing, talking, and other activities. A word of caution if you elect to develop a curriculum or use an existing one: be careful not to so tightly pack your agenda with activities that you do not allow for spontaneity, or for going "off-track" when the situation warrants.

Non-directive groups may include activities or topics, but these are frequently derived from the topics or interests that the young people bring with them to the group each session. At The Dougy Center, an opening circle is held where participants share their name, age, and who died, and anything else they would like to say. Sometimes a topic evolves naturally from this circle, and other times an activity is proposed from an activity manual (The Dougy Center, 1990). An unstructured time follows, where children select from a range of activities in different areas of the Center, including staying in the "Talking Room," going outside to play, punching a bag or throwing soft objects in the "Volcano Room," painting, drawing, mask-making, clay and other art media, dressing up, puppetry, sandtray or water play, playing air hockey or foosball. Through their play, children work through and process their worlds. The teen groups tend to stay in their circle and talk, though sometimes all or some of the group will go in the art, volcano, or sandtray areas.

4. Should groups be adult-directed or peer-run?

Not surprisingly, the answer to this question involves an examination of the population and one's philosophical beliefs about how children and teens most effectively learn, change, and grow.

Most existing programs fall into one of two categories. They either have adult-directed (usually curriculum-driven) groups, or they include a combination of adult staff and/or volunteers who allow the children or teens to direct the content of the sessions. Your decisions about whether to provide curriculum-driven or non-directive groups will likely determine the answer to this question.

5. How do we determine which children and teens are appropriate for groups?

Some young people function better in group settings than others, and some would benefit more from individual attention than group settings allow. There are several ways to determine whether children or teens are appropriate for groups. One way to is to give them an informed choice by orienting them to what the group involves, and allowing them to choose whether or not they would like to participate. This allows them to regain some sense of control after the loss of ability to control their world and prevent the death from happening. At The Dougy Center, we suggest that parents ask their child or teen to participate at least once before determining that they don't want to participate further.

Some children or teens are unable or unwilling to engage in groups because of shyness, fear, emotional problems, or other factors. Although they should not be forced to participate, we have found at The Dougy Center that many children deemed by others as "inappropriate" for groups have successfully engaged in groups when given clear boundaries (mostly rules about safety), and leeway for leaving the group if and when they need to. Some children, especially those who have witnessed traumatic deaths, have difficulty focusing, sitting still, or being polite to others. When they have difficulty focusing, we allow them to focus their attention elsewhere. When they can't sit still, we let them stand, jump, leave the group, or go to the Volcano Room. Being rude, engaging in put-downs of others, and other difficulties are framed as safety issues, e.g. "It doesn't feel safe when you call other people names, and we want everyone to be safe here." Occasionally, behavior "contracts" are developed when behavior violates the child's own or other's safety, but that has been rare.

A related issue is when children or teens are "ready" to participate in a group setting following a death. We propose that if they agree to participate, they are ready, regardless of whether it has been a week or a year since the death. Although some professionals have suggested that grievers not participate in groups for several months following a death because they tend to be numb, The Dougy Center allows the participants to decide for themselves if they are ready. If they choose to express their numbness in the group, it's okay with us.

One teen, a sixteen-year-old whose boyfriend shot and killed himself in front of her, became a runaway and stopped attending school, despite her previous straight-A record and extracurricular involvement. Her mother frequently saw her only when she showed up for her group at the Center, dropped off by friends. Janice would fall asleep in the opening circle, and sometimes sleep for the entire 1½-hour session. Although some facilitators protested that she was "not doing her work" and was not "here to sleep," the staff allowed her to sleep, knowing it may have been the only safe place in her life to do so. She slept for several months, and when she "woke up," it was with a fury: She began to write poetry, re-engage in life, and went on to graduate from high school and attend college. She later told The Dougy Center staff that if we had not permitted her to sleep, she would have stopped showing up, and may well have lost her way.

6. Age-related issues: What ages should we work with, and should we group by age?

Most professionals in thanatology agree that even infants are capable of grieving. At The Dougy Center, we provide support groups for children beginning at the age of three. They're a bit more labor-intensive than the fifteen-year-olds, but no less capable of expressing what they feel and think. In fact, many of them are more open, and sometimes more articulate, than older kids. Because play is the "work" of children, younger children often express what they're thinking and feeling through their play. At The Dougy Center, children draw, paint, give puppet shows, set up scenes and stories in sandtrays and sinks with toys, dolls, gravemarkers, and other props, use dress-up clothing of firefighters, police, emergency personnel, and play with dollhouses, among other activities. In such play, they often reveal their fears and fantasies. Three-year-old Jerome's sister drowned in their bathtub when his mother left them alone to take a phone call. For months Jerome would fill up the kid's sink in the playroom, undress a doll, and place her carefully in the water so that her head was above it. "See," he'd say, "she's going to be okay!"

We have found it helpful to group children and teens by age as their developmental issues tend to be more similar. But it is not necessary for you to do so. Younger kids can learn from the older ones, and vice versa. Exactly how you decide to group them is less important to the success of the group than what you do in the group. The Dougy Center's teen groups include teens from the age of thirteen to nineteen. At one point the staff planned to split the teen groups into thirteen to sixteen-year-olds and seventeen to nineteen-year-olds. Fortunately, we had the good sense to ask group participants what they thought. Most of them protested and explained that they liked having the age range. If we were going to split them, they suggested we split them by death of a parent and death of a sibling or friend. A few of the younger teens did want to have their own groups, and we ultimately added a "Middlers" group for ten to fourteen-year-olds, leaving thirteen and fourteen-year-olds the option to be with younger or older kids. One thirteen-year-old suggested we call the group the "Awkwards," because, she explained, "We're at that really awkward stage."

We also conduct a monthly group that includes three-year-olds up to twelve-year-olds, with a separate teen group. What matters is not rigid age grouping, but doing something to address the issues of these kids. *Don't get hung up on the incidentals.*

7. Can we run groups with mixed losses—parent and sibling, impending death and post-death?

The simple answer to this question is yes. If you don't have a large enough population to divide children and teens by age, or by type of death, then by all means run mixed groups. Some programs choose to mix groups even when they have large populations.

There are some advantages to having various options. We run specific groups for children impacted by violent death and by suicide, but children do not have to participate in those. They can be in a parent death group, or a sibling death group, or a mixed group. Sometimes they will start in a parent death group and then move to a "Healing from a Suicide" group. In some ways it seems more difficult for the parents or adult caregivers to adjust to mixed-loss groups. For example, it may be difficult to be the only parent whose child died in a group where spouse death is most prevalent.

Some programs have support groups for children or teens who are dealing with the terminal illness or impending death of a family member, as well as groups for them when the death has occurred. It is difficult to mix these populations since the issues are very different, but clearly both populations can benefit from group support. If you elect to hold both kinds of groups, you will need to think through whether participants in the impending death group stay with their peers after the death, or whether they move to a new group.

8. What locations or settings are most conducive to effective groups?

While it's nice to have a homey, comfortable setting in which to run groups for children and adolescents, the setting is much less important than the people and the atmosphere created. Effective groups can happen in borrowed halls, churches, homes, or school classrooms. If you have the luxury of designing or building your own site, by all means do so with kids, warmth, and homeyness in mind. Try to avoid a cold or inhospitable atmosphere.

Some families have expressed resistance to attending groups in hospitals, churches, or funeral homes. For some, the hospital is a painful reminder of their loss. Those estranged from or disillusioned with the church may react negatively to that setting. And funeral homes may remind them of the finality of their loss. But effective programs can be run in any of those settings. It's up to you to create a welcoming, engaging experience through the people you work with and programs you run.

9. What size group is most effective?

This depends on what ages you're working with, how much adult assistance you have, and how much individual attention you intend to provide within the group format. In general, the younger the child, the more adult assistance required, or the smaller a "manageable" group can be. Most of the groups at The Dougy Center have up to fifteen children or teens, with adult assistance ranging from a one-to-two ratio for three to five-year-olds, a one-to-three ratio for six to twelve-year-olds, and a one-to-five ratio for teens. You may have larger or smaller groups depending on your setting, the activities you include, and how much adult assistance you have available.

10. Should we include parents or adult caregivers in these groups, or in our program?

If at all possible, absolutely. Resiliency studies suggest that adult influence is important in children's success, and other studies (Worden, 1996) suggest that one of the most influential predictors of how children will survive parental death is how the surviving parent is coping. Many programs include an adult component which is therapeutic and educational in nature. Concurrent adult groups allow parents and caregivers some time off from parenting, enable them to discuss with other adults the challenges of raising grieving children, and provide the opportunity to both seek and give support and advice.

Whatever you decide to do for or with grieving children and teens, do something. Too many children still get the wrong messages from the adults around them. Morgan and Dylan, brothers whose father was murdered, were told by a family friend a month after the funeral to "forget your father and get on with your lives." Their school counselor suggested an extended weekend at the beach so that they could "recover." While a getaway weekend isn't a bad idea, it took over two years of attending a group with others who'd had a family member murdered, completion of the trial, and consistent support from teachers, coaches, family, and friends before they felt their lives had regained a sense of balance. "We'll never forget our father," they said, "and we'll never be totally over it. There's no such thing as complete recovery. It's like you're changed forever, and it takes a long time to adjust to life without him. We'll go on, but we won't go on in the same way we would have with his love and support."

What you do—or don't do—to help grieving children and teens will have a lifelong impact on their lives.

Donna L. Schuurman, EdD, is the Executive Director of The Dougy Center for Grieving Children in Portland, Oregon. She serves as 2nd Vice President on the Board of Directors of the Association for Death Education and Counseling and is writing a book for adults who had a parent die in childhood.

12

Magical Dreams, Visions of Reality
Guidelines for Developing a Grief Center for Children

Rebecca Sloan Byrne

For over thirteen years, I have dreamed of starting a center to serve bereaved children, adolescents, and their families. Today that center is a reality. The St. Louis Bereavement Center for Young People opened in December 1997. You may have similar dreams. But how can you start? How can you make those dreams a reality? The following chapter will provide the answers to some of these questions and many more. Yet we can't answer all questions and concerns; as our center develops, we continue to learn. But as we share this story, we hope that you may learn from our successes and mistakes so that your dream for a center can become a reality.

Formation of a Non-Profit Corporation

You have two basic choices in beginning a center. One is to create a center supported by client fees. We chose not to do so. We wanted our center to be able to solicit contributions and to serve young clients independently of their abilities to pay for services. This entailed creating a non-profit corporation. The first step in starting a non-profit corporation is to seek an attorney who specializes in corporate or, better yet, non-profit corporate law. The time commitment for the attorney is minimal—

maybe four to five hours. The attorney should first explain the pros and cons of establishing a non-profit versus a for-profit corporation. You may be asked that question in the initial stages of development and you want to be confident of the decision. The attorney will also need to provide information about the process of incorporating in your state. Each state may have a slightly different procedure. A resource to help familiarize yourself with the procedure is the *Martindale-Hubbell Law Directory* (1995). It provides a synopsis of each state's process and can be found in almost any library or in the office of an attorney.

Secondly, a name for your organization needs to be chosen and a search completed through the office of your Secretary of State to verify its availability. The sooner a name is searched and reserved, the less likely the name will be rejected. Holding the name generally entails a fee of around twenty-five dollars, which may need to be renewed after a given time. When the name of the organization is definite, Articles of Incorporation must be filed, which means giving information such as name, address, phone number, name of person forming the corporation, names of board members, and corporate officers. Turn-around time for this process can range from a couple of days to a couple of weeks. This process signifies the existence of a non-profit corporation. It does not entitle contributors to a write-off on taxes. It does not entitle the organization to make purchases without being charged sales taxes. Additional paperwork must be completed to obtain these benefits.

As soon as possible after incorporation, the organization should obtain tax-exempt status. You will need to file for 501(C)(3) status, Form 1023, with the Federal government. The paperwork can be found at most Internal Revenue Service offices. Completing the forms for this recognition can be time-consuming and tedious, but it allows you to be tax-exempt and to provide a deduction for contributors. In addition, most foundations require such IRS status to dispense grants. In order to obtain such IRS status, you will need to provide a detailed strategic plan that includes a one- to three-year budget and bylaws.

Strategic Plan

A thorough, detailed strategic plan is vital. It is the first tangible plan of what the mission, vision, and goals of your center are and how they will be supported. It is the initial introductory information that will be given to potential board members, volunteers, and major contributors. The first impression of the organization will be based on the strategic plan and the person(s) leading the start-up and development. Most parties assign more credibility if the plan appears businesslike in presentation and style. There are many parts of the plan, such as:

Background information: This should consist of needs-assessment results, national and local statistics, and pertinent but precise and simple grief research. National statistics can be found in the research, but local statistics are hard to capture. The best way is through the Office of Vital Statistics, US Census Bureau and the Coroner's Office of your area. Most likely, you will need to apply national statistics—such as 83 percent of children that die have a surviving sibling, or one of every six kids will experience the death of a parent before the age of eighteen—to the local numbers. This information will *not* reflect the quantity of children and teens that are grieving the death of a friend, grandparent, neighbor, or teacher. Also, the statistic for a child's death only accounts for one surviving sibling for each death. Please remember, "Once bereaved, always bereaved."

Mission statement: This document states the goals of your organization. The least amount of words with the clearest explanation is ideal. It must be known verbatim by absolutely every single board member, staff person, and volunteer.

Vision: This is a statement revealing the overall large picture or dream for the organization. It usually reflects the impact expected on the community and population served.

Guiding values: These consist of a few statements that convey the underlying philosophy or ethics that will guide decision making.

Needs statement: This should be a paragraph that shares the results from the community needs assessment and why the organization is necessary. Be clear and precise about what "hole" in the community the organization will fill.

Problem statement: This consists of a few sentences that specifically explain why the target population will benefit from the services or programs offered.

Organizational assumptions: These assumptions list the beliefs held true by the organization. These beliefs or assumptions are the foundation for the design and implementation of services and programs.

Organizational objectives: These objectives share the overall goals to be met through the variety of services and programs.

Support services description: You must provide a description of the services to be implemented in a detailed yet concise manner. Be able to list and explain each service and program to anyone who asks. Outline which programs or services will be implemented and when (i.e., *start-up*—in the first year of operation; *short-term*—in the second and third years of operation; *long-term*—in the third through fifth years of operation).

Client population: This element should answer the question: "To what target audience does the organization plan to offer services and programs?"

Organizational goals: Goals provide specific details on how many particular services or programs will be offered in a specific period of time.

Critical success factors: This is a list of factors that will influence the organization and its ability to meet the mission.

Metrics for gauging success: These explain how the organization plans to evaluate the effectiveness of the services and programs in meeting the mission.

Marketing strategy: A strategy describes how the organization plans to market its services and programs, who it will target, and in what order.

Budget: You need to provide a detailed budget that spans all aspects of the organization.

Funding sources: Include a list of the methods and sources from which the organization will seek funds.

Personnel: Describe the staff and briefly share their background, talents, and expertise.

Board of directors: List the current members of the Board of Directors and their expertise. Describe the plan for further development, i.e., types of talents needed, characteristics of members desired, time span for expansion, ideal membership number, and turnover pattern. Clarify the role of the Executive Director in relation to the Board. Existence of liability insurance should be stated. If there is a plan for an advisory board or subcommittees, that should be stated as well.

Bylaws: Include a copy of the organization's bylaws. They are the "rules of the road" for governing a non-profit corporation. A framework for writing bylaws is available in *How to Form a Non-profit Corporation* (Mancuso, 1996) and *Starting and Running a Non-profit Organization* (Hummel, 1997).

When the strategic plan is completed, it will need to be revised at least once a year. The changes should reflect the state of programming in existence, in current implementation, and in development. Any details of the plan that need to be deleted or enhanced should be incorporated. For the sake of understanding the history and growth of the organization, save every revision of the strategic plan. It is helpful to have summaries of the plan that do not include the budget or bylaws. This version is more applicable for sharing with potential volunteers, while the entire plan is necessary for recruiting board members and major financial contributors. Examples of guiding values, organizational objectives and organizational assumptions are written below.

Guiding values

- We believe that all people, regardless of race, economic, social, or spiritual affiliations are entitled to all bereavement services.

- We value the full range of human diversity and seek to involve a variety of populations in our staff, board, volunteers, and clientele.

- We inquire about, listen to, and respect the opinions, thoughts, concerns, and desires of the children, adolescents, and families we serve in relation to their bereavement needs.

- We strive to conduct our services and ourselves with integrity, honor, and respect.

Organizational objectives

- We will provide emotional support to grieving children, adolescents, and their families.

- We will introduce or enhance healthy coping strategies in the face of loss through death.

- We will educate teachers, health care professionals, and the community at large about the grieving process in children, adolescents, and their families.

- We will increase awareness of the needs of grieving children, adolescents, and their families.

- We will provide opportunities for families to meet and support each other.

Organizational Assumptions

- Children and adolescents grieve.

- Education and support can assist children, adolescents, and their families through the grieving process.

- Everyone grieves in his or her unique way. There is no right or wrong way to grieve unless it harms self or others.

- Death and dying are subjects not easily addressed.

- Skills to cope with death, dying, and bereavement can be learned. A strong foundation of knowledge, confidence, and hope will help the individual adapt to future losses.

- Children and teens have the ability to heal themselves, especially if given love and support.

- Group settings are conducive to the grieving process for many children, adolescents, and adults.

- One never "gets over" the death of someone they love, but instead learns to live with the loss. Grief is a lifelong process, whereby a new, revised relationship with the deceased is established.

- In one way or another, unresolved losses eventually present themselves.

Development of the Board of Directors

For the establishment of a non-profit corporation, most states require that the Board of Directors consists of at least three persons. At initial start-up, the most important persons to fill those positions should be ones who have passion for the cause, energy to act, and determination to succeed. They will energize you. They will lead you in the right direction. Trust and believe.

Initially, the board members will most likely be a working board. They may have a hand in every aspect of the organization. In time, they should evolve into a group that oversees only major organizational decisions and sets general policy. The number of Directors should be enough to ensure a wide base of support, yet small enough so that business can be conducted in an orderly and expeditious manner. A number between nine and fifteen is ideal. An odd number assures avoidance of ties in voting results. Persons who should be sought for the Board of Directors can include: attorney, tax expert, professional fundraiser, marketing/public relations expert, clergy member, psychologist, physician, bereaved adult, or school official. They should possess qualities such as commitment, initiative, effective communication skills, integrity, solid networking ability, and resourcefulness. Length of term, turnover pattern, voting procedures, age and residency requirements, frequency of meetings, attendance requirements, and process for removal of a director should all be outlined in the organization's bylaws. For board meeting processes and procedures the best and most commonly used resource is *Robert's Rules of Order* (1996). Schedule a "highly encouraged" annual meeting where the past year's accomplishments and struggles are outlined. Plan for the upcoming year—schedule programs, set new goals, and identify strategies for further upholding the mission.

Due to time and energy restraints, establishment of an advisory board should be considered. For the first year, the Board of Directors may need to meet every week to every other week. The advisory board could meet four to six times a year but serve as an avenue for gathering "ambassadors" for the organization and for developing a base of volunteers. The advisory board will be a working board that exists separately from the Board of Directors, yet acts as a sounding board or gives advice. There is no set limit on the number of members. On average, one third of the board will attend each meeting. It too should consist of a variety of backgrounds and expertise.

Design of Programs and Services

What are the needs the organization aims to meet? Overall, the needs of grieving children, adolescents, and their families are simple, yet complex. They need a safe, comfortable environment where they can address the pain of grief. They need to feel normal. They need to develop or enhance effective, healthy coping strategies. They need to feel they are not alone but are supported by many. They need to have a path of open and honest communication between family members.

What programs or services could be developed that would target fulfilling those needs? Below is a listing of possible programs or services. Please know that there is no perfect way to implement support. Identify your population, your needs, and your resources, then make a decision. A few programs should be chosen for start-up while others can be implemented as organizational expertise and resources grow. Depending on that growth, as well as finances, volunteer base, and staff, it may take years to initiate all of the chosen options. The frequency or availability of a program should be based on the need revealed by the target population. Remember that *any* support you offer to the families is very likely more than they would have had otherwise.

Family-centered support groups: There are many questions to consider. Should the format be closed and time-limited or open and on-going ? If time-limited, how many sessions per set? At what interval do the groups convene? Eight to ten sessions per set are most common. Closed or open, groups often meet once a week to twice a month.

Some other questions to consider are: What is the role of the facilitators? Is it educational, facilitative, or a mix? There should be a lead and a co-facilitator for each group. Are the kids always separate from the adults? Are they together as a family during some of the sessions? Are the groups dependent on talking or are they activity-based? Is there a focus for each session? How do you keep the adults aware of what is happening in the groups while preserving confidentiality? What is your route of communication with all facilitators? What is the process for reporting safety issues for a particular member?

Bereavement camp for kids: This activity provides a relaxing, peaceful, safe place for kids to meet other grieving kids. It attracts many who otherwise would be hesitant to attend a support group and can be an opportunity for substantial media coverage for your organization.

Resource library: The library provides print, audio, and visual resources for kids, adults, and professionals.

Community referral service: This service helps persons with a need outside of the scope of the mission.

Teen weekend retreats: These can offer a private support experience without parents or guardians. Other programs for kids and adolescents can include slumber parties or a "hang-out" space for social gatherings.

School support and education: Your organization can facilitate support group access for those who otherwise would not be able to attend. Educate and support school staff about how to respond to a grieving student. Offer guidance in the development, implementation, and evaluation of a crisis intervention team.

Holiday support: This service acknowledges the pain that may acutely exist before and during the holiday season.

Family social events: These provide an opportunity for families to meet other grieving families and to share their losses in an informal manner.

Impending loss support program: This program assists families in resolving unfinished business, building memories, living more fully, feeling empowered, and "saying goodbye."

Family weekend retreats: Retreats offer fun and support in a relaxed, peaceful environment.

College-age support groups: These groups offer grief support for this population.

Speaker's institute: This can provide a repertoire of presentations on death, dying, and bereavement topics for the community at large.

Gender-specific support groups: These acknowledge and support different grieving styles.

Loss-specific support groups: Groups can offer support for survivors of suicide, homicide, AIDS, and other specific types of loss.

Pet-loss workshops: These workshops acknowledge and memorialize the death of a pet.

Logistic support: This service allows meals, transportation, camp clothes, and luggage to be offered to families who otherwise would not be able to access or enjoy the programs.

Death, dying, and grief research: Research can validate programming, services, philosophies, and approaches, and establish unmet needs of kids and families.

Mentoring service: Mentoring can assist new organizations in establishing centers to support grieving children, adolescents, and their families.

Grief resource development: The organization can create print, audio, and video resources for education and support of grieving families and the community at large.

Host Children's Grief Symposium: This service focuses on planning and executing a conference of the National Children's Grief Symposium.

Recruitment and Management of Volunteers

A strong base of volunteers is essential for success. The best way to recruit volunteers is to reach out to community groups such as church groups, boy and girl scouts, sororities and fraternities, high schools, civic groups, and corporations with community involvement requirements. Any marketing or public relations measure that increases community awareness will attract volunteers. Once a volunteer commits to helping the organization, explore her time and talents, then ensure that a task is given as soon as possible. Follow up to evaluate each volunteer's experience.

It is advantageous to assign smaller, shorter jobs to more volunteers than to assign larger, longer tasks to fewer volunteers. Every volunteer linked to the non-profit can serve as an ambassador, a fundraiser, a marketer, and a recruiter of other volunteers. Very soon after establishing a small network of volunteers, designate one or two persons to organize, assign, evaluate, and recognize volunteers. An annual volunteer appreciation event does much for fostering an ongoing relationship of support. Incentive packages work well for motivation. The more volunteers feel welcomed, needed, and appreciated, the more they become committed to the organization.

It is critical to develop and implement policies to properly screen, train, and supervise volunteers. The screening should assess, among other things, a volunteer's motivation for service. Naturally, volunteers will often exhibit diverse motivations, some of which may not be in line with your mission. Be aware of state and local regulations that govern adults who work directly with children and adolescents.

Development of Financial Support and Stability

It is vital that every person affiliated with the organization feels comfortable in helping to seek financial support. The worst that can happen is that an individual or institution reports that they are not in a position to contribute. Avenues to explore for financial support include private donations, corporate sponsorships, grants from private and public foundations, and community fundraisers. There are a number of resources that can help make fundraising easier. They include: FC Search, The Foundation Center's Database on CD-ROM (version 3.0, 1998), *The Foundation Center's Guide to Proposal Writing* (1997), *The Foundation Center's Guide to Grantseeking on the Web* (1998), and *National Guide to Funding for Children, Youth and Families* (1999). Many community fundraisers that are well established choose a new organization to support each year. Be alert to newspaper, television, or radio advertisements of fundraisers and contact them for information. Funeral homes may wish to link with programs that can enhance their aftercare services and their community outreach. Recruit financial sponsorships for each support group member or camp attendee.

Organizational Support

The network of support for performing the business of the organization can vary. As for the staff of the charity, some do not have any paid employees when the services are initiated, while others already have an executive director, director of development, and office personnel. The decision on what to have in place before start-up depends on the financial situation, the availability of volunteers, and the amount and complexity of services initially offered. If there are no employees, you will need a solid core of volunteers, and it is likely that programming will be limited when the center opens. Within six months to a year, there should be a strong push to hire long-term, knowledgeable, committed individuals for staff positions.

Usually, organizations begin with the executive director position. Following her or his employment, the next position filled might be office manager or director of development. Other positions to consider as the need and finances dictate include: program director, director of volunteer recruitment and training, director of community outreach, director of school support and education, camp director, adolescent coordinator, and building manager. Any position can begin on a part-time basis and evolve into a full-time position as the organization grows and its needs change.

Ideally, a permanent site for operation should be secured. Families need a location that is familiar, comfortable, and safe. It should present itself as welcoming and warm. The site should be open for walk-ins as much as possible. Offering a peaceful, serene resource library space where families can find a moment of calm can be healing. The staff offices should be located in the organization's space as well. Support groups, intake meetings, social events, volunteer training, community presentations, and board meetings could also take place there. Home visits can work well for the impending loss program but it is difficult to be fully flexible when there are limitations in the tools that can be transported. It is vital when working with children, adolescents, and their families that a variety of creative expression modalities are available, so the space where counselors and clients work is critical.

The organization may need to begin in less than a dream house. If it is not yet possible to obtain your own Center, research donated space at churches, community centers, hospitals, office buildings, or schools. They often have rooms that can be suitable for support groups, training sessions, and meetings. But be aware that churches and hospitals may be uncomfortable sites for some grieving persons. Investigate your county's procedure for handling foreclosed properties. Be alert to any available in your desired area. Even though it causes confusion, programming can rotate between locations. Consider all the factors and make a decision that best suits the organization at that time. If there is no affiliation or contractual agreement with the host site, make sure those you serve are aware.

Establishing a Marketing Plan

How will your organization get the word out about its existence, its services, and its needs? How will you access grieving families most efficiently and effectively? Your marketing plan addresses these questions. For The St. Louis Bereavement Center for Young People, the initial marketing areas included school counselors and social workers at their district meetings, fellow community organizations that also target a young population, and practicing pediatricians. From there, the efforts extended to physicians in the areas of intensive care, emergency medicine, hematology/oncology, cardiac, and HIV/AIDS care, funeral homes, and businesses that cater to children, adolescents, and their families. Businesses should include children's museums, zoos, restaurants, play areas, science centers, and any location where kids and families frequent. Often there is a bulletin board or other place where brochures can be placed. In addition, there are a variety of other outlets for information, including:

- Yellow pages listing (this can be provided for free if there is a promotion)
- Brochure distribution
- Speaking engagements
- Newspaper articles
- Television or radio spots
- Public service announcements (radio stations provide a certain amount of these at no cost)
- Community resource books (published by mental health centers, hospitals, funeral homes, and schools)
- Internet website (can very likely be developed and maintained by donation)
- Conferences, expositions, booths (especially if the audience attending is somehow linked to your target population—women, parents, kids, hospice workers, and mental health professionals)
- Marketing tools (especially refrigerator magnets, can opener grippers, notepads, or other useful items)
- One-on-one meetings
- Direct mailings (December can be most productive for mailing. Focus on the kids and have the participants write from a personal viewpoint.)
- Billboards on major highways or thoroughfares

Conclusion

In summary, the adventure of watching a dream evolve into reality can be exhilarating, if at times exhausting. Yet you can be a critical medium to help provide grieving children and adolescents a safe and peaceful place as they adapt to loss.

Rebecca Sloan Byrne is the Executive Director of the St. Louis Bereavement Center for Young People, which provides comprehensive support services to grieving children, adolescents, and their families. She served for thirteen years as a pediatric nurse and designed, implemented, and coordinated a hospital-based bereavement support group for children and teens.

PRACTICAL SUGGESTIONS

Talking to a Grieving Child: A Guide for Classroom Teachers

Be simple and straightforward.
A simple statement such as, "I'm sorry your Mom died," is much more effective and heartfelt than a long, fruitless attempt to comfort. Avoid euphemisms and use a normal tone of voice.

Listen and respect the child's feelings and fears.
Allow the child the right to his or her grief. You will not make children feel better by denying their feelings. Instead, allow them a safe place to talk. Help them identify people who can help them.

Be patient with repetition.
As they tell the story of their loss, it helps make it more real.

Be sensitive to the child's feeling of being different.
Extend attention carefully. Many children will resent being singled out. Be aware of classroom activities, such as creating gifts for mothers or fathers, that can accentuate loss and feelings of isolation. Such projects can be easily reframed as creating a gift for a special person.

Give the child a sense of control.

In extending support, give the child options on how you can best help.

Recognize that grief can affect schoolwork.

Grief not only affects the ways children feel but the ways they think and behave. They may need a little more time or support during this period. You may have to help them set priorities and solve any difficulties that may arise as their family copes with loss. At the same time, recognize that children do have a need for a constant sense of structure, as their own lives may feel more chaotic in the aftermath of the loss.

Watch for manifestations of problems and refer if necessary.

Students exhibiting problems such as accidents, substance abuse, truancy, self-destructive behaviors, anxiety, depression, severe regressive behaviors, apathy, aggressiveness, delinquency, or significant changes in behavior or performance ought to be referred to a mental health professional.

13

The Role Of Death Education in Helping Students to Cope With Loss

Robert G. Stevenson

Many adults think of childhood as an idyllic time, filled with joy and innocence. While this image may be well-intentioned, the reality of life for most children is quite different. Life brings changes to every child and many of these involve loss. Perhaps the most profound loss a child must face is the death of someone they love. Because some adults try to maintain that image of innocence and joy, they would like to believe that children do not need any special knowledge about death and grief, which may leave children isolated and forced to cope on their own when a death occurs. Schools and teachers can play an important role in helping students to examine loss and grief before such a crisis occurs. This chapter presents the views of one educator/parent of the benefits of the classwork that has come to be called "death education."

Students and Death

Why? For most of the 25 years I have spent as a death educator and counselor, the most frequently asked question has been, "Why?" When it follows a loss, or a death—one of the most profound losses—it is even more poignant. Why did she die? Why do things like this happen? When some educators attempt to answer these questions, others arise. Why are *you* teaching this in school? Why do you think you are qualified to teach this topic? If the lessons take place to prepare students to cope with loss the question becomes: Why teach this to children before they need to know it? All of these questions are legitimate and reflect concern on the part of students, educators, and parents. They deserve honest answers.

This chapter deals with the last of the *Why?* questions. Why teach this to children before it is necessary to know about death or loss? If this question is not answered satisfactorily, the topics of death and loss may well be removed from the school. If this happens, the other questions may not have an opportunity or a place to be voiced. In fact, the best place to discuss death is clearly at home in a family setting. Religious communities also have an important role to play for many families. However, they do not always fulfill this task. Many caring adults seek to spare children the pain that we know accompanies the loss of someone precious. In seeking to shield students from this emotional and spiritual pain, parents and caring adults may try to avoid the topic. Worse, when forced to address it, they may resort to platitudes or dismiss the serious questions their children pose because they do not feel confident about how to answer.

If it were possible to spare children this pain, it would be tempting to do so. However, loss is something that many students confront almost daily. It may be the loss of a feeling (such as safety or self-confidence). It may be the loss of future plans (failure to achieve admission to a certain college or to earn a spot on an athletic team) or the loss of a condition or state (such as good health). Or, it may be the loss of a person (through death or divorce). All of these losses have things in common, including ways the student may view the loss or choose to cope with it. The coping skills which can help a student to face smaller losses—smaller, at least, to others, if not to the student—can also be used to cope with the losses caused by death or divorce.

The reality is that students, family members, teachers, and principals do die, and parents do divorce. Students learn of the deaths of community members, of the siblings of classmates, or of famous people with whom they feel a connection. Yet, many schools act as though grieving students, when they return to the classroom, should return to business as usual. Students may even be disciplined by parents or teachers for a drop in grades after a death occurs. The grief of these students can then be complicated by guilt that they experience for not maintaining their previous level of academic achievement, when, in fact, they may be performing quite a feat just by returning to school and functioning at any level at all.

Death or loss education is not just for children; it must also include professional staff as part of the target audience. Many educators—both classroom teachers and counselors—do not understand how grief affects children. They are not aware that grades often fall after the loss of a loved one, or that such a drop can take place even years after the loss when children muster their strength to postpone their grief. Unable to cope with a loss, a student may exhibit behavior changes or self-medicate with alcohol or drugs. How often do educators try to deal with the manifestations of unresolved grief without touching the real cause—the pain of the earlier loss?

It is not simply that students fail to inform teachers about what is happening to them. The students may not, themselves, be aware of the components of grief or how it is affecting their lives. The most difficult time for anyone to study the effects of grief and to try to learn how to cope (or to help others cope) is after a loss occurs. If schools are to play a positive role in helping students to cope with the losses they will inevitably encounter—or with the deaths of loved ones which may occur—we must take action before such a loss occurs and not after the fact.

An illustration of how not to address grief can be found in the aftermath of the 1986 Challenger space shuttle disaster. In many schools, educators wanted to do the "right thing," but were themselves in shock. Televisions had been turned on in classrooms and common areas so that students could watch another American "triumph" in space, including the trip of Christa McAuliffe, the first teacher in space. As these televisions replayed the explosion over and over, few people did anything. The whole spectacle was simply unbelievable. Teachers and students watched the screen to see some glimpse of the shuttle emerging from the blast. It was not to be. In the school where I taught, there was no general announcement of any kind. The next day there was a moment of silence followed by one teacher's poetic tribute to Christa McAuliffe. However, unlike this female teacher, not all of the students had identified with Ms. McAuliffe. Some were angered by this assumption about their feelings. They personalized the loss by identifying with one or more of the other six crew members, and they took their omission from the tribute to be a personal slight. When a bulletin board was posted to honor all seven astronauts, some of the anger finally dissipated. By the end of the second day, the school had finally started to respond, but why had nothing been done on that important first day?

The answer is that it takes time to identify what has happened and it takes even more time to decide on an appropriate way to respond. All of these decisions were being made in the midst of the crisis. In accordance with state regulations, this school has two fire drills every month, as does every public school. In over 35 years of existence, this school has never had a serious fire. However, it has suffered the deaths of students, parent, teachers, and other national figures and still had no idea how to respond to an episode that prompted community grief. A caring faculty and an involved parent-teacher organization had never, in any meaningful way, attempted to develop a planned response to such losses.

The students in my death education class helped to construct guidelines for dealing with death in the school. Because a death education course was already in place, the students in that class had discussed and thought about many issues related to death and grief. These students asked other students and teachers to recall the questions they had when the tragedy took place. The guidelines were built around these questions.

Who should tell the students that something has happened? The students believed that it should be someone in authority. However, it should *not* be done over the public address system or in an impersonal school assembly. The best person seemed to them to be a classroom teacher or counselor—someone with whom they had developed a prior relationship. At the time of the Challenger explosion, nothing was said until the next day. Students felt that teachers or administrators should have said something to clarify what had just happened. This could have helped control rumors and avoid some of the anxiety caused by feelings of uncertainty about what students had, in that case, just witnessed.

Where should the students be told? An individual student should be told in a private place where he or she may remain after hearing the news. The school nurse's office or a counselor's office was recommended. When the loss affects the entire school community, a school-wide announcement should be made in individual classes by the teachers. If possible, all classes should be informed simultaneously. This would, clearly, necessitate prior planning.

What should be told to the students? The student answer to this was a simple one—the truth. Tell them what happened and do it in an honest, direct manner.

How should the students be told? The students offered several suggestions. They said such information should be kept simple. The meaning of words should be clear. Platitudes should be avoided. The educator should be sure that students understand what has been said. Misunderstanding can lead to hurtful rumors. Allow student questions and answer them as honestly as you can.

These questions formed the basis for a later protocol that was designed to assist educators dealing with the need to inform students of a death. The school community had come through a traumatic event together and, by discussing their individual experiences, gave future students and teachers a better way to deal with such a crisis.

What is Death Education?

The label "death education" has been applied to a wide range of student experiences. It does not simply refer to any course in which the word "death" is mentioned or discussed. An English class that is reading Shakespeare's *Hamlet* or *Romeo and Juliet* may not be dealing with this in a context of death education. Death education is defined as a formal curriculum that deals with dying, death, grief, and loss and their impact on the individual and on humankind. After a quarter century of death education courses in schools, it has become clear that educators and students can benefit from having the study of death and loss as a part of the curriculum.

Benefits for students

It is essential to look at the impact of death and loss education on students. After all, it is the effect upon students that is the ultimate standard by which any such program should be judged. What, then, are the specific benefits to students of studying these topics before a death occurs? My quarter century of experience in teaching courses dealing with loss and death has shown that such a course produces several positive benefits. These typically include:

Preparation for coping with future losses The study of dying, death and grief can serve as preparation and mitigation in helping an individual or family to cope with loss. The Federal Emergency Management Agency (FEMA) works with preparation for disaster prevention and recovery on local, state, and federal levels. FEMA has identified four phases in dealing with any emergency. They are Preparation, Response, Recovery, and Mitigation. Preparation includes actions taken to help prevent negative consequences from a possible emergency. Response includes actions taken during the emergency. The Recovery phase includes all actions taken to restore a situation to "normal" (or as close as possible) after an emergency. The Mitigation phase includes those steps taken to reduce the negative impact of such an emergency in the future. When there are crises that may occur more than once, mitigation is perhaps the most important part of the cycle. This same cycle can be applied to the losses an individual will encounter in life.

Death education courses can help in all four phases, but they are most effective in prevention and mitigation. Information received in death education classes can help students to understand what they are experiencing and what may be expected of them when a loss occurs. As Prevention, students are given knowledge of what to expect if they attend a funeral or memorial observance. When this knowledge is put into practice, it becomes part of the Response phase. The experience of grief can be frightening and some student attempts at coping with the experience may prove ineffective or even counter-productive. Students may manifest their anxiety through questions about seemingly small details. What should I wear? How should I behave? What will I see? What will I be expected to do? By knowing these things in advance, students report feeling less anxious about saying or doing something inappropriate. As Mitigation, such knowledge can help prevent a loss from turning into an even greater tragedy through ineffective or destructive attempts at coping or through inappropriate words, dress, or actions.

By examining how individuals have coped with past losses, the course can help the student to develop more effective coping styles to use when losses occur in the future. Knowledge of the elements that are present in grief can assist bereaved students in recovery. For example, it is important for students to know that an inability to concentrate can sometimes be the result of grief and should not cause the person to feel guilty about any perceived "lowering" of academic performance.

Is there a guarantee that this will work for every student? Sadly, the answer is no. However, by presenting students with the option of taking such a course, every student will at least have the opportunity to develop coping styles that may mitigate the negative consequences of future losses.

Improved communication For many years in this country, death was a taboo topic. As students study and discuss death, the taboo falls away. Such discussions take place not just in the classroom, but in the home as well. In follow-up questionnaires, majorities of students and parents identified improved communication as the first and greatest benefit of death education. Channels of communication, once opened, were used to discuss other topics that may have formerly been taboo as well.

Increased knowledge and academic skills The academic tools used to measure increased knowledge (in the areas of psychology, sociology, history) included testing of student knowledge in each area, measuring improvement in academic skills (such as reading, essay writing, and forming effective generalizations) and problem-solving strategies. The increases shown by the students in death education classes were greater than the improvement shown by those same students in the English, history, and social science courses they were taking at the same time.

The topic of death is of such importance to students that their interest in this subject takes them far beyond the "limits" they had previously placed on themselves. Student research was on a sufficiently high level that one school's death education students wrote and published several articles for professional journals. Death education students made presentations at medical conferences at Columbia-Presbyterian Medical Center and at Columbia and St. John's Universities in New York City. I watched in appreciation as one student sat discussing the impact of grief with a doctor at Columbia during a break in the presentations. The doctor stopped the young man and asked, "Are you a medical student, or are you just an undergraduate?" In fact, this young man was a "mainstreamed" special education student who, in a death education class, had finally "found his voice." Effects will clearly not always be that dramatic, but they are overwhelmingly positive.

Lessening of death-related fear and anxiety This is an area with "mixed" results. For students who reported a high degree of death-related fear, there was a lessening of such fears. As one student put it, "I used to think about death all the time, but I could never talk about it. Now I talk about it all the time, so I don't have to be afraid of it anymore." Students who had not previously thought much about the topic at first reported an increase in death-related fear, then a reduction in such fear as time passed and they had an opportunity to process the experience.

Greater feelings of personal control of life Children and adolescents often feel that their lives are beyond their control. The emotions associated with grief can magnify such feelings of helplessness. It is interesting to note that silence on the part of adults in the face of grief also magnifies such feelings. Are adults not acknowledging the student's loss because they too are "helpless?" Is it because there is nothing to be said that will improve how the student feels and the situation is thus "hopeless?" Or, worst of all, is the student guilty of some transgression and adults say nothing because this student is "worthless?" Feelings like helplessness, hopelessness, and loneliness are part of the emotions present in normal grief. When they are combined with worthlessness, they represent the emotions present in many suicide attempts. Feelings of guilt and anger from unresolved childhood grief have been found to be a factor in adult suicide attempts. Silence may reinforce and strengthen these very feelings. It is clear that silence is not an effective way to deal with student grief.

Students who have learned the physical and emotional effects of grief report that they still hurt after a loss, but they also feel less isolated and afraid. By understanding what it is that they are experiencing, they say that they feel their lives to be less "out of control" when a death or other major loss occurs. My grandmother was fond of saying, "Happiness shared is happiness multiplied. Sorrow shared is sorrow divided." Death education classes can be a safe place to "share sorrow," and they have the ability to help students develop an awareness of the support that can be there for each of them in the future when other losses do occur.

Life is felt to be more precious Although not at the top of the list, this point is made by every group of students who take death education classes. Students say that each day becomes more precious to them and that they are less likely to take it for granted. Students' behavior may or may

not bear this out, but this may be one of those cases in which what someone believes to be true can actually be more important than "reality."
Students in post-course evaluations speak of telling family members that
they love them, visiting relatives that they may have avoided previously,
and becoming involved in public service projects and in charity fundraising. These student stories of stronger family "bonding" run counter to the
criticism that death education courses undermine family authority. If anything, students who have looked at death say they appreciate life, and see
the importance of family in that life.

Greater appreciation of cultural diversity In looking at the ways in
which people mourn the dead and express their grief, students can study
in a practical way the similarities and differences among cultures. Very different ceremonies can have the same goals—removal of the deceased's
body, recognition (and, possibly, celebration) of the life that has been
lived, acceptance that that life is now ended, and beginning of the grieving process of the survivors. Since death and grief are experiences that
are truly universal, studying the cultural expressions of grief gives students
a basis on which to build greater appreciation of cultures other than
their own.

Possible therapeutic effects When we look at the possible benefits of
death education, it is also important to recognize the limits of such courses. Death education courses are just that: academic courses with established curricula and trained teachers. Even if some students experience
therapeutic effects, these courses are not therapy for "troubled" individuals. As one psychiatrist put it, "When we teach, what we 'cure' is
ignorance." In this case, it is ignorance about the nature of grief. Some
students in a death education course may have problems that would best
be dealt with in outside counseling. When this occurs, the school has
counselors available (and, in some schools, psychologists and consulting
psychiatrists). In addition, there are mental health and counseling centers
in the community that work with schools and regularly accept referrals,
when these are made in consultation with parents or guardians of
the student.

Clearly, because of the strong emotional component of death
education, there is a great need for teachers who are properly prepared to
deal with this sensitive subject. Anytime there is the ability to offer great

help to students, there is also the possibility that inappropriate action can cause great hurt. Schools that institute death education courses should maintain a program of evaluation and revision to monitor such courses. The school should seek input from educators, counselors, students, parents, and community members in evaluating the course and its place in the school.

Death Education's Place in the Curriculum

Everything contained in this chapter is intended to use with death education programs in secondary and elementary schools. The high school course that provided much of the information upon which this material is based was developed in 1972 and taught by me from 1972 until my retirement in 1997. Just as one cannot take college material and bring it into a high school classroom without evaluation and modification, high school content and methodology cannot be moved into elementary school without similar evaluation and adaptation. My course began as a nine-week social studies elective and was expanded to 18 weeks (one semester) and paired with a psychology elective to give students a full-year program. In schools that cannot devote an entire course to issues of loss and grief, modules have been developed for use within health, social studies, English, and science courses. Family-living courses often are given the task of dealing with this topic. In New Jersey the state mandated some time ago that school family-living courses must teach the "full life cycle" from birth to death. However, the state never offered suggestions or materials to help educators implement their directive. Death education units were found to fit the bill quite nicely. Death education courses on a high school level, whatever their "parent" discipline, are never unrealistic. However, as a practical matter, units or modules covering one or more aspects of loss and grief can be placed in a curriculum within existing courses to at least begin to deal with this important topic.

On an elementary school level, complete units or modules on loss or grief have not become popular with educators. However, books that deal with themes of death or loss in an age-appropriate context are used regularly. The discussion that often follows such reading has been found to have positive benefits for the students. In every death education class below the college level, it is important to encourage students to discuss with family members what they are learning in class. At the elementary school level, it is essential that parents be informed when material related to loss and grief is being used in school. This allows parents to be supportive to their children and to monitor the impact of this material on them. It also avoids possible negative reactions that can occur when such topics are discussed without the knowledge of parents.

Summary

Why teach children about death and dying? The answers start with the fact that knowledge is better than ignorance. If that is not true, then our schools have no function at all. Our schools have been charged with educating the "whole child," not some type of disembodied intellect. Students do experience loss and the deaths of those whom they love or with whom they identify. Grieving students will manifest different behavior in school and it is beneficial for students and teachers to know more about such possible behavior. Each of us is unique in many ways. Death education helps students to see that individuals experience loss and express grief in many different ways. By doing this, they can come to appreciate their uniqueness, instead of feeling lonely, misunderstood, or "weird." It is important for them to know that, no matter what their reaction, others too have felt or reacted this way and have still gone on with their lives. Death education will not shield students from the pain of loss. But experiencing such a class has helped many students by sparing them additional, unnecessary pain. It is said that knowledge is strength. That, by itself, is often not true. However, understanding what that knowledge means to each student and how each can use it in his or her life—that is real strength. It is a real gift that educators can offer to their students through death education.

Robert G. Stevenson, EdD, designed and taught a high school death education course for 25 years. He currently works in a residential alcohol/drug rehabilitation program and teaches graduate counseling courses at Mercy College in New York. He is an active member of both the International Work Group On Death, Dying, and Bereavement and the Association for Death Education and Counseling.

When a Student
or Staff Member Dies:
An Action Plan for Schools

Schools are advised to have a protocol or action plan should a member of the school community die. This plan should be periodically reviewed and modified. Central to any plan is that a crisis team consisting of administrators, teachers, and support staff should be formed and trained. A telephone chain is helpful, as all staff, as much as possible, should be informed prior to coming to school. This team will be the key to any effective response. Here are suggestions for the components of such a plan.

As soon as they are informed of the death, the crisis team should meet.
The initial work of the team will be to determine the correct information, as well as the wishes of the deceased's family. Once information is clarified, the team can plan to respond. In this response, the team should identify students, faculty, and staff most at risk. In assessing risk, the team should remember that not all strong attachments are positive. Both enemies and friends may be affected.

Be sure information is accurate.

Rumors are much less likely to occur when the information shared is accurate, uniform, and complete. Inform classes in a matter-of-fact tone.

Encourage discussion.

Recognize that the day will not be a normal day. Students and staff will need to discuss and review the life and death of the person, as well as process their own reactions.

Have help available.

It is helpful to have counselors available for students and staff that seem most affected by the loss. These counselors should reach out to students and staff with strong attachments. But they should also allow students and staff to self-select into counseling should they feel a need. The death of someone can raise a sense of vulnerability in people with no visible connection to the deceased.

Encourage students and staff to reach out to the family.

Students may need help in knowing what to say and what to do. School personnel should definitely have a presence at the funeral.

Shape a group response.

It may be helpful to students and staff to respond as a group. Depending on the needs, circumstances, and culture, responses can include contributing for flowers, or memorializing in other ways.

Inform parents.

Parents should receive a letter informing them of what has happened, how the school responded, how they can help their children, and where they can receive help.

Handle the deceased's personal effects, such as papers, in a careful manner.

These papers should be offered to family. In some cases, family may not really know what they want in the early phases of grief. It is better to hold personal effects for a year, even if the family does not express initial interest. Never send them without warning to families, and *do* remove the family from any automatic communications. For example, in one case, parents continued to receive absence notes after their daughter died.

Finally, do not ignore the needs of staff.

Their needs and grief must be recognized even as they reach out to others. The emphasis on staff is critical, as they can easily be overlooked.

Part III

Special Losses

This section, emphasizing the unique nature of distinct losses, provides a challenge to an editor. Of the many losses that children and adolescents experience, how does one select which particular losses should be singled out for review? Many other losses—such as the loss of a parent by divorce, probably one of the more common losses children and adolescents experience—are worthy to be included. The natural selectivity of this section does not mean to imply that the losses considered here are the most important or critical. Rather, they serve as models, reminding us of the ways that individual factors in *any* loss, such as the relationship or circumstances, affect the process of grief.

The chapters in this section explore two major relationships in the lives of children—parents and siblings. Silverman's chapter reminds us of the crucial role of parents in the life of a child. Davies stresses the role of siblings. Siblings share special relationships that are not always appreciated. Siblings can be friends as well as kin and they often share sets of experiences that provide a special bond. Only my sister and brother, for example, can fully appreciate references to shared family experiences, such as vacations or memories of relatives. And both siblings and parents remain part of our identity. Being Dot or Franky's kid brother shaped who I am today. And my son constantly reminds me how much I share characteristics of my dad.

Silverman's and Davies' chapters stress another critical fact—the death of a parent or child can radically affect the functioning of a family, further complicating grief. These chapters are further illustrated by the poignant *Voices* contributions of Whitehead and Kaskeski. And Goodridge reminds us of the loss of a grandparent. Their pieces also speak to the variety of critical relationships, both kin and non-kin, that children and adolescents experience.

The remaining chapters consider how the circumstances of loss influence grief. Carroll and Mathewson review the unique nature of military losses, in an excellent consideration of both facilitating and complicating factors. Support, shared experience, and ritual assist survivors. But the sudden nature of loss and the secondary losses that follow complicate grief. Both Martin, in his chapter on suicide, and Sheras, as he considers violent and traumatic loss, further develop this theme. And both illustrate the crucial roles that schools can play in responding to loss.

Beyond the ways in which the individual nature of the loss complicates and facilitates grief, other themes emerge in this section as well.

Loss Affects Children Even at Young Ages

Both Silverman and Davies note that even young children are affected by loss. Even if they cannot fully comprehend death, they can recognize and respond to changes in their environment. Just short of four when his father died, Whitehead still shares memories and feelings about that event.

With Each Loss, There Are Secondary Losses

Secondary losses are losses that follow the initial loss. For example, when Kaskeski's dad died, she had to move out of a supportive environment into another culture. Both Silverman and Davies remind us that the illness and death of a sibling or parent may entail a range of secondary losses, such as the decreased involvement of other family members. Traumatic losses challenge our sense of safety, a point emphasized in Gordon and Doka's theoretical note on resonating trauma.

Losses Continue to Affect Children Throughout Life

Silverman's chapter strongly addresses this theme, even as it is recognized throughout the book. Loss is part of human development, and as we continue to develop, we revisit these losses. As Silverman and Davies both stress, we continue to maintain a relationship, albeit a changed one, with a deceased parent or sibling. Whitehead's *Voices* piece illustrates that point. Though his father died many years ago, he wonders how he is like and unlike him, a normal adolescent quest for identity. Even in adulthood, these losses will continue to be reviewed and restored, for these attachments never really end. Our task, then, is never to help children and adolescents get over or even through a loss. Rather, it is to assist them as they continue to live a meaningful life even in the face of loss.

14

When Parents Die

Phyllis R. Silverman

This chapter describes some of the factors to consider in understanding children's reactions to the death of a parent. Any intervention that might be offered to help bereaved children and their families needs to be responsive to these realities in the bereaved child's world. We need to match any help offered to what the bereaved are actually experiencing, to their resources, and to the social context in which they are living.

Findings from the Harvard/Massachusetts General Hospital Child Bereavement Study provide the data for this paper. The Child Bereavement Study at Harvard/MGH examined over time the impact of a parent's death on children ages six to seventeen. Both children and their surviving parent were interviewed, in their homes, approximately four months after the death, as well as one and two years later. A community sample from the greater Boston area, 125 children in 70 families, was recruited through the funeral directors who served them at the time of the death. Interviews with respondents were audiotaped and included many open-ended questions, thus allowing them to tell their story in their own words (Silverman and Worden, 1992, 1992a, 1993; Worden and Silverman, 1993, 1996; Silverman, Nickman, and Worden, 1992; Silverman and Nickman, 1996; Normand, Silverman, and Nickman, 1996; Nickman, Silverman, and Normand, 1998; Silverman, 2000).

Factors to Consider in Understanding
Children's Reactions to the Death of a Parent

Grief as a transition, not an illness

In talking about grief in children or in their surviving parents there are many ways of understanding what they are experiencing. In fact, there is no right way or wrong way to grieve. Sometimes it is easier to cope with the situation if we have a theory that explains the experience. One approach that until recently has dominated our thinking looks at grief as primarily an inner psychological phenomenon. The feelings of sadness, of confusion, of longing, and the anxiety about the vacuum in one's life are seen as something to be expunged as quickly as possible. In this view, grief is seen as an illness, and the negative consequences of this illness can be prevented by helping the child express his or her feelings. People who see grief this way talk about "recovering" and "bringing closure" to the experience within a limited period of time. If the child doesn't do so, they are seen as being at risk of developing serious emotional problems. In many ways this view is often incompatible with the actual experience of bereaved families. They find that there are too many other things happening as they struggle with the loss and its impact on their lives.

In another view, grief is understood as a life-cycle transition, albeit unexpected given the family's place in the life cycle. This view focuses on the broad range of issues and tasks that the surviving parents and their children have to attend to as they move in time away from the death (Baker and Sedney, 1996; Silverman, 2000). When viewed as a life-cycle transition it is easier to see that grief is more than the expression of extreme feelings. More than a life is lost when a parent dies. Not only has a person died but a way of life is lost as well. The self they were in this relationship is also gone. It is a time of loss and change in the family's life. The goal of help is to enhance the mourner's ability to find ways of living in this moving, changing situation.

One of the findings of the Child Bereavement Study is that grief does not end at a given time (Silverman and Nickman, 1996; Silverman 2000). It is not something that children can simply put behind them or "get over." The bereaved, both the surviving parent and their children, often feel isolated, as if something is wrong with them, when their experience does not coincide with the advice they are given to "seek closure," to "put the past behind them," or to "let their grief go." A mother of teenage boys reflected on how she felt a year after her husband's death:

People keep telling me I will feel better, the children will return to normal. I wondered what was wrong with me when nothing was the same as before. What was I doing wrong? I finally realized that everything was different—we would be okay, but never like before. I stopped talking to most people. They didn't want to hear about our pain, about the ups and downs and all the changes we were dealing with.

In fact, as children mature and as a result of their experience, they develop a greater depth of understanding of the death. An eleven-year-old reflected on how he has changed:

I didn't think I would ever feel better; I couldn't concentrate or think about anything. I thought the world would end without my mother. I wouldn't talk to anyone. I can't believe that one year later, I still miss my mother and I feel sad but I can study and I'm getting along with my friends. I'm lucky they stayed with me.

Children will revisit the meaning of their parent's death many times over their lifetime. They will experience the loss in different ways at various stages and phases of their lives, such as graduation, marriage, or the birth of a child. This is not an expression of unresolved grief. Their accommodation and adaptation is a dynamic, ongoing process.

Children are often facing, for the first time, the fact that people die. To some extent children lose their innocence and the expectation that their parents can protect them from all the vicissitudes of life. They need to learn to make room for this fact of life in their experience. They need to learn to deal with unusual feelings with which they have had little experience, and to live in a world that has changed for them in ways that they could not have imagined.

Life does not stop while they deal with their feelings and sort out what is happening. The family has to find continuity with the past while constructing new ways of living together in a single parent bereaved family with a changed family system. They need to develop a new sense of what is normal, given the changed circumstances.

Children do not grieve alone. Children are part of a family, all of whom have been affected by the death. One mother observed, shortly after her husband's sudden death, that every time his father's name was mentioned her nine-year-old ran into his room:

> *He hid under the bed and who could blame him, I was ready to join him there. I guess I looked okay on the outside, I needed to be there for the children, but if someone could see inside, they would feel the tumult, the terror.*

The family that both the children and their surviving mother or father once knew is gone. A way of life is lost. In the words of a thirteen-year-old girl, "I couldn't imagine how we would get on without my father. Nothing seemed right." One father felt as if he were in someone else's house. Another mother talked about her fears:

> *Everything changed. They had gotten used to his being there after school since he couldn't work anymore. My husband was a nurturer and he really enjoyed listening to all the day's news. I wasn't sure I could handle it alone. He gave me balance and a bit of humor. That's gone.*

The gender of the surviving parent makes a difference. Men and women, not invariably but often, approach their grief in somewhat different ways (Silverman, 1980, 1988; Cook, 1988; Worden and Silverman, 1992; Silverman and Worden, 1993; Silverman, 2000; Martin and Doka, 1998). In considering the effects of the death of a parent, differences in terms of the roles of mothers and fathers in the family need to be considered as well (Boerner and Silverman, 1999; Silverman, 2000). Women seem to relate more to the emotional needs of the family and are more responsive in providing children with support and care. Even when the women worked and fathers were accustomed to helping in the house, in this study population women were the ones who cared for the emotional needs of the family and made the house into a home. Most children reported that they were not used to talking to their father about the details of daily life or confiding about their friends. This was most often the role their mothers played in their lives. In most families where the mother is the surviving parent there seemed to be fewer changes in the family's daily routines (Silverman and Worden, 1993). In the words of one mother, "I just went on doing what I always did—not much changed in that sense."

Several mothers, in anticipation of their own deaths, recognized their husband's limitations in nurturing their children and advised them to remarry so the children would have a mother. Yet fathers did rearrange their lives to care for the children, taking jobs that were closer to home or that had less demanding hours. Many fathers recognized that they had a good deal to learn about parenting. One father talked about his twelve-year-old son. His older children were grown:

I had a lot to learn. I wasn't sure I could do it. He was so close to his mother, her baby. We've come a long way. We now talk, we do things together. I'm here for him and we are managing. He's doing good in school and he has lots of friends who he brings home.

Women, too, have a good deal to learn about keeping the family together and keeping the household going. They need to learn to parent alone. Many of the women in this sample had lived with their parents until they married. The mother of a school-age child and a teenager talked about her concerns:

My husband knew how to take care of all the little things in the house. He was always there to back me up. I don't know how I can be alone. I think there is always the worry. Can I hang on to the house? Am I going to raise my kids well enough? Can I get a job with mother's hours and health insurance to carry us through so I can be with the children as much as possible?

Whether it was mother or father who was the surviving parent, at some point after the death both had to come to the realization that they had to learn to be a single parent and this job required new skills. The content of what they needed to learn was not the same, depending on their role in child care in the family before the death. It is not simply gender that made the difference in what was lost for the family with the death. There was no longer a division of labor that balanced the differing qualities of each parent.

The nature of the death

When a death is expected it is impossible to protect children from knowing what is happening. They see and they hear. Even in the case of a long illness, death is most often experienced as unexpected. While the shock of a sudden unexpected death is very profound, in the Child Bereavement Study families, at the end of two years, this did not seem to be a factor in how children and their families accommodate to the loss (Silverman and Worden, 1993).

What does seem to be an issue for some children is how they understand what caused the death. This understanding can have repercussions on their own future physical and emotional well being. For example, several mothers died of cancer at the same age as their own mothers had died. For their daughters this knowledge created a fear and anxiety that needed to be named and legitimated. In one family where these fears were not recognized, the girls developed antisocial behavior that in many ways was self-destructive. It was as if they did not see much hope for their own futures. In contrast, in another family the genetic issue was addressed openly. The children were involved in learning self-care skills and in developing an attitude that would promote their involvement in the care of their own bodies. They understood there was no magic bullet but they didn't feel helpless and trapped. In a family where the father died as a direct result of alcoholism, the mother had taught the children to see their father as a caring, loving man who had an illness. The children were able to see that there were two sides to their father. They could see the tragedy of his illness and how he fell victim to it, and they understood that nothing they could have done would have prevented this outcome unless their father changed. In contrast, in one family the mother was clinically depressed, but this was never explicitly acknowledged. The children had no idea that their mother had an illness and how this related to her death. They saw themselves as somehow to blame for her being upset and sad all the time, and this was reflected in the ongoing tension in the family.

The view children have of their parent's death and its repercussions for them depends on the surviving parent's ability to face the reality of what has happened, to give it words that accurately describe the condition, and to communicate this to their children to give them accurate information abut how the death affects them (Silverman, Baker, Boerner, and Chait, 1999).

The child's age and stage of development affects their sense of who died and what is lost. The typical research into children's understanding of death examines the child's responses to questions about the finality, universality, irreversibility, and causality of death (Koocher, 1976; Smilansky, 1987; Speece and Brent, 1996). When a parent dies, children grapple with the qualities of death almost immediately. However, their understanding is not simply related to age but to their experience (Bluebond-Langner, 1997). What children experience as lost with the death, how they talk about their parent, and how they understand his or her place in their lives may be more critical than the researchers' theoretical focus on children's age-specific understanding of death (Silverman, 2000).

Children's ability to know the other and to take the role of the other, to reflect on their own behavior and to see how they interact with others, increases over time as they grow and mature (Kegan, 1982, 1993; Selman, 1989). Younger children see their parent as someone who does things for them, who meets their needs. They need their parent to keep their world together and provide them with stability and certainty. They do not yet have the ability to experience their parent as a person with needs of her own. Each stage brings with it a different ability to understand and reflect on the world and oneself, and therefore to reflect on the meaning of the death. As the child matures they begin to set aside their own needs and become aware of the other person as someone with needs of her own, and by adolescence the child should be able to construct a relationship in which he can find a place for his own needs and the needs of others as well. With the death of his or her parent, children, depending on their age and stage of development, will have lost very different people (Silverman, 2000). For example, a child of seven says she is sad because "Daddy will not be there to throw me in the air when he comes home. We snuggled when we watched TV. Now I have no one to snuggle with."

At this age children have lost someone who did things for them, who gave them pleasure, who was there in the service of their needs. A child of ten will ask "Who will help me with my homework, who will play baseball with me?" As they get a bit older children are beginning to be more aware of their own needs, not only for someone to do things for them but with them. They can use words to state in a more abstract fashion what their parent provided them.

A child of twelve may say of her mother, "She was a good cook, I could talk to her about anything." At this age she has an awareness of individual parental qualities—but still as they meet her needs. By the time they are teenagers, when a parent dies, children talk about losing a friend. "We were really just getting to know each other." "The house is really empty without her voice and her laughter." There is a sense that what is lost is the developing interaction with the parent whom the child was just beginning to know. Older children can recognize what the deceased lost as well. As the child gets older his very sense of who died changes (Silverman, 2000).

Constructing a relationship with the deceased

Children seem to find comfort and solace from remembering and constructing a relationship with the deceased (Silverman and Nickman, 1996; Normand, Silverman, and Nickman, 1996). They do not live in the past but remain connected to the deceased in various ways that change as they develop. For example, a ten-year-old's construction reflects his understanding of what his father wanted for him: "I always do my homework, he would be furious if I didn't do well in school."

His father still serves as an appropriate agent of control in his life. An older child can see his behavior differently: "It is important that I do well in school. It meant a lot to my father and it's like I am carrying on his memory in what I do."

The older child can take the role of his father and the part he (the child) plays in their relationship so that in a sense he becomes what we have called his father's "living legacy" (Normand, Silverman, and Nickman, 1996). Nickman, Silverman, and Normand (1997) observed the role of the surviving parent in helping their children find a place for the deceased in their lives. Parents' ability to help the child in part depends not only on how they view the mourning process, but on their understanding of where the child is developmentally.

The family system shifts and changes. The family drama centers on the ability of the system to deal with change. To a large extent how this takes place depends on the surviving parents' ability to orchestrate and guide the shifting scene at a time when their own resources are taxed beyond belief. The ability to do so depends on how they experience their own grief and how they understand their children's behavior. They will have difficulty if they do not see the connection between their children's age and stage of development, and the child's reaction to the death. Those parents who can involve the children in the family drama, who recognize their children as mourning and needing care and support, seem to have an easier time finding ways to shift gears and appreciate their own competence to act in the new situation (Silverman, 2000).

It is not easy for parents to recognize their children's needs as mourners. Many parents worry about whether or not the death of one parent will impair their children psychologically. While parents often focused on their concern that their children were not letting their feelings out, they were very relieved when children carried on as before with few displays of disruptive or atypical behavior. There seemed to be at least two perspectives from which the parents responded (Silverman and Gross, 1996; Silverman, 2000). There were parents who were more *child-centered* and others more *parent-centered*. These patterns are not really mutually exclusive. Parents moved from one position to another with many gray areas.

Parent-centered families These parents seemed to be centered on themselves and their concerns about how they would react given the pressure they now feel. They focus on the deficit in the family. Children in these families often talked about their parent's wish for them to behave and not to be disruptive. These parents often rationalized that the child's reactions were due to a developmental growth spurt rather than the death, ignoring that it was probably both. For example, one mother suggested that her six-year-old's nightmares were simply related to his age. In this way she minimized the impact of the death. Some parents could not separate their own reactions from those of their children, and it was difficult to know whose grief they were talking about. Most recognized their importance to their children, and they were indeed doing the best they could under the circumstances. From the point of view of physical care, all these children were well cared for. There was a sense of continuity in their lives, and they were going to school and continuing with their routine activities. There was not, however, a real sense of connection to how much the loss meant to them, and they did not feel legitimated as mourners.

Child-centered families Parents with a child-centered perspective focused on how the family had to change to deal with the new situation. Child-centered parents were often proactive as they thought about their children's needs and could set aside their own needs for the moment. A mother of a six-year-old reported how worried her child was about whether or not the Easter bunny would come after her father's sudden death. The Mother said that her older children wanted to be alone and needed time to be with their friends. This left the mother with space to focus on her six-year-old. Nonetheless, she was also aware that she was in no condition to deal with her young daughter's wish to make Easter eggs at the same time that she (mother) was arranging a funeral. She invited her niece to come and to color eggs in the mother's kitchen. She thus provided her child with the security of being in her own home and seeing that life goes on. This mother understood what was needed. She understood that focusing on the Easter eggs was what a six-year-old needed in order to feel secure in a world that had suddenly fallen apart in a way that she could barely understand. The mother was able to mobilize resources to help her meet her child's needs while respecting her own limitations.

Child-centered parents were aware that their children needed to learn to talk about the deceased as well as about the feelings they had never experienced before. One mother found a way to encourage her teenage sons to talk about their father and to help them validate some of what she thought they might be feeling. She invited them into a conversation, not about feelings but about their father. Talking about the deceased can often be more valuable than talking directly about feelings (Silverman and Nickman, 1996). Parents in this group were very clear that they would need to learn new ways to do the job of raising their children alone. Some were unsure how long it would take, but they knew that learning and change were involved. A father of an eight-year-old boy described the shift in his thinking from focusing on his own grief to recognizing his child's needs:

> I worked overtime for six months after the death. I ignored what was going on at home, as long as things were quiet. I realized one day that I had a young son to raise and it was my responsibility, not that of his older brother and sister. It was bad enough he lost his mother. He needed his father now.

Resources for Coping

Coping and adapting are dynamic processes as the bereaved family deals with the rhythm of their lives and the vicissitudes of their new and changing situation. None of us can deal with these changes without a little outside help. Thus, families found resources in others in their community, in themselves, and with each other (Silverman, 2000). The rituals and belief systems that frame their lives are also resources, as are clergy. Since children spend so much of their day in the classroom the role of the teacher is critical in helping bereaved children cope. In many communities there are additional resources that extend beyond the immediate helping network of the family. The mental health professional can be such a resource. Often when no specialized resources exist, as, for example, a center for bereaved children, parents themselves develop these resources. Often the role of the professional is to facilitate this process and collaborate with families to provide the range of services that may be needed in their community (Silverman, 2000). At times, to accomplish their goal may involve changing attitudes about death and grief in the community as well.

What do children need to help them adapt to their new situation? Children need to live in an environment that provides them with care, continuity, and connection (Silverman, 2000). *Care* is a synonym for social support. Children need to know that there is someone to be a guide for them, to teach them, and to provide feedback about how well or poorly they are doing, to "be there" for them—to meet their emotional, social, and physical needs. Children need to be listened to and to be recognized as active partners in the family drama. Is their voice heard? The spoken as well as the unspoken word? The nature of the surviving parent's response to the child's communication becomes very important. A child dealing with stress needs the safety of knowing that there is some continuity in their lives between the past, the present, and the future. *Continuity* provides the child with a sense that the family will carry on and find its way. Children need an explanation, regardless of their age, of how the family will manage. They need reassurance that family, friends, and others will be there for them, that while the family had a past it also has a future. *Connection* means both that the child is included as part of the family and the family drama and that there is a connection to the deceased and a place in the family for him or her. While the relationship has changed radically the deceased parent is still part of the family and part of the child's identity (Silverman and Nickman, 1996).

For parents to meet their children's needs is an enormous task. It comes at a time when the parents themselves are preoccupied and grieving and have little energy for the demands of single parenthood.

Children need:

- *to have their grief legitimized*
- *to be able to learn in manageable segments so that they are not overwhelmed*
- *to learn a vocabulary that can help them describe and live with the changes in their lives*
- *to talk about who died, both positive and negative qualities*
- *to develop ways of honoring the dead and recognizing that their parent can be both present and absent in their lives*
- *to be included, in ways appropriate to their age and stage of development, in the family drama.*

Parents need:

- *to recognize that they are dealing with change in their lives and in their very sense of self*
- *to learn new skills appropriate to their new role as a single parent*
- *to learn how to talk to their child(ren) about who died, the nature of the death, their common grief, and how they will build their new lives together.*

There is no easy prescription to ease the pain but we can make learning easier when support and understanding are available to the family. There are ways of helping so that people feel less alone and become more competent to deal with the many faces of the bereavement process. The examples below for teachers and mental health professionals can help inform the work of other helpers as well.

How teachers can help:

- *Get as much information about what has happened as possible from the child's surviving parent, a close friend, or another relative.*
- *Ask what the family would like from the school and what they think would be most helpful to the child.*
- *Find out about funeral rituals and mourning practices and whether classmates can, with their parents' permission, be appropriately involved.*

- *Talk with the class about what has happened and allow them to react; suggest ways for them to be helpful and provide comfort to their classmate.*

- *In talking to bereaved children, listen to their story. Don't tell them how they feel or should feel, let them tell you how they, in fact, do feel. Some children don't want any special attention and some don't want to talk. Respect these differences.*

- *Be aware of how children react in age-specific ways. Avoid stereotyping, generalizations, and giving unsolicited advice.*

- *Recognize the long-term repercussions for children and that from time to time they may be upset long past the time when you think they should be "over it."*

- *Create a place in the school where children can retreat if they need quiet time for whatever reason.*

- *Children may need space to grieve by withdrawing from the class either physically or emotionally, or by being actively involved in the class. Respect the fact that they may know what they need and when they need it.*

- *Create a peer group with other teachers to talk about your own concerns about dealing with death in the classroom. Develop helpful guidelines and a curriculum that would facilitate this process.*

How mental health professionals can help:

- *Do not assume you understand the needs of the bereaved or where they are in the process.*

- *Encourage children and their surviving parent to tell their own stories. Let them be your guide and teacher.*

- *Rather than looking for pathology and what is wrong, focus on helping people recognize the impact of the death on their lives and help them to find ways of changing and adapting.*

- *Ask both children and their parent to tell you about who died before you ask about their feelings. What did they lose with this death?*

- *Examine with the surviving parent what is involved for them in assuming the role of single parent.*

- *Ask questions that help both the surviving parent and the children look at their belief systems and how they make meaning of what is happening to them, so that they can understand how these affect their behavior and appreciate their ability to act on their own behalf.*
- *Learn to stay with the pain in the family, don't try to take it away.*
- *Legitimize the need to remember and connect to the deceased.*
- *Accept the paradox that the bereaved cannot live in the past but that the past is part of the present and the future.*
- *Recognize that some problems have their roots in the family's pre-death experience and may need more traditional therapeutic interventions.*

Helpers need to be able to look at the full picture, some of which has been described above. Their emphasis should not be primarily on how people feel and on the deficits in their lives. Rather, they need to help the bereaved hear their own story, assess their situation and help them develop appropriate resources as needed (Silverman, 2000).

Phyllis R. Silverman, PhD, is Professor Emerita at the MGH Institute of Health Professions and an Associate in Social Welfare in the Department of Psychiatry at Massachusetts General Hospital and Harvard Medical School. She is Co-Principal Investigator and Project Director of the Child Bereavement Study.

The Child Bereavement Study was funded by the National Institute of Mental Health grant # MH-41791 and by grants from the National Funeral Directors Association and the Hillenbrand Corp. The author was co-principal investigator with J. William Worden. In addition the author was project director and is directing a continuing analysis of the data.

V · O · I · C · E · S

I Never Knew My Dad

Keith Whitehead

To tell you the truth, I never really knew my dad. My dad's name is Michael John Whitehead. He died when I was only three years old. The worst part of it is that he died the day before my fourth birthday. That was in 1989. Most of what I know about my dad I hear from stories from my mom or from my godfather. My godfather was my dad's friend ever since my dad was about seven years old. He had been sort of a big brother, and they became close friends. Before my dad died he asked his friend to do him a favor. The favor was to help take care of me like a grandparent.

The stories include good, funny, and bad things, sad stories about when he was ill. But I guess that is the same with everyone. From these stories, I picture my dad being like me in a lot of ways. One of my favorite stories goes back to when my father was twelve years old at this winter camp. The kids would sled down this big hill. There was one counselor who they thought was mean. When he was coming up the hill they would steer their sleds like they were aiming for him and he would jump out of the way. My dad was one of the youngest kids there. So when the counselor saw him aiming he decided to call my dad's bluff. Dad just smiled and ran right over him. I like that story because I am like that in a way. My friends kid that I don't bluff. I guess that's one thing I got from my dad.

I miss my dad at all different points. Mainly I think of him when my friends and their fathers do things together, like play sports. I wonder what he would be like, if we would be close or not. Every so often, my friends ask me questions like "Where does your dad live?" or "How tall is he?" I think they ask me the last question since I want to play college or maybe pro basketball. All I say is that he died. They say "sorry" and probably wish they never asked about him.

I wish I could remember him a little more. Even the things I do remember, I do not remember exactly. One sad thing I remember is going to visit him when he was sick. At the time, I was too young to understand he was dying so it did not really faze me then. Because I was so young, I didn't even get to go to his funeral. And since we moved, I cannot go to the cemetery. We do some things to remember him. For example, we light a candle at church. And when I was confirmed I took his middle name as my confirmation name. So now I am Keith Michael John Whitehead after my dad. Well, like I said, I really don't know my dad that much from experience. But I still miss him a lot.

Rest in peace, Dad.

Keith Whitehead is fourteen years old and in the ninth grade. He likes aggressive rollerblading, hip-hop music, and snowboarding.

15

Sibling Bereavement: We Are Grieving Too

Betty Davies

From the time a new baby enters the family, a special bond develops between the children. Older siblings take great pride in being the "big" brother or sister and help to care for younger ones, often teaching them new skills and socializing them to the outside world. The younger ones look up to their older brothers and sisters, seeking advice and assistance as they learn about the world. Siblings share household tasks and philosophize together about the wonders of the world. They share secrets from their parents and other adults. Siblings protect one another, support one another, and ally themselves against parents and others. Siblings also see each other as competitors, teasers, and antagonists. Such is the ambivalent nature of sibling relationships. Siblings, therefore, play significant roles in each other's lives. The death of a sibling is a potentially traumatic event.

Despite the impact of a child's death on brothers and sisters, many adults react as if children have no feelings about death and consequently assume that siblings do not grieve. If, on the other hand, adults are aware of children's capacity for grief, they often act to protect the children from sorrow. Whether acting on faulty assumptions or misguided intentions, the result for siblings is the same—they are often excluded from the family's mourning. Such separation only adds to siblings' confusion and to their sense of loneliness and isolation even in the midst of everyday activities. As a result, siblings are often the most neglected family members when another child dies.

Siblings' Bereavement Responses

Siblings' responses to the death of their brother or sister vary considerably. Because children do not usually verbally express their feelings and concerns in the ways that adults do, we have to look for other signs of their reactions. The most obvious way is to observe their behavior. Children may have sleep disorders, such as trouble going to sleep, fear of the dark, nightmares, or walking and talking in their sleep. Many children have difficulty eating—they may lose their appetite or overeat. These behaviors are considered normal in adults who are grieving; they are also normal reactions for grieving children.

Several studies have shown that the most common problems for children include fear and anxiety, crying, withdrawal and clinging, indifference, sadness and loneliness (Davies, 1983, 1985, 1999; Birenbaum, 1989; Birenbaum et. al., 1990; McCowan, 1982). Some children also are nervous, and others misbehave by not listening to their parents and becoming irritable and belligerent. Changes in school work are also common. We must pay attention not only to the child whose school work declines, but to the child whose school work improves markedly. The latter may reflect a child who is trying very hard to fulfill unrealistic self-imposed expectations, such as attempting to spare his parents further distress. Both responses are indicative of children coping as best they can with a situation that they find troubling and worrisome. What is significant about these responses is not whether or not any one response occurs, but the intensity and duration of the response and whether other responses are also present.

Finding that bereaved siblings' responses include behavior problems is not surprising. To find no changes in their behavior would be to deny the significance of the event for siblings. However, some children have more difficulty than others, and it is important for adults to be alert to the needs of these children. In some studies, about 25% of bereaved siblings demonstrated behavioral problems at levels comparable to those of children referred to mental health clinics; in the general population, behavior problems of only 10% of children reach this level (Davies, 1983, 1985; Birenbaum et. al., 1990).

Unfortunately, there is no certain way to identify those children whose behavior is a sign that they are in trouble, but the following behaviors may signal those children who may require further attention: Watch for children who are persistently sad, unhappy, or depressed; who may be persistently aggressive or irritable; who complain of being lonely and who have withdrawn from their involvement with activities, hobbies, or friends; who seem to worry a lot; who are persistently anxious or nervous; who may be having ongoing eating difficulties or recurrent nightmares; who do not seem to feel good about themselves; and who may be doing poorly in school. It is important to remember that we are looking for persistent changes in the child's behavior and for a pattern of problems. No one problem by itself is necessarily an indication of trouble. Though not requiring formal intervention, most bereaved siblings can benefit from opportunities to talk about their responses, not only at the time of the death, but for many years following.

The impact of sibling bereavement lasts for a lifetime. Years following the death, many bereaved siblings report that they still think about, talk to, and miss their deceased brother or sister. They often experience renewed and intense grief on occasions that would have been significant in their lives together, such as graduations, weddings, the birth of babies, career challenges, and even retirement in their later years. It is helpful to warn parents and older siblings about the recurring grief they may experience, and to reassure them that such reactions are common and are not signs of emotional disturbance.

A child's death not only has the potential of negative effects on surviving siblings; psychological growth often results as well. In one study, bereaved siblings scored higher than the standardized norms on a measure of self-concept (McClowry, Davies, Martinson, May, and Kulenkamp, 1987). Many siblings felt they had matured as a result of their experience, and they felt good about their abilities to handle adversity. As one teenage boy commented, "I have a better outlook on life now; I mean, I realize how important life is as a result of my sister's death." Interviews with parents also indicated that they perceived their children as more sensitive, caring individuals who had matured as a result of their experience with death. Many parents described their children as more compassionate and aware of other people's problems. In the words of one mother about her fifteen-year-old daughter, "She has learned a lot from her brother's death.

It hasn't been easy, but she has gained such insight about life and death. She has been exposed to things that most kids her age are not. She had to grow up faster, and she is very sensitive and patient. She is so much more tolerant of others as well."

Major Sibling Responses

Most of the sibling bereavement literature focuses on the types of responses described in the preceding section, particularly changes in children's behavior. However, a recent conceptualization of four encompassing sibling bereavement responses provides an expanded view (Davies, 1999). The first—"I hurt inside"—focuses on the emotional and psychophysiological reactions that are common to all who grieve, including siblings. The hurt stems from the vulnerability of being human, of loving others and missing them when they are no longer with us. The hurt that siblings feel includes sadness, anger, frustration, loneliness, fear, irritability, and all the many other emotions that characterize grief. Unlike adults who often talk about their emotional responses, children manifest their hurt in other ways. They may cry, withdraw, misbehave, fear the dark, seek attention, or overeat.

The second response category is "I don't understand." How children begin to make sense of death depends in large part on their level of cognitive development. Children under the age of two do not perceive death as such, but they are sensitive to separation from those who are familiar in their everyday lives. Even a child of eighteen months will miss his brother or sister, and at some level, feel abandoned by the older child who never returns. Egocentricity and magical thinking characterize the way in which young children view the world. Consequently, they are particularly vulnerable to feeling responsible for a brother or sister's death, especially since siblings sometimes wish the other would "just go away!" Children often believe that the dead will return, a perception that is reinforced by television where the same cartoon characters reappear time and time again after disastrous deaths. Consequently, young children expect that their deceased sibling will return as reflected in statements such as, "Johnny will come for my birthday—I know he will." Young children also perceive that the dead remain functional; this explains questions of "How will Marika eat in her coffin? Will there be toys in heaven for the baby to play with?"

School-age children become much more logical in their thinking. They are intrigued with how things work. They are increasingly interested in the details of death, asking pointed questions about graveyards, funerals, and body decomposition. By about age nine, they understand the biologic explanations about death, that is, the heart stops beating or the brain stops working. They understand the seriousness of terminal illness, but death is not yet a personal entity. Death happens to those who are old or very sick, but is not supposed to happen to children. A sibling's death therefore may be the cause of considerable worry.

Children over twelve years of age begin to accept the reality of personal death, at least in a theoretical sense. Young people realize that they can die, but do not usually believe it can actually happen to them. They now have an understanding of death as universal, inevitable, and irreversible. As siblings grow and develop new ways of viewing and understanding the world, they will have questions about the death. Each new phase of development will bring more questions and the desire to rehash the story yet again. This is a normal phenomenon and not a sign that the child is "dwelling" on the death.

Siblings need explanations about what has happened to their brother or sister that take into account their level of understanding. Similar explanations are required to help with their confusion about their own responses and those of others in the family. With the death of their brother or sister, their worlds have been forever changed, and they struggle to adapt to their new situation. Younger children especially may be frightened by the sometimes explosive and intense nature of their parents' anger, and often attribute parental outbursts to something they have done. Confused by their parents' reactions, and wanting to make things right again, siblings want to help but do not know how. They ask questions that are ignored or followed by long, awkward silence. Without careful explanations from the adults in their lives, siblings begin to feel as if they are different from the others; they feel separate and alone. Over time, as roles and responsibilities realign within the family, siblings may feel as if there is no place for them anymore. They may find solace outside of their family, but often their experience with death makes siblings, particularly adolescents, feel very different from their peers. They feel as if "I don't belong"—the third category of sibling responses.

Sometimes, siblings feel as if the child who died was their parents' favorite child; they may feel as if they are the ones who should have died instead. Often, such feelings of inferiority were present before the death and are only compounded after the death when parents direct intense emotion and longing toward the deceased child. No matter what they do or say, surviving siblings cannot seem to make their parents happy again. They feel as if "I'm not enough." Such siblings do not feel special in their parents' eyes.

For some siblings, a factor contributing to their feeling of less worth is their sense of responsibility for the death. This can happen easily when the death is the result of an accident in which the surviving child was involved, such as when a toddler drowns in a pool while under the supervision of an older child, or when a teenager is killed in the car her brother was driving. But it can also happen when the death follows an illness. For example, Tom's brother had cancer and was susceptible to infection. When Tom got the chicken pox, his brother was exposed to the virus, also developed chicken pox, and died. Tom's mother attributed her older son's death to Tom, as did his classmates. No one helped the family help Tom to alleviate his feeling of responsibility; Tom felt very much alone and unloved. He felt he could never undo the damage that had been done. He was certainly "not enough."

Another factor contributing to a sibling's sense of "I'm not enough" is a feeling of displacement by the addition of new family members, particularly other children who the siblings perceive as substitutes for the one who died. For example, four years after the death of their older son, Mr. and Mrs. Jensen adopted a boy who was about the same age as their surviving son, Jim. They thought it would help alleviate some of Jim's loneliness. Upon being informed of his parents' plan, Jim exclaimed, "But I don't want a replacement for Bob!" Jim felt, and rightly so, that no one could ever take his brother's place, yet he perceived this was what his parents were trying to do. He felt as if he was "not enough"—otherwise, why would his mom and dad need another son?

In other families, despite their own grief, parents interacted with their surviving children in ways that made the siblings feel special. These parents indicated that they loved their surviving children just as much as the one who died, and they did not even hint at blaming surviving children for the death. In addition, these parents took pride in all of their children, not necessarily for their accomplishments but just because of who they were. They also were explicit about telling their children how much they were loved. Such children did not feel as if they were not enough; they were confident of their parents' love for them and for the child who died.

Sibling Responses in Context

Sibling responses to the death of a brother or sister do not occur in isolation but within the context of many interrelated variables. Categorized into individual, situational, and environmental variables, they include those factors listed in Table One. No one category of factors, nor any one individual factor, accounts for the total experience of any child. However, some variables play a central role in how siblings respond.

Table One—Factors influencing sibling bereavement (Davies, 1999, 50)

- Individual Factors
    - Age
    - Gender
    - Health status
    - Dependence
    - Temperament
    - Coping style
    - Self-experience
    - Past experience with loss and death

- Situational Factors
    - Cause of death
    - Duration of illness
    - Place of death
    - Time elapsed since death
    - Involvement

- Environmental Factors
    - Shared life space
    - Centrality
    - Family environment
    - Parent/child communication
    - Parental grief
    - Family functioning

One factor that influences sibling response is whether the death is sudden and unexpected, or if it follows a downward illness trajectory. The death of a child from a progressive life-threatening illness implies that the deceased child had undergone a long course of treatment, often over many months or years. We assume then that families have anticipated the death of their child and that this somehow makes it easier for them. However, this is not the case. Even in the context of a prolonged illness, death is always a surprise and a shock. All parents hope that their child will be the miracle child who will recover at the last moment. They struggle to put aside their fears of death. Siblings also tend to appraise the situation in positive ways (Brett and Davies, 1988). As a result, there is always an element of the unexpected in a child's death, even if it is only, "We thought she would make it until the holidays," or, "I thought he would wait until I got home from school."

Closeness between siblings is another variable that influences sibling bereavement response. The closer the relationship between two siblings, the more difficulty the surviving child will have following the other's death. Closeness may override age and gender similarities. Though often hesitant to do so, family members can always identify which siblings were closest to one another. In one family, the fifteen-year-old brother was much closer to his four-year-old sister than were either of his two older sisters. He was the one who accompanied his little sister to the cancer clinic. When she was feeling very ill, he was the only one who could get the little girl to eat or drink or lie still during bone marrow aspirations. They shared a special bond. Upon the little girl's death, it was this boy who exhibited the most behavior problems and was the most withdrawn. The adolescent boy greatly missed his little preschool sister.

Environmental variables, particularly family social climate and level of functioning within the family, also play a critical role in affecting sibling bereavement outcome. Children react strongly to these factors since they are dependent on their families for the information and support they receive. Adults can go elsewhere should they choose to; children cannot. Openness within the family about sharing thoughts and feelings is especially significant in sibling bereavement. Children learn from their parents, and other adults, about grief and how to manage it. If they see their parents openly expressing their sadness through tears, if children hear conversations in which their parents talk about their sadness and how they deal with it, then children learn effective ways of expressing and managing their own sadness. The Martinez family, for example, openly shared their tears and sadness, and laughter and joy. In fact, Mr. Martinez described a family rule—"Never cry alone." Whenever family members felt sad and tearful, they were encouraged to find another family member to cry with. That way, the sadness could be shared and the inevitable loneliness that accompanies sadness could be reduced. What a different message the Martinez children received as compared to children in families where tears are not tolerated with messages of "That's enough crying now—we'll have no more of that!" Sometimes, regardless of the family attitude about crying, children will avoid tears or other visible expressions of grief in order to protect their parents.

Sibling bereavement responses occur within a broader context as well. Since families do not live in social vacuums, their culture and community values and priorities also contribute to the context of sibling bereavement. However, whether within the family, or outside of the immediate family, it is the interactions siblings have with the adults in their lives that are critical.

Adults' Interactions with Bereaved Siblings

Parents are often overwhelmed with their own grief. They feel burdened by their own reactions, by the multitude of arrangements that need to be made, and by having to care for their surviving children. They frequently do not have the energy to pay attention to their children's specific needs. They may not understand the changes in their surviving children; they may not realize the importance of sharing their own reactions with their children, and of being patient with them. Sometimes they berate or belittle the children's unique ways of responding to the death, and children hurt even more. They may themselves be consumed with their own pain and grief. But parents are doing the best they can in the midst of one of life's most difficult situations. Parents themselves need support and guidance so that they can tend to the needs of the surviving siblings. It is helpful for both parents and siblings to enlist the assistance of other adults who are familiar to the grieving children. A favorite aunt, uncle, family friend, or teacher can be asked to spend time with, and provide individual attention to, the child.

Adults who are meeting the needs of grieving siblings can think of the four major sibling responses as a way of guiding their time with the children. For children who "hurt inside," the goal is to help children accept whatever emotion they experience and to manage those emotions in appropriate ways. This is easier said than done. It means comforting and consoling the child. It means helping them to understand the reality of death and the feelings that arise. Since children seldom verbalize their thoughts and feelings—at least not in adults' terms—it's important that caring adults watch for changes in the child's behavior and respond sensitively. Children who are hurting inside do not need lectures, judgment, teasing, or interrogation. They need someone who is consistent and honest, and who is willing to share his or her own thoughts and feelings with the child. Helping children who "hurt inside" is a two-way process.

To help children who "don't understand," adults need to remember that confusion and ignorance are additional forms of hurting. Therefore, adults must continue to comfort and console. Adults have a responsibility to be aware of what children understand, and to offer honest explanations that fit with the children's developmental capabilities. Caregivers must be open to children's questions, giving them the freedom to ask whatever they want without fear of ridicule. Helping children understand is not just providing information about facts and events; it is also giving information about feelings, about what to expect and what not to expect.

Adults can do much to prevent siblings from feeling as if they "don't belong." Encouraging children to help in some way in the activities of caring for an ill brother or sister, or involving them in the rituals surrounding death, is reasonable when individual choices are also respected.

Helping siblings to feel as if they are valued, loved, and considered to be special by the adults in their lives is the best way to help children avoid feeling as if they are "not enough." If adults interact with bereaved siblings in ways that comfort their hurt, clarify their confusion, and involve them in what is happening, it is unlikely that bereaved siblings will feel as if they are "not enough."

In my interviews with children, I often ask what advice they would have for adults. Repeatedly, they say, "Don't forget that we are grieving too." Their words capture well the most important message. Though sibling grief may be a difficult, long, and lonely journey, it is not one that siblings must travel alone if the significant adults in their lives acknowledge the impact of sibling bereavement and are willing to walk alongside them on their journey, comforting, consoling, involving, and validating.

Betty Davies, RN, PhD, is professor and chair at University of California San Francisco's School of Nursing, Department of Family Health Care Nursing. She is a clinician, an educator, and an active researcher focusing on the care of patients and families with life-threatening illness and on child and family bereavement. She is a member of the International Work Group on Death, Dying, and Bereavement and the Association for Death Education and Counseling.

V · O · I · C · E · S

How I Got To Know Grandma Bootsie Before It Was Too Late

Leah Goodridge

She liked wrestling. No, she *loved* wrestling. Whenever a show was about to come on, she'd make this big deal of it. She'd spread the sheets, make sure all the snacks were ready, turn off the overhead lights, and then turn on the lamp. Yep, that was her thing. Every now and then she would go "oooh" and "aaah" with amazement at how the burly wrestlers nonchalantly took a beating.

She was a fun grandmother. Hip, I might add. You could tell by the name she told me to call her: Grandma Bootsie. I remember when she used to spread her nice bed sheets and I had to wait for like ten minutes; she had to do it perfectly. Then, finally, she'd hop in and I'd hop in after her, and we'd cuddle.

Those were the good memories. Those were the priceless times—the good days when I felt so safe...so surrounded with love and care.

But little did I know those good memories would soon be clouded over with bad memories. The phone rang. My mom picked it up. "Hello?" Her face looked worried. I heard a man's voice on the other end of the receiver. The voice said, "I'm marrying Robin." It could have been my uncle. It could have been my cousin. It could have even been my grandfather. But somehow, even at four years old, I just knew that that scratchy, unclear voice was my father.

I don't have as many memories of my father as I do with my father's mother. But as I recollect, he was this "cool cat." You know, the type that would say, "Hey kid, you want that pony? I'll getcha that pony." After that phone call, I don't remember ever seeing him again. As I grew up, I made excuses for it. Ya know, maybe he had money problems. Maybe he's sick. Or maybe he got married and had another kid, and left me fatherless.

It's so funny how love could so soon turn into hate. After the realization that my father simply just didn't want me as a daughter, I hated him. I hated him, and everyone associated with him, like his mother. He stopped contact with me. And I guess between all those father-mother quarrels over the baby (which was me), I never really got to say goodbye to Grandma Bootsie.

Years passed and birthdays flew by—seven, eight, nine, ten. My father was invisible. Grandma Bootsie was, too. Then came age sixteen. My mom and I were in the car. We were talking about something insignificant, something petty. Then she casually said, "Your father wants to see you."

I was shocked. My father? My initial first thought was, "I don't want to see him." But then all these feelings overtook me—all the thoughts that probably every fatherless child wonders. Do I look like him? Does he like the same foods as me? You know, it's weird. All the hate just disintegrated, just like how the love had. The hate was replaced with curiosity, wonder, and eagerness. The naive little girl came back, and I started to think, "Maybe it wasn't his fault."

I went to see him. It wasn't anything like I expected. We sat, and I listened to his reasons for becoming the Invisible Man. I sat and I listened and I learned. And I realized this: I learned to sing without him; I learned to dance without him; I got into a notable private school without him; I became a beautiful A student without him; and I spent fourteen birthdays without him.

Then it then came to me. It didn't matter if I was the worst person in the world. It didn't matter if I was the best person in the world. None of that mattered—because he still would have left. He didn't even give me a chance. It's not me; it's him.

So I stopped contact with my father and Grandma Bootsie promptly. I didn't even give him a chance. Might not have been the right thing to do, but in my sixteen-year-old mind it was. Then, seventeen came. I hadn't seen or heard from them in a year, on account of my refusal. And to be honest, I rarely thought of them.

Then, one day my mom told me that Grandma Bootsie was sick. She had had a stroke, and she wasn't doing too well. Mom insinuated that I should go and see her. My response? No. I didn't want to see her, I told my mom. Why should I go see her? The conversation ended, but the topic lived on. My other grandmother then hinted that I should visit her. My response? Negative. Nope.

Weeks passed. Months passed. I still refused to visit her. I'd never been in this situation before. I wasn't a heartless person; I was a scared person. Then one day, the topic was brought up again. "You should really go and see her," my mom said. "Nah, I don't think so," I replied. "Leah, she got her leg amputated. Grandma Bootsie is dying." I froze. I didn't say it then, but I agreed to go and see her.

On the day of the visit, I can't really say I was nervous. I don't know if eager would be the word either. Who is eager to see an ill person in a nursing home? "Casually anxious" would be the term. We drove to the nursing home. On the way there, I thought she would look the same as fourteen years ago. Soft, brown hair. Topaz eyes. We took the elevator up. We walked down this long corridor. And then I saw her.

I hardly recognized her. Her hair was gray and stringy. She didn't have the same face. She was so thin and frail. My mom walked up behind her and touched her hand. "Grandma Bootsie? It's me—remember me?" She let out this long, agonizing cry. Tears streamed down her eyes. She didn't see me yet. She was so disturbed that the nurses had to carry her to another room.

And then, my mom pulled me by my hand and said, "And this is Leah." Silence. Shock. I felt uneasy. She didn't say one word. For a second, I thought maybe she didn't know who we were. But then she cried again. And held my hand. Looked at my fingers. She wouldn't let go.

I motioned for my mom to leave the room. "Hey," I said. She responded with a funny noise. "Um, yeah, so I know it's been a long time." Again, she responded with a funny sound. I came to realize that Grandma Bootsie was unable to talk. She would let out noises that sounded like "we-bee-bee-bee." I looked closely at her face. My God. I looked just like her. The same eyes, same nose, same chin.

I felt horrible after the first visit. Horrible that I even hesitated to come. She kept mumbling something that sounded like "we-bee-teen." Then she held up ten fingers and then four. Fourteen years. And she cried again and I held her hand. It was then that I realized that it wasn't her fault.

None of this was her fault. She certainly didn't cause the disappearance of my father. That was his choice. But although he wanted no contact with me, she had always wanted to stay in touch. She had tried to call and I'd refuse to talk. My stubborn sixteen-year-old mind thought she abandoned me too. And that's when I realized, that just like how my father didn't give me a chance, I almost didn't give her a chance.

I visited her several times after that first visit. I'd visit her in the morning and leave in the afternoon. She would cry a lot and point to her amputated leg. It hurt watching her cry. I'd try to get her mind off the pain by talking about things that were going on in my life. One day, when I tried this, I was looking up at the ceiling. When I turned back to face her, she was sleeping. I laughed.

Another time when I went to see her, she was irritated. I didn't know why but I soon found out that she wanted to be lifted from the wheelchair and into the bed. The nurses ignored her cries. They couldn't understand her. I summoned all the strength I could muster and I lifted her into bed. She was weak. When she was finally on the bed, her face was turned down towards the floor and she could see my toes through my sandals.

She made a questionable sound. "Wee-bee?" I looked up. "What is it?" She pointed to my toes. "You like the nail polish, Grandma?" She pointed to my toe rings. She looked at them with curiosity. I said, "Oh, those are toe rings." She tried to repeat the term. I moved my foot closer so she could see them. She laughed.

It was the first time that I saw her smile. "What, Grandma Bootsie, what's so funny?" "Wee-bee-bee-bee," she rambled on in this sassy tone and snapped her fingers at me. I laughed too. I knew exactly what she was thinking. It was something she always said when I was a little girl: "You too much for me, girl!"

I'd try to make sure and visit Grandma Bootsie as much as possible. Between work and classes, I didn't have much time to spare. But I managed to see her about every week. After the toe ring incident, every time she saw me walking down the hallway into her room, she would look at my toes, playfully roll her eyes and then laugh. I'd laugh too.

These are the good times. These are the priceless times. When I feel so safe....so surrounded...so loved.

Leah Simone Goodridge is a seventeen-year-old high school senior. She is a scholar in the Arthur Ashe Institute for Urban Health's Science Academy and a member of the Arista Academic Honor Society.

Reprinted with permission of the Arthur Ashe Institute for Urban Health, Inc., 450 Clarkson Avenue, Box 1232, Brooklyn, NY 11203. Funded in part by a grant from the Open Society Institute.

16

The Military Model
for Children and Grief

Bonnie Carroll and Major Judy Mathewson

Have you ever heard the term "brat?" You might think it's slang for a child who is acting up, but in the armed forces it's an affectionate nickname for those children who have become a part of the American military from birth. They are the proud offspring of our nation's military members, serving in their own way by living a life dictated by the missions of national defense policy. They have learned that constant moves, gaining and losing friends on a regular basis, adapting to exotic cultures, and coping with foreign languages are the norm. The profile of Women's World Cup Soccer star Mia Hamm says it all—it lists "All over" for her home town, and then goes on to explain that she was an "Air Force kid." That term applies to thousands of children around the world, and their story would not be complete without an examination of how they cope with one very harsh reality of life in the military—the tragedy of sudden death.

Imagine sitting in your Department of Defense Dependent School (DODDS) classroom overseas, your fifth school in eight years of elementary education, listening to your math teacher but preoccupied with the global situation and its impact on your family. Your dad is "TDY" (on temporary duty) serving in a war zone, and you are worried for his safety. Quite a load for a thirteen-year-old to carry, but one that all the kids in your DODDS class understand. They share your pride but also your concern.

Then one day it happens. The door to the classroom opens and the school nurse steps in. Everyone is tense and fears the worst. A name is called, but it's not yours. Susan collects her books and heads for the door. She glances back and you do your best to give her a reassuring smile. You don't see her again, because the news that came that day was that her father had been killed in a land you can't even pronounce, near where your own dad is serving. You have a mixed reaction of sadness for her and fear for yourself. How close it was to being you! You hear later that Susan left quickly with her mom and little brother for the States for a funeral at Arlington National Cemetery. They came back to Germany only long enough to pack up their belongings and figure out where to go. Rumor had it they wound up back in the little Midwestern town where Susan's mom had grown up, to live with Grandma for a while and try to "sort things out."

You can't imagine what this must be like. What would Susan do? How would she make friends? Would these new friends understand what life is like in the military, moving every few years, being part of a global mission, living on a base and going to schools with kids who had lived similar lives? How could you be taken away from everything familiar, from all your friends and from the world that you had grown up in, right when you need familiarity and support the most? It's all too much to comprehend, and you say an extra prayer at night for the safety of your own father and for a quick end to the fighting.

In this chapter, we will examine the traumatic loss experiences of the children of our military, and the ways in which they handle the stresses and challenges they face. We'll share with you the tremendous strides that have been made in recent years through organizations such as the Tragedy Assistance Program for Survivors (TAPS), including its annual Kids Camp in Washington, DC, as well as the support offered to families by the armed forces.

The military does a wonderful job of memorializing those who die in service to this nation. It is part of our culture, even if viewed from afar. It is a familiar scene in so many war movies—the widow in black clutching the tiny hands of her children as the folded flag is presented and taps is played. In the world of cinema reality, this is the last time we see the stoic widow. We are not privy to the struggle ahead as she forms a new life for her family.

For children, understanding the ceremonial aspects of a military memorial brings context to an event that has shattered their young existence. It is the final pronouncement that their parent was part of a greater whole, that the work he or she set out to do will continue, and that there is an enduring strength that will gently guide the family through the difficult days ahead. In his commencement address at West Point, General Douglas MacArthur spoke of the "long gray line" of soldiers who had gone before and now stood in silent watch over soldiers during battles yet to be fought. There is continuity to a death in the armed forces, and the ceremonies children participate in provide a foundation in this understanding that is critical to their ability to cope.

The burial services are filled with tradition, and they can sometimes be overwhelming, especially for children. In one case, a family was left unprepared for the many ceremonial aspects of the graveside service. While the family had been forewarned about the folding and presentation of the American flag, the mournful playing of taps by trumpeters in the distance, and the flyover of three aircraft in a "missing man" formation, they were not aware there would be a 21-gun salute. This salute consists of three volleys, each fired simultaneously by seven riflemen, and on this day, it was to take place on a hillside behind the seated mourners. One military-caliber rifle is loud, but seven fired at once are deafening. The family is sitting in their chairs at the graveside on this sunny, quiet afternoon when the first volley sounds, and everyone is startled. Grandma, sitting in the front row, is so startled that she faints, falls forward, and almost goes headfirst into the open grave. As people are now scrambling to grab at her ankles and pull her back from the brink and it seems things can't get more chaotic, a little boy in the back row jumps up and announces with childlike certainty, "They've shot Grandma!" This is certainly a scene you wouldn't see played out at your average civil burial service.

While military memorial services are steeped in traditions, it is often from children that we hear the most honest descriptions. Garrett Schmidt, only nine years old at the time of his father's death in an Army C-12 crash, remembers the services this way: "The funerals are mostly when everyone cries and when everyone remembers how many good times they had with the person. When the soldiers brought in the coffin and laid it down, many people including me laid down flowers and other nice things.

Yes, the funeral is always one of the hardest parts, and there's never a funeral when no one sheds a tear." He went on to describe the burial: "After the funeral, the triangular-shaped flag was given to us from the soldier. The taps song was played from the trumpet. In the future you never actually get over it, you still get sad and emotional once in a while. But you do feel a little better after a few years. If I think back, I could remember a lot of things he taught me like how to ride a bike, how to tie my shoes and how to read. My dad was a great guy and I wish he were here in person. But I know, in my heart, he's always there with me."

Garrett's view of the funeral is simple—those who cared about his dad were given a chance to remember the life that was lived; those he served with in the military honored the life he selflessly gave his nation; and Garrett himself held close the memories he had of his dad. But in the end, we are left with the knowledge that our loved ones remain always in our hearts.

The armed forces present children with many challenges, not just those related to the death of a parent. They face loss every few years—in some cases, every few months—as their parent's assignment changes and they must move to become part of another mission in another corner of the world. This can be a time of excitement and exploration, but it can also be a time for tremendous grief over the loss of friends who have shared childhood adventures; the friendships forged with neighbors living next door on base housing; the security and comfort of a bedroom fixed just so; the familiarity of teachers who know who you are and what you can do; even the style of clothes that was "cool" in one location, but out of style in another. Each move requires a new start, and each new start requires energy and effort.

Remember your first day of anything, whether it was school, a new job, or joining in any existing group dynamic. You wore your new clothes and hoped you didn't do anything to stand out more than you naturally would. You were the outsider and worked to make a positive first impression. Imagine going through this process over and over again, throughout your childhood. The military helps children adapt in many ways, but there is no way to break through that initial awkwardness.

Departures are even more difficult. Striving to find a constant in their lives, children begin to form identities that are closely tied to their parents' jobs. If Dad is a fighter pilot, you have grown up hearing jet noise and watching aircraft blast through the sky, and you see yourself in a flight suit someday. If Mom is an Army nurse, you've lived near a military medical facility and the kids you played with may also have been part of a hospital family. If you had a parent who served on a Navy ship, you long to head out to sea and experience the adventures in foreign lands that you have heard about. When you move away, you lose everything except for two things—your family and your identity with that part of the armed forces that you belong to.

Moving forces you to re-evaluate your belongings and keep only things that are "worth packing." One child related the trauma of arriving at his new home in the United States after living in Germany for four years. He discovered that the movers had lost his carefully packed box of his most special toys. As an adult, he has made it a hobby to search out and replace the G.I. Joe, the Curious George, and the Slinky he lost. What you have and can carry with you becomes a bit of who you are when life is so transient. You have no "family home" to return to, and no real sense of roots. So, you must find a way to fill that void with the experiences of life as a military brat. And when you lose part of that life through a death or through a divorce, you are losing more of yourself than many can understand.

In the first days after a death in the military, each service has a Casualty Affairs office that assigns experts to the family in the areas of benefits and mortuary care. The family support organizations, volunteer groups made up of local service families, rally to comfort and care for those affected in the early aftermath. There is a wide range of benefits and entitlement available to the family, and experts on hand to assist. The officers in charge, the chaplain, and the medical and mental health service professionals can provide tremendous support. For a time, this support is the focus of the entire installation.

This time, however, is actually very short. In a typical situation, the memorial service is held within a week. Then, as President Clinton said during the memorial for those killed in the Khobar Towers bombing,

"It is now time to move forward." The family is given 180 days to move out of base housing, but in reality, this often occurs within a few weeks. If a child is attending a DODDS, they have somewhat of a cushion in the care and understanding received in the immediate aftermath. If the military dependent is attending an off-base civilian school, the impact can be more difficult, in that teachers and counselors may not understand the military culture.

For the family, what was once a paycheck now becomes a complex web of entitlement and death benefits granted from the military and the Department of Veterans Affairs. Children often watch as their remaining parent, who had never been able to start a career due to the constant moves, finds a new place to live and a new career to sustain the family. Once the dynamics change so dramatically in a military family due to a death, families sometimes find themselves in total chaos and uncertainty in determining new family roles. The child who was once the little son of the "hottest fighter pilot on base," proudly wearing Dad's patches on his tiny flight jacket and sleeping in his flight suit pajamas, now finds himself "the man of the house" with no father to look up to.

One such boy could not have been prouder when his father was named "Army Aviator of the Year." Shortly thereafter, Dad was killed in a test helicopter crash, and the family moved—away from the Army around which he had grown up, away from the sound of rotor blades, and away from the other kids who were envious of his father's national distinction. No one in his new school understood. No one had had a parent die. In an attempt to be "normal," he would shrug off inquiries about where his dad was by parroting what he heard so many classmates say: "My parents are divorced. Dad doesn't visit us." It was accepted. But it wasn't the truth and left him feeling hollow inside.

Eighteen months after his dad's death, this boy attended the TAPS Kids Camp while his mom went to the National Military Survivor Seminar. He finally found kindred souls in his fellow brats—kids who could relate. As he sat in a circle listening to other stories of proud boys and girls who had lived the life he knew so well and then lost it all, he finally found a kinship. When it was his turn to speak, he shared without hesitation the pride he had for his father, the shock of hearing he had been killed, the fear of moving away, and the confusion of his new school. Everyone understood. It was liberating and normalizing.

The TAPS Kids Camp, held annually over Memorial Day in Washington, DC, offers opportunities for children between eighteen months and twenty-one years to meet other young people whose parent has died while serving in the armed forces, regardless of the cause of death. The Camp honors the deceased military member and becomes a personal tribute from the surviving children. While the youth are attending their Camp activities, the surviving parent is networking with other National Military Survivor Seminar attendees, learning about grief and loss, post-traumatic stress, and benefits they may qualify for as military dependents, all in a factual and helpful atmosphere. The children are safe and cared for by trained adults who understand the importance of group support for kids experiencing highly personal and emotionally traumatic life-changing losses, including both a parent and a way of life. The losses are overwhelming, but the children are simultaneously nurtured and educated about the process and emotions of grief.

The children participate in organized grief work activities facilitated by bereavement specialists who have a connection to the military. Members of the Honor Guard squads from the Army, Navy, Marines and Air Force serve as mentors. Volunteers also participate, ranging from the Chief of Army Casualty for the Military District of Washington, who entertains the children with balloon animals, to the wife of a former Secretary of the Department of Veterans Affairs, who lovingly guides the children on a tour of the funeral home she directs. The Honor Guard volunteers attend training prior to the camp that includes a discussion of coping strategies to best support each child's age, stage of understanding, needs, and loss.

Gwen Perry-Crawford, volunteer social worker, made the following statement after her involvement: "TAPS has been a gift to everyone involved—parents, volunteers, and most especially the children. The friendships continue over the years as each youth follows his or her own path of healing. Knowing they are not alone in their pain, it is safe to reach out and talk about what might have been."

As research suggests, mourning for a childhood loss can be revisited at many points in an adult's life, often during important life events: graduation, marriage, or the birth of a child. By addressing the loss issues now and recognizing the complicating factors of a death in the military, we are giving these children healthy coping tools, a support system upon which they can rely, peers to lean on, and mentors to look up to.

At the camp, each adult TAPS mentor and facilitator pairs up with a child to serve as a role model, a sort of "big brother or sister," and a loving ear for the children. Activities include artwork, aerobics and body-work, and a discussion of the children's losses and coping strategies to create a new life without a parent in the military. The children also participate in ceremonies that honor the culture and traditions so integral to their lives in the armed forces.

Five-year-old Georgianna Eyre shared, "My daddy died in a plane crash on February 4, 1997. I was very sad. Sometimes I am still sad. But my mommy found TAPS and I got to meet other girls and boys who had lost a parent too. I had fun at the Kids Camp. We got to play games. I got to make some things to help me remember my daddy. I made a memory book and a dream catcher. The dream catcher catches the bad dreams and lets the good dreams come through. Now I have a lot of new friends. Thanks TAPS for making a fun Kids Camp!"

From the moment the young people arrive, they are honored as survivors of an uncertain future and their grief is recognized in a safe and secure environment that allows them to find their similarities as military dependents. Nineteen-year-old Gabrielle Tarmy related, "Personally, I had no friends who had lost a parent. I was facing a very dramatic change in my life. However, my family and I have dealt with and overcome each new situation and change with the bravery my father instilled in us. At TAPS, I met others like me, celebrating their fathers and saluting them for their bravery and hard work. We got to express our love for them, and make friends who shared the same experiences and feelings. We got to know that we are not alone. TAPS allows us to share our loss and show our appreciation for those we love."

As part of the grief work, the youth learn about all the emotions of grief, to know that their feelings are normal ones in reaction to the abnormal situation of a sudden, traumatic death of a military parent. Addressing their emotional, spiritual and physical needs, the TAPS kids write letters to their surviving parent to tell them how much they appre-ciate them, as well as how much they miss and love the parent who has died. Additional healing occurs during story time, when our Chaplain shares stories such as the soaring eagle who spirals ever higher until he is no longer visible to the eye, but is still powerful and alive. A balloon release also gives the children a chance to see in yet another tangible example the way their messages go up and up and up, until they disappear from our limited physical sight.

Tears are respected as children show pictures of their deceased parents and identify the particular branch of service and how their parents died. Six-year-old Rachel Thomas described her experience this way: "My papa died in a plane crash on September 22, 1995. I remember that morning, I was sleeping and then my mom screamed. When I went into her room she told me an Air Force plane went down and my papa was flying that day. Later my mom told me that papa was dead. I don't like remembering it but my mom says it's okay to cry. It's been a long time now and I'm doing really well. Going to the TAPS Kids Camp helped me a lot. It helped because all the kids had lost a mom or a dad, too. It wasn't embarrassing to cry and if I was sad everyone understood why. I used to just keep everything inside but at the TAPS Kids Camp, it exploded. That was ok because everyone understood. Since then I have been feeling a lot better. I still miss my papa, though. Thanks for everything, TAPS!"

The TAPS Kids have an opportunity to learn about the great sacrifices their parents made as members of the military and the price of freedom by touring Arlington National Cemetery, the Vietnam and Women's Memorials, the Pentagon and the Caisson at Fort Meyer (home to the horses that pull the funeral carriages). They have also been special guests of the Headquarters Marine Barracks and treated to private performances by the United States Air Force Honor Guard Silent Drill Team and the Joint Forces Color Guard. It's all part of learning that their parents' contributions to the military were important, recognized, and honored.

Allison Burris, at age four, was immensely proud of her father's service. She shared, "My daddy was Major Andrew Scott Burris. He was a soldier in the 82nd Airborne Division. My mommy and I were very proud of him. My daddy was my best friend. He played with me all of the time and made me feel like I was the most important little girl in the world. Everybody said that I had the best daddy ever. My daddy was killed June 13, 1997. My mommy had to tell me that my daddy was an angel and he would always be with us but that he could never come home and play with us again. My mommy and I cry a lot together. We both miss him very much. I pray to my daddy all of the time but I wish that he could come back. I miss him very much. At the TAPS Kids Camp I got to meet a lot of other little boys and girls whose mommy or daddy is in heaven so I don't feel like I am the only one who doesn't have a daddy. I love my daddy very much and will never forget him."

During one camp, the children created a special wreath and participated in the formal wreath-laying ceremony on Memorial Day at the Tomb of the Unknown Soldier. While the other Veteran Service Organization wreaths were made out of silk flowers and all bore a striking resemblance to each other, this wreath stood out. The children lovingly made it out of small hand prints, traced and cut out of red, white, and blue construction paper, which were inscribed with secret messages to their deceased parents—messages they must have felt certain would reach their destination if left in such a hallowed place. One of those messages showed a previously unspoken appreciation: "Dad, thank you for the camping trip," and another offered a blanket apology: "I'm sorry I wasn't better." Each completed something left undone or unsaid and in doing so, eased some pain.

Two of the children, elected by their peers for this honor, placed the wreath with great pomp and circumstance, accompanied by uniformed Honor Guardsmen. After they carefully laid the wreath, the Honor Guard rendered a dignified salute, a send-off to the messages and an honor to the recipients. The spectators, heretofore silent, erupted in heartfelt applause of support and love for these precious survivors.

The camp also includes fun and friendship-building opportunities, such as a private dinner at a local restaurant and pool parties at the hotel. By the end of the camp, the young people come to understand that their parents were heroes for their service, regardless of the cause of their deaths, not only in the hearts of their families, but in the eyes of a grateful nation.

Amanda Tarmy, age ten, wrote, "I went to the TAPS Kids Camp, a place where people who have lost a loved one in the military can go to be together. TAPS helped me a lot, because now I know there are other people going through all the changes and differences I'm going through too. In TAPS, there's also fun stuff like going to the Capitol and White House and seeing two parades and on and on and on. A hard thing was leaving all the friends you make, but at the end of the trip you say, 'Hey! I just realized I'm a survivor.' So when you learn that, and you will, just always remember that."

That is the message—that we can survive the pain, cherish the memories, and gain strength from walking side by side down this difficult road called grief with those who understand and care. There is much that can be learned from our military culture, including honoring the lives that were lived rather than focusing so much on the death that occurred, and finding comfort and kinship in the genuine understanding of those who have experienced a similar loss. The dignity and ceremony of a military burial service, with all its history and traditions, provides a tangible and visible symbol of honor, dignity, and respect for a life lived. It also provides a fitting final salute that brings closure to one chapter and, with the help of programs like TAPS, a beginning to a new chapter of healing and comfort.

As the folded flag is ceremonially presented by the soldier to the family and the casualty case file is completed, the military gently passes the emotional care of the survivors to TAPS, knowing they will be in the safety of an understanding group of those who have been there before them. General John Shalikashvili, former Chairman of the Joint Chiefs of Staff said, "We [in the Defense Department] cannot do for you what you can do for yourselves, and that is gently guide those who come after you through this journey called grief." The children are proof of the tremendous power this empathy has to heal and comfort.

From these children, we learn hope and gain inspiration. These children have faced the loss of everything familiar in their lives—a parent they loved, a lifestyle that was all they knew, and a close circle of friends. Yet they have survived. In writing about the father who died when she was a small child, a woman now in her late forties writes, "He was a soldier and he was my hero." She came to know this man through the stories his comrades told and the battles he fought. She defined his life by the moment of his death, when he saved others during combat. Though her father was not there to applaud at her graduation or walk her down the aisle when she got married, he was a vital part of her life, and his military service was an integral part of who he was.

For children, the military provides a life that may include stresses such as moving and changing friends and schools. Through these experiences, however, these children are often provided with the gifts of a broad mind and an easy spirit, to help them adjust to separation, to make the best of wherever they may be, and to learn to care for those around them.

Bonnie Carroll, founder and president of the Tragedy Assistance Program for Survivors, Inc., is a Captain in the Air Force Reserve currently serving as Chief, USAF Casualty Services, and is the widow of Brigadier General Tom Carroll, US Army.

Major Judy Mathewson is a special education transition coordinator at Chugiak High School in Eagle River, AK. She has served for fourteen years in the Air National Guard and is currently the Executive Officer for the Air Commander. Major Mathewson is a certified Bereavement Facilitator and is the Director of the TAPS Kids Camp.

V · O · I · C · E · S

A Military Death

Elizabeth Kaskeski

My name is Elizabeth. I'm eighteen years old and I grew up in the Air Force. My father Chuck Kaskeski was in the service for over eighteen years, when he died suddenly of a heart attack. I have one little sister named Ashley, three cats, and one dog. My father passed away a little over two years ago. I was sixteen years old and Ashley was just about to turn eleven. The sudden shock of his death was very overwhelming. Just like any death would be. It was extremely hard to deal with and I often felt like no one could truly understand what we were going through. On top of my father's sudden death, we really had no close friends where we were living. We had moved to Kirtland AFB only six months before, and our family felt more alone then ever. I would like to point out, however, that my father's squadron was very helpful and generous to us with anything we might need, and we are very appreciative of that.

A couple of months after my father died we decided as a family to move back to Florida. Florida is where my mom's side of the family lives. The move was yet another big rock to climb. For the second time in one year I changed to another high school. This was also the first move that we ever did without my father. I think moving to Florida was one of the hardest moves I ever had to deal with, for a couple of reasons. One reason was that this was the first place that I had ever lived that was non-military. I found the kids in my new school were not used to "outsiders."

They had all grown up together. They all had their cliques and their memories. I was just an intrusion. And finding my place was much more difficult than in a military community where the kids are used to other kids coming and going.

Another reason was I had to face things that I had never faced before on a military base. I never realized people could be so cruel! Depending on who I was talking to, other close-minded people would give me looks. Prejudice was a big surprise to me. These were all changes I had to learn to cope with after my father's death.

Now that I look back on it, though, I realize that I have grown. I think moving so many times in my life helped prepare me for what I would face later on. I know that if I did not grow up in the military I would not be the person I am today. Dealing with constant changes, like leaving my friends and making new friends, has helped me to become more outgoing and open-minded.

Overall I would say the military has been more of a positive experience for my family and me than a negative one. I miss the military now. I miss the people and the atmosphere of it all. I miss hearing stories from other kids who have been all over the world. I miss sharing my stories. And I really miss relating. I believe that only other military children can truly understand another military child. Most of all I miss my dad. And I also thank my dad. I thank him for the lifestyle that he gave me. And I thank every military person out there who also helped me grow up. I truly think we are all one family.

Elizabeth Anne Kaskeski is eighteen years old. She is in her first semester of college. She works full-time and volunteers with the Jaycees.

17

In the Aftermath:
Children and Adolescents as
Survivor-Victims of Suicide

Terry L. Martin

Marcy

She asked me if I wanted to join her for a bowl of oatmeal. I replied "No, I am going to take a shower and get ready to go." Those were the last words we said to each other. When I got out of the shower, I found her. She was still alive. I tried to make her breathing easier but there was nothing I could do. When I realized what happened, I called for help. I didn't know whether to feel mad or hurt. I was out of it; I didn't know how I felt. It was a day I will never totally heal from. Life must go on, especially now. All of her hurting is over. She will feel no more of anything. It's a lot tougher to keep on living. (Note: Sixteen-year-old Marcy shared this entry from her diary with me shortly after her nineteen-year-old sister shot herself in the head. Although Marcy continues to improve through counseling, she still has occasional flashbacks, nearly four years after the suicide.)

Sarah

Sarah was eleven when her mother hanged herself in the living room while the rest of the family slept. After a brief, intense period of grieving, Sarah appeared to adapt to her mother's death. When she turned eighteen, Sarah hanged herself in her bathroom. A letter of rejection from her mother's alma mater was found in her nightstand.

Carol and Amanda

Carol discovered her husband, Jack, dead from an overdose of sleeping pills on their kitchen floor. While in the throes of her initial grief, an additional crisis arose—Carol discovered she was almost three months pregnant. After exploring her options and feelings through counseling, Carol decided to have the baby.

As Amanda grew, Carol spawned a myth about Jack's "accidental" death. Shortly after her seventh birthday, as Carol lay dying from a recurrent brain tumor, Amanda learned the truth of her dad's death. Now, two years later, at the behest of her custodial grandparents, Amanda is exploring her feelings about her father's as well as her mother's death. Her most pressing question: "How could my daddy kill himself, while my mommy wanted so badly to live?" The counselor has no answer.

These cases, and many others like them, reveal the profound and lasting legacy left to child and adolescent survivors of suicide. This chapter examines the grief of children and adolescents after the suicide of a family member or peer.

While there is, finally, a growing body of literature on children and adolescents as suicide *survivor-victims* (Shneidman's 1973 eminently useful term), the findings are inconclusive. This is hardly surprising considering the nature of the topic, the difficulty in securing samples, and the inherent subjectivity of the researchers. Ultimately, the reader is reduced to evaluating the information in light of his or her own clinical experiences with children and adolescents touched by suicide. Thankfully, these encounters are relatively rare for most counselors. This, too, confines our understanding to a small, self-selective sample. Perhaps the best we can hope for is to remain vigilant to the potential risks faced by these child and adolescent survivors and await improved and reliable data from our research colleagues.

We begin by briefly reviewing the problem and then sampling the literature. We will then examine the aftermath of suicide, counseling issues, and sources of support.

The Problem: Kids Killing Themselves
Adolescent suicide

The most recent vital statistics report from the Centers for Disease Control (www.cdc.gov) confirm a grim reality: American teenagers continue to kill themselves in record numbers. In 1997, the suicide rate for people aged sixteen to twenty-four years stood at 11.4 per 100,000. This translates to 4,186 young Americans killing themselves. Sadly, suicide remains the third leading cause of death in this age group.

While adolescents may not commit most of the suicides in the United States (that dubious distinction belongs to elderly white males), the three-fold rate of increase in adolescent suicides since 1960 is alarming. These numbers may represent only the tip of the proverbial iceberg; it is estimated that the numbers would triple if all adolescent suicides, which are often recorded as accidental deaths, were reported as suicides.

Adolescent suicide is a multidimensional problem, and the causes should not be oversimplified. However, there are a few predictors that appear again and again in the literature (for a more detailed analysis, see Orbach, 1988; or Stillion, McDowell, and May, 1989):

1. Psychiatric disorders, found in more than 90 percent of adolescents who commit suicide, with affective disorders, especially depression, heading the list

2. Personality factors, including aggression and a global sense of pessimism

3. Cultural factors, such as race, ethnic group, or a culture that features "pro-death forces"—where choosing death is preferable to living a life with intolerable problems, especially since one is entitled to a good life (Barry, 1989)

4. Situational factors, like family violence, family losses, and the dissolution of the family. Having a parent who killed himself or herself is a special risk factor.

Suicide among children

Thankfully, suicide among children younger than fourteen years old remains rare. However, statistical data about suicide in this age group is suspect, since many fatal childhood accidents could, in fact, be suicides. An oft-quoted study looked at suicide among children from Minnesota, five to fourteen years of age, and found rates increasing since 1980. Nationwide, the estimates vary, but the Centers for Disease Control now lists suicide as the sixth leading cause of death among children aged five to fourteen years. In 1997, 307 children died from self-inflicted injuries.

Why would a young child want to end his or her life? An early study (Bender and Schilder, 1937) noted the following as contributing to suicide among children:

1. A wish to escape a difficult life situation

2. A desire to be reunited with a deceased loved one

3. An attempt to gain affection and attention

4. A method for demonstrating "independence," or a way of punishing those who "interfered" with the child

5. Spite.

Literature Review: A Small Sampling

An initial report from a recent longitudinal study (Brent, et al., 1993) found that adolescent siblings of teenage suicide victims were seven times more likely to experience the onset of a major depression within six months of the death when compared to a matched group of non-bereaved controls. Subsequent findings from the same study (Brent, et al., 1994, 1996) did not find the siblings at any greater risk for depression than controls, although siblings who were younger than the suicide victim fared worse than older siblings. These siblings did, however, continue to grieve. Recurrent depression continued to be a problem among nonrelated friends of the suicide victim even after much of their grief had subsided. The authors speculated that this was because the siblings were allowed and encouraged to show more overt grief behaviors than the friends of the suicide victim. As for younger siblings tending to have more psychiatric disorders than older brothers and sisters, the authors suggested that older teens were more likely to spend less time at home; therefore, younger teens bore a greater share of the family's burden of grief.

Additional studies have verified the psychiatric impact of suicide on child survivors. Among a sample of children aged five to fourteen years, 40 percent of those surviving the suicide of a sibling or parent reported symptoms of post-traumatic stress (Pfeffer, et al., 1997). By contrast, a study comparing suicide- vs. non-suicide-bereaved children did not find any evidence of post-traumatic stress, but found more overall symptoms of psychopathology among the suicide-bereaved children (Cerel, 1999). Additional studies have found significant levels of aggression, withdrawal, and anxiety (Cain and Fast, 1966; Shepherd and Barraclough, 1976).

While much of the literature provides alarming insights into the plight of child and adolescent suicide-survivors, many recent studies do not support the notion that child survivor-victims of suicide fare any worse than children experiencing other types of deaths or than non-bereaved controls (see, for example, Brent et al., 1996).

To summarize the research:

1. Children and adolescents who lose parents or siblings to suicide bear not only the burden of intense grief, but may be vulnerable to psychiatric disturbances.

2. Children and adolescents surviving the suicide of a peer may or may not experience intense grief and may or may not be vulnerable to later psychiatric problems.

3. Suicide-bereaved children and adolescents may not be touched by the suicide beyond normal grief.

The reader should remember that clinical and case study reports are considerably less ambiguous than research studies and highlight the qualitative differences between child survivors of suicide and survivors of other types of death, viewing suicide as a complicating factor. An investigation of how suicide differs from other forms of death might dispel our confusion about the impact of suicide on children.

The Aftermath of Suicide

What happens to children and adolescents after a significant peer or family member commits suicide? We begin by examining the social cost to survivor-victims and then review individual psychological reactions.

The social cost: Suicide as stigmatized death

Stillion (1996), after reviewing the recent literature on attitudes toward survivors of suicide, concluded that, when they are compared to survivors of other kinds of deaths, suicide survivor-victims are more likely to be viewed negatively. Doka (1989) recognized this stigma when he referred to suicide as an example of a "disenfranchising death." Suicide may especially brand older children and adolescents, who base their growing sense of self-worth and identity on the approval of others, particularly their peers. Grief, in itself, marks the child or adolescent as "different" from his non-bereaved peers. Grief in response to a suicide magnifies this difference by stigmatizing as well as marking the child as "different." This has important implications for the type and degree of support available to the child, as well as his or her social standing among peers, and his or her sense of isolation from others.

Individual psychological reactions

Rando (1993) identified a constellation of psychological reactions to suicide which are independent of age:

1. Anger, guilt, and shame
2. Concern for one's own tendency toward self-destruction
3. The desire to search for understanding
4. The need to resolve unfinished business (the consequences of being unable to say goodbye)

How do these reactions manifest during childhood and adolescence? First, children and adolescents are in the process of learning self-control. In particular, adolescence is a time for developing control over such feelings as anger, jealousy, lust, and melancholy. Anger and rage in the wake of a suicide may overtax the adolescent's recently acquired ability of self-control. But while we may forgive children their tantrums, adolescents are expected to be adultlike in their expressions of feelings.

Both teens and children are vulnerable to feelings of guilt. Children, with their residual belief in magic, may blame themselves for causing the suicide: "I should have behaved better," or "I should have been nicer." In one case, after a seventh-grade boy hanged himself, several of his female classmates became concerned that they "caused" the death. Apparently, this young man had approached a number of girls about going to a school dance and had been rejected each time.

By contrast, adolescents, with their fragile sense of omnipotence (which usually coexists with self-doubt), may chastise themselves for their inability to detect and prevent the suicide: "I should have known this might happen and I should have stopped it."

As noted above, suicide stigmatizes the survivors. Shame becomes a familiar, though unwelcome, companion.

Children and adolescents tend to suffer great anxiety over uncomfortable or painful feelings since their perception of time differs from that of adults. Bad things may seem to last forever for the child or adolescent. Add to this the effects of limited life experience, and the individual child or adolescent may believe that he or she will never feel any differently—or better—than he or she does now.

Second, adolescents, in particular, often fear their own impulses. When the suicide victim is a peer, the teen may realize that he or she, too, is often stressed and unhappy, and may wonder, "How do I know that I won't do that?"

Third, late childhood and adolescence marks the beginning of the individual's existential quest. Questions about meaning abound: "Who am I?" or "Why am I here?" or "What shall I become?" and "What is important to me?" Add to this the search for answers to the suicide—which is often doomed to failure from the start—and the older child or adolescent may become confused and frustrated, giving up the search for meaning.

Fourth, having unfinished business with others may be a requirement of adolescence, since this is also a time for establishing a sense of independence from one's parents. Many adolescents find that the only way to feel free of their parents is to create friction and an eventual "gap." This "individuation" is accompanied by a large measure of ambivalence: "I want to be free of you, but I need reassurance that you will always be there for me." Adolescents and parents often find themselves in the perpetual state of having "pending" relationships with each other. Suicide prevents the eventual reconciliation and mutual respect as both parent and child move through life.

Children and adolescents may also have fluid relationships with their peers. It is common for children in middle school to switch allegiances from one person or group to another several times a month. Thus, having unfinished business with another during adolescence may be a developmental imperative.

A special burden:
Suicide survivorship and the search for identity

Adolescence is, above all, a time of self-discovery, of establishing an identity. The chief task at this stage of life is to resolve the conflict of identity versus identity confusion (Erikson, 1950). Different aspects of the search for identity manifest during the three phases of adolescence (see Fleming and Adolph, 1986). During the initial phase (usually age eleven to fourteen years), most of the adolescent's efforts are directed toward achieving emotional separation from his or her parents. When death intervenes, especially the suicide of a family member, the young adolescent may respond in polar-opposite forms or patterns. For instance, one adolescent may regress, "acting-out" or failing at school as a way to gain the attention and comfort he or she so desperately needs. Another adolescent may strive to become the perfect or "parent" child. Sadly, this child is often neglected since his or her behavior is generally approved. In fact, premature assumption of adultlike behaviors (and responsibilities) may signal an "identity foreclosure" (Marcia, 1966), where the child gives up his or her attempts at self-discovery and passively accepts others' definitions of himself or herself as his or her own.

In phase two (age fourteen to seventeen), the teen's focus shifts to achieving competency, mastery, and control. As noted previously, the intense emotional responses to a suicide may overburden these nascent efforts at self-mastery. Suicide may also teach the adolescent that he or she is helpless. Abramson, Seligman, and Teasdale (1978) suggested that there are two types of "learned helplessness" (a generalized expectancy that events are independent of one's own responses): universal and personal. In universal learned helplessness, non-suicide bereaved teens may find solace in perceiving that no other person could have avoided or prevented the death. Unfortunately, the suicide-bereaved teen may experience personal learned helplessness, as he or she believes that someone might have anticipated and prevented the suicide. This results in apathy, problems with persistence, and loss of self-esteem.

The final phase of adolescence (age seventeen to twenty-one years) centers on the adolescent's ability to commit to something or someone, and to establish intimacy with another. As Fleming and Adolph (1986) rightly point out, intimacy and commitment require a sense of "I am not alone," and "Others understand me." As a survivor-victim, the adolescent may believe that "No one can possibly understand what I have been through," and "I am alone and unlovable." This can lead to "identity diffusion" (Marcia, 1966) in which the adolescent remains in an "identity crisis" and actively avoids any form of commitment.

In summary, the suicide of a significant other may thwart the adolescent's search for self and thus threaten, suspend, or damage his or her identity.

Counseling the Child or Adolescent Survivor-Victim

Many of the same counseling methods or techniques that are effective with young people generally are equally applicable to child and adolescent survivor-victims. Stevenson (1998) has suggested the following guidelines for parents and educators:

1. Talk about the death.

2. Provide factual information and confront rumors.

3. Stress positive solutions to dealing with the pain of loss.

4. Acknowledge the changes wrought by the suicide.

5. Commemorate the death, but do not romanticize it.

6. Focus on remembering the individual, not the act.

7. Be vigilant for anniversary reactions.

8. Deal with caregiver stress (for parents and educators).

Below is a list of additional guidelines to help young survivors of suicide. The reader should remember that developmental differences among children and adolescents are always a first consideration, especially in trauma (for more, see Eth and Pynoos, 1985).

1. Be vigilant to the survivor's increased risk of suicide. Use age-appropriate assessment tools and observations as ongoing aspects of the counseling process (see Pfeffer, 1986).

2. Confront defensive myths. Children often find it necessary to cushion the impact of death by fantasizing that it has not happened. With time and support, most children adapt to their losses. However, in the wake of suicide, denying the reality of death may be supplanted by denying the cause of the death. Gentle yet persistent reality checks by caring adults can enable the child to gradually accept how his or her family member or peer died.

3. If, or when, the reality of suicide is accepted, be prepared to treat anxiety and/or profound feelings of sadness. Suicide is a sudden, frightening, high-grief death, and affective responses may be intensified.

4. If there are recurrent flashbacks, nightmares, or phobias, the child may be experiencing Post-Traumatic Stress Disorder. Although there are a number of useful and effective treatment modalities (e.g. hypnosis, guided fantasy, cognitive restructuring), not all counselors will be comfortable in confronting PTSD. Identify available resources in the community and make a referral.

5. Children often gain a sense of mastery or control by recreating real or imagined traumatic deaths through play. Post-traumatic play in the wake of suicide should be monitored very carefully, since the act of pretending to kill oneself may become self-reinforcing.

6. Be alert to changes in the child's family. It is generally held that "as the family goes, so does the child's adjustment." The same may be true of the child's peer support group. Counseling the entire family and/or group counseling should always be considered.

7. Should intense anxiety and/or depression persist beyond a reasonable period of time (as individually determined on a case-by-case basis), consider referring the child to a pediatric or adolescent psychiatrist for additional evaluation and psychophar-macological treatment. There are times when appropriate and judicious use of medications can assist the counseling process and the child's recovery.

8. Include the child in discussions about terminating counseling. Suicide ends a relationship suddenly; thus, ending the therapeutic relationship should be handled gradually and cautiously.

9. Finally, recognize that different patterns of grieving may first appear during late childhood and early adolescence. And while the child's gender may influence his or her grief responses, it does not necessarily determine them (Martin and Doka, 1999).

Sources of Support

There are numerous books, organizations, and groups to meet the needs of grievers, but few target the needs of the suicide survivor. Of the resources available to suicide survivors, only a handful are designed for children. Much of the available support is in the form of books, pamphlets, and newsletters. Suicide survivors' groups are an important resource. The American Association of Suicidology maintains a referral list on the Web of 350 self-help groups for survivors of suicide at www.suicidology.org. However, a survey of 149 suicide support groups (Rubey and McIntosh, 1996) showed clearly that most groups consisted of adult participants.

School systems may be valuable resources. Many school districts have crisis response systems or teams in place. Most of these crisis plans for intervention include training in suicide postvention. Many schools now offer bereavement support groups, but a general bereavement group may not meet the needs of a suicide-survivor.

Hospices, too, may offer support to child and adolescent suicide survivors. For example, many hospices hold special camps for bereaved children (Cable, Cucci, Lopez, and Martin, 1992). However, while some of the participants may be suicide survivors, these and other general programs for bereaved children do not identify nor target the special needs of children or adolescents surviving the suicide of a loved one.

Conclusion

There is much that we still do not understand about the impact of a suicide on a child or an adolescent. At best, the suicide-bereaved child may be no worse off than a non-suicide-bereaved child. However, it is equally likely that in the wake of suicide, children may be especially vulnerable to pathological reactions as well as increased risk for their own acts of self-destruction. If so, timely and effective intervention is the best antidote for these young survivor-victims.

Terry L. Martin, PhD, is an Assistant Professor of Psychology and Thanatology at Hood College in Frederick, MD. He is a licensed clinical professional counselor in private practice specializing in adolescent behavior and grief therapy.

18

Grief and Traumatic Loss: What Schools Need to Know and Do

Peter L. Sheras

Death intrudes on us all. Even though grief and loss are part of life, for children and adolescents it is untimely, out of place, unnatural, and disorienting. For most young people, it is the province of old age, grandparents, or chronic degenerative illness, not associated with immediate family, friends, and school. For school-aged children, death is very often traumatic because it is not "supposed" to happen. Many other losses may be experienced as traumatic and can represent the "death" of a relationship, the sudden disappearance of love and support, or the significant change in an expectation. Whenever such an event occurs, it shakes children to the core and causes them to doubt the reliability of most everything. "If my friend, who is just a kid like me, dies, how can I trust anything to be as expected?" Children are not supposed to die, and those closest to them—parents, friends, or teachers—are not either.

When death occurs, routine is disrupted and predictability goes out the window. Matthews (1999) describes the losses experienced by young students as impacting the actual or perceived physical or emotional safety of every child. Further, it is incumbent upon school personnel to be knowledgeable of how the grief related to traumatic loss is played out in the academic setting. In American society, children and adolescents can most frequently and reliably be found at school. Although dealing with death and loss is often considered to be a major function of the family and the spiritual or religious community, all but the most immediate experiences of this emotional upheaval are played out in school.

The school life of students is influenced strongly by events at a variety of levels. It is at school that young people are most likely to find both a significant peer group and adults with whom they regularly interact. For small children, teachers and administrators are surrogate or auxiliary parents, while for adolescents they can represent role models, emotionally supportive adults, and in some cases confidants. Schools have access to grieving or traumatized students, and they are also in a key position to help their charges deal with the immediate and long-term effects of loss. School can be, and needs to be, a healing environment for these young people.

A trauma can be defined as a violently experienced injury or wound or a shock which has lasting effects. In the case of traumatic loss, students respond with a "fight or flight" reaction, either acting out their feelings or withdrawing from them. Common reactions include an increase in daily fears and fears about the near future, regression in school performance and classroom behaviors, an increase in anger, guilt, or shame, disturbing memories or flashbacks, the appearance of physical symptoms of anxiety or illness, and, finally, coping difficulties including nightmares, social withdrawal, or extreme moodiness. For those who may already be a bit psychologically unstable, losses can prove to be devastating. Even to the most resilient, at least some periods of significant reaction or dysfunction can be expected.

In order to deal most effectively with traumatic loss, schools must be prepared to deliver interventions for involved students, to follow-up immediate interventions with postventions, and to work to prevent further problems related to the inadequate resolution of the emotional issues surrounding loss. These three functions, *intervention*, *postvention*, and *prevention*, form the components of an appropriate school response. For these to be accomplished, school personnel must be trained to understand the dynamics of grief and traumatic loss for individuals and in groups, and they must know how to respond based upon this knowledge. Being familiar with what might be considered *dimensions of loss* or characteristic distinctions about how grief affects children and adolescents becomes essential. While there is not space to cover these dimensions in depth here, it is useful to identify some of them and their impact on how schools treat grieving youngsters.

Dimensions of Loss

An event that produces a grief reaction in a school-aged child or teen is often unique and complicated. How a school responds depends upon who is affected and at what level. Below are some of the important factors to consider and how a school's response might differ depending upon the case.

Emotional proximity

How close is the child emotionally to the loss? Frequently, judgments about proximity have to do with whether or not the loss was a close friend or relative. It is assumed that the closer the death, the more impact there will be. The loss of a best friend, classmate, or parent, for instance, would be more devastating than the death of someone barely known. It is important to remember, however, that sometimes a person has a strong reaction because of an association to an event not obvious to observers. In one case, an eighth grader died from a long battle with cancer. When students were invited to come to the school guidance office for support if they wanted, many of her close friends came to share their strong feelings of grief. A number of other students came as well, however. They did not know her well but were experiencing similar reactions because they were facing other issues of grief and loss in their lives. One had a grandmother at home ill with cancer, another had lost a brother in an auto accident the previous year, while another had a friend commit suicide two years earlier. For them, there was emotional proximity of a different, but just as powerful, sort.

One role of the school is to identify and support all those whose reactions are strong and who are feeling close to those just lost. In the first moments following a loss, members of the school crisis team or the guidance staff should try to judge who is most influenced by the tragedy and make sure that help is available. This may mean communicating with other schools where siblings or friends may be. In a case where a high school student died in an auto accident, the school needed to work with a local elementary school because the victim was a popular babysitter for more than fifteen students in the first and second grades. These youngsters were upset as much as the peers of the victim in eleventh grade.

Group, individual, or system-wide

Death or traumatic loss can be felt not just by an individual, but throughout an entire system. Interventions cannot occur just in schools without taking into account family and community systems. Grief responses to catastrophic events such as floods, earthquakes, or school shootings are experienced in many venues. When schools seek to help a student deal with issues at school, they need to bear in mind that the reaction at home, or in church, or on the street may make resolving loss issues more difficult. A child may feel like he has a place to talk at school but when he gets home, he must take on a different role or cover up his feelings. Entire communities, families, and classrooms may grieve over the loss of an individual (Nader, 1997). A school-based intervention must take into account where and how else grief is being handled in these larger settings. Does a religious service help for a particular child, or raise even more questions?

Peer or adult victim

It is important for a school to consider who has been the victim—an adolescent, a younger child, or an adult. The response of the survivor may be very different depending upon the age of the victim. For many adults it is most difficult to help a student understand why a child has died. While upsetting, the death of an adult, especially an older one, can be very painful but not as deeply disorienting. It might cause children to grieve and be upset but not question everything else about the world around them. It is important to remember that helping young people through grief is not necessarily getting them to understand why the loss happened, but to help them express what they feel about what happened. After all, who really does understand why these events occur? School personnel, as representatives of teaching institutions, are in a good position to tell students that some things cannot be explained but must be described and talked about anyway. There are differences that students feel when a peer dies as compared to an adult. Speaking out about their feelings, thoughts, and reactions about who has died can be important.

Predictable or unexpected

Were the traumatic events predictable or not, sudden or of slower onset? When a school knows that a teacher is terminally ill, or that a hurricane may be two days away, there is some time to prepare. Consider the case of an elementary school teacher diagnosed with a rare and terminal blood disorder. As the school year progresses, students observe their beloved teacher become weaker and weaker. She misses a few weeks of school to be hospitalized for treatment and returns feeling better, only to begin declining again in a few months. When she decides to tell her class, it seems almost violent to them.

Many times, it is human nature to avoid talking about such unpleasant possibilities, hoping that ignoring them eventually will, somehow, make them less likely to occur. Classroom discussions and pre-planning (e.g., introducing a future teacher before the present teacher has left, or in the case of violent weather, talking about a school evacuation plan) can help students feel less anxious about what the future holds. Helping students name their fears can aid them in preparing and help them feel more in control. If a school has a crisis team or a crisis plan, for instance, it is helpful for students to know that such preparations have been made. Even small children like to know that adults have planned to take care of them. They may not need to know all the subtleties of such provisions, but they need to have a sense that someone is looking out for them. These kinds of preparations can be very important in creating a feeling of safety among the student (and adult) population of a school.

Child or teenage survivor

How a school responds to a crisis related to a traumatic loss also depends upon the age or developmental stage of the survivors. Preparing and intervening with elementary school children may be different than for middle or high school students. Until about age nine, children may not yet comprehend the full reality of death. As children become older, their conception of death becomes more adult-like. Children want to know more about why death might occur and be comforted by more cognitive explanations. In middle and high school, students seek a broader understanding of events, the right and wrong of it, and even the physiology of death.

One must remember that the youngest children may react to loss with reduced attention, fantasies, mistrust of adults, and uncharacteristic behaviors. After age nine or ten (a bit later for boys than girls), reactions can include anger at the arbitrary unfairness of life, self-criticism, blame, self-blame, and even symbolic or psychosomatic symptoms. These students often appear to regress to more childlike behaviors. Older teenagers are more likely to be judgmental, moral, or suspicious, and may seek to deal with their anger by violence, suicidality, substance abuse, or general loss of impulse control (Peterson and Straub, 1992). School interventions must take into account these developmental considerations (Pitcher and Poland, 1992). Group interventions, focusing on peer group sharing, for instance, may be more helpful for older children, while comfort and reassurance might serve younger children better.

Single or multiple loss

The number of victims may also be an issue for those dealing with grief in schools. Some events include more than one person or more than one event. Losses may be multiplied to include the loss of people and the loss of familiar surroundings or routines. A school arson might include grief related to those who died and also the loss of the school building, books, lockers, a playground, and the school routine. These multiple losses may require interventions to deal with a variety of issues. Some need to be explored together, and some separately. If a student loses more than one friend, the grieving process may be complicated significantly. "Survivor guilt" might need to be addressed, for instance, if a number of teenagers die in an auto accident when one person decided not to ride in the car that night, or couldn't fit in the back seat. A group intervention, often easier to accomplish at school than in any other setting, might be useful in dealing with this sort of grief, where other survivors could share their similar feelings.

Actual or perceived

Traumatic losses can be actual or perceived. In either case they can be very real to a student. While perceived losses may not seem as significant to an observing adult as to the student, they can be every bit as emotionally difficult. The redistricting of schools, or changing of boundaries, for instance, can create the perception of the loss of friends; in fact, they actually have been lost. Re-assignment of teachers or the change of a school principal can feel almost like a death to the most sensitive students. For elementary school children, when bonding to a teacher is significant, these sorts of events may be more important than adults think. A teacher who leaves in the middle of the school year on maternity leave, for instance, may be mourned by students very deeply. School interventions which acknowledge this significance are important. Taking the time to bring a teacher back to visit or corresponding with her as a class may help to relieve negative reactions to this perceived loss.

In the case of traumatic loss, that which is perceived and what actually happened may become confused. In an attempt to find a reason to explain how a tragic event occurred, people's wishes and desires may cloud the facts. When a third grader was killed in a head-on auto accident while riding with his uncle, his classmates assumed he was not wearing his seat belt. When they were told that he was wearing it, they did not believe the teacher. They perceived that their friend must have "made a mistake" and that is why he died. They could hope, then, that if they wore their seat belts all the time, such a thing could never happen to them or to others they loved.

Human-made or natural

Survivors of losses and disasters often react differently depending upon whether the event was a natural disaster or a result of human actions. When loss is by a natural cause, there is often a sense of having little or no control, of being a victim of circumstance or of a global event. When other people are responsible for an act of violence or even a mistake (e.g., forgetting to wear a seat belt), students may have different feelings. These events might have been prevented in the past or could be prevented in the future. While school interventions may focus on accepting what has happened, it is important to reassure students that in the future they might have some power in protecting themselves from tragic events. In the face of a great loss, it is expected that people feel some loss of control. Schools can show students how to understand natural disasters better, for instance, or even diseases that kill students, or how fires start. Some insight will allow them to feel more powerful in the future, even though they have felt powerless about the traumatic loss they have just experienced.

Regaining a sense of power over events might also take the form of designing memorials or rituals, or actually taking on prevention efforts as a school or as a group. It is important to remember that certain kinds of memorials may not be appropriate in cases where suicide or other self-destructive deaths have occurred. Physical plaques or planted trees may serve as an encouragement to other desperate students who feel invisible or unacknowledged. Decisions about permanent memorials need to be considered carefully. Are they honoring a life that was taken from them or inadvertently recognizing an act that was impulsive or even hostile where the person had control? Although it may seem stigmatizing to separate out those who may have died at their own hands, the grieving process may be different. Those who consciously decide to commit violent acts against themselves or others are seen as controlling their own destiny, whereas those who are the victims of such acts could not choose to be hurt and, therefore, could not save themselves. This is a very complex issue, however, and schools need to consult their own legal staff as well as mental health professionals.

School as an Intervention Setting

We rely on our educational institutions for many things. Our children spend a large part of their developmental years in school and under the influence of teachers (Stevenson, 1995). Schools are logical and convenient places to help students deal with grief responses, whether the events that produce these reactions are related to school or not. Sometimes, as in the case of school violence, schools are the places where traumatic events take place. In many cases, however, schools are merely the venues where grief experienced elsewhere is played out. In these cases, schools may be one of a number of places where grieving takes place. It is useful to realize, then, that schools are not the sole intervention agents, but part of a larger system helping to support young people experiencing grief and traumatic loss. They must not only be prepared to provide service, but to help coordinate it.

There are many types of interventions practiced in schools. They represent a toolbox full of techniques to be applied to the unique circumstances of each traumatic event. Depending upon the dimensions of loss involved, they can be used to great effect, especially when coordinated with other parts of the survivor's support system. Below are some examples of types of interventions in schools.

Classroom interventions

Classrooms are the most common venue for students and are therefore the most natural place for grief interventions. In many cases, following a tragedy, people find out about what has happened in class. If friends are involved and are either at school or absent because of these events, peers find out about it in class. Classrooms are a place for discussions about grief and are often the first line for teachers to identify students dealing with grief. Some schools include death education as part of their regular curriculum (Wass, Miller, and Thornton, 1990). In a school with good intervention programs, teachers are well trained to discuss grief and loss.

Individual interventions

Schools must be able to respond to the individual needs of their students. Individual counseling through the guidance department is the most common way to deal with emerging issues of loss or preparing for anticipated grief. Intervention agents for the individual are most frequently the school psychologist, school social worker, and the guidance counselor (when appropriately trained). Schools need to be certain that their guidance and professional mental health staff are equipped and trained to help individuals deal with grief responses.

In the case of traumatic losses, it may be necessary to bring in additional professional support when the school personnel are either overwhelmed or over involved. One school told students they could meet with counselors in the aftermath of a suicide, and 300 high schoolers came to the guidance office. Another very small community school suffered the death of three popular students in an auto accident, including the child of a teacher. It was difficult for the school staff to deal with its own traumatic loss. Outside helpers were useful to support them in supporting their students. The role of these outside groups is to support the school and students by providing only the counseling and support that is needed, not to "take over" the response. The more familiar faces that can be there to soothe the anxieties of students, the more feelings of support will be felt.

Group counseling

Group counseling can provide the most effective setting for intervention for grief and loss. Facilitated by mental health or guidance staff, these groups can allow students to share the feelings they hold inside, their concerns, fears, fantasies, and even plans for revenge. It may be the case that ongoing groups to deal with anger management or problem solving will be helpful in the aftermath of a loss. Continuing grief groups led by psychological, medical, hospice personnel, or clergy during or after school can provide positive ways to help students express themselves. It is important to note that groups are not for everyone. Merely bringing everyone together to "talk about it" may create a circumstance where there are too many participants to allow for sharing, too great an opportunity for children to "hide out" quietly, or sometimes a chance to literally leave the room without sufficient qualified staff to go after them. A counseling group is not just a discussion. It has a purpose and a direction. It needs to be facilitated by qualified leaders who understand who will benefit and to look for warning signs of significant depression.

Working with parents

When there is grief and trauma in the student population, schools must reach out to involve parents. This is not just a good idea, it is essential. Schools need to be supportive of parents' efforts to deal with their child's grief while allowing them privacy at the same time. Often it is helpful to send information home to parents about signs of childhood and adolescent grief and suggestions for resources in the community available to them. Individual parents must always be notified by the school if there is concern about their student's reactions or well-being. Do not assume that parents know what to do about funerals or visitations. Some guidelines might seem redundant to some parents but are welcome information for many who may be overwhelmed by grief themselves. It is appropriate for schools to send home some suggestions about attendance and behavior at such events. Parents may need some information about how to help their child face a circumstance they have never experienced. A parent meeting at the school to answer questions is usually a good idea. Anything that will foster good communication and cooperation will decrease the possibility of later difficulties (Cornell and Sheras, 1998).

Working with other helpers

In addition to partnerships with parents, schools need to have existing or developing relationships with others who can help with understanding and dealing with grieving. Local clergy, mental health professionals, physicians, hospice workers, The Compassionate Friends, or other support groups can be of great help. Some communities have volunteer crisis debriefing groups or crisis networks that can be of service. The school crisis team should find out about these resources before an event occurs and utilize their services when it seems helpful.

Rehabilitation

A number of programs in schools are using models such as rehabilitation to provide grieving students with a kind of formal and structured support (Goldberg and Leyden, 1998). Such programs can be drawn from a variety of mental health or grief theories and allow students to progress through a structured set of experiences to achieve some sense of closure or expression of feeling. In many cases, school groups are short-term, reactive, and crisis-oriented, and do not allow students to deal with the continuing feelings they have as they move through their grief. The structure provided may also be reassuring to participants and encourage them to continue their grief work.

Schools as Postvention Agents

Loss and grieving responses are not often short-lived for those most impacted. Postvention serves to continue aspects of intervention, assess progress, and deal with the longer-term impact of losses, identifying those who might experience continued risk for lethality (Leenaars and Wenckstern 1996; Komar, 1994). Effective postvention can serve to reduce the likelihood of post-traumatic stress reactions as well.

It is also important to realize that postvention activities serve to support the adults in the system, to encourage them to deal with their own reactions to the loss and to their need to be continuously supportive to their students. Good postvention includes components of periodic follow-up with staff and faculty, continued risk assessment of students, acknowledgment of anniversaries and strategies to deal with them, and debriefing at regular intervals for school personnel.

School as Prevention Agents

It has often been observed that it is very difficult to start prevention initiatives until something catastrophic has happened. It is often the case, however, that a crisis is a prevention opportunity. Schools need to be ready to institute preventative and proactive programs whenever they can. Often it is only in the aftermath of a crisis that such an opportunity comes. Prevention activities can take many forms. Some school systems already have prevention programs that may be in need of updating. There are many ways to approach prevention and many activities available at all academic levels (Peterson and Straub, 1992). Below are listed some types of prevention initiatives for schools to consider.

Good and thorough follow-up

After a loss or a violent act, there is always the issue of preventing such things from happening again. Learning about exactly what happened and working to defuse future situations is, in many ways, prevention. Students at risk for depression or violence need to be followed and kept from falling between the cracks or between the services available to them. A school crisis team should write a report about their performance in the crisis to be used to help develop future prevention plans.

Learning about death and grief

Don't be afraid to talk about death and teach about it. Death education programs, even in elementary school, may help prevent prolonged grief reactions. Grief cannot and should not be prevented, but it can be constructively concluded if children are knowledgeable about how people routinely handle it. There are good school and classroom activities available that can be very helpful (Stevenson, 1995; Perschy, 1997; Pitcher and Poland, 1992; Peterson and Straub, 1992).

Understanding loss in life

Help students understand that loss is part of life. This can be done through discussion and through modeling by adults. Help children realize that losses are survivable and that even though they may be painful there are positive lessons to be learned. Do not help them deny loss, but deal with it. Work with students to let go of self-blame if it is part of their grief reaction. Help them learn from more minor losses in school (e.g., new teachers, graduation, new facilities) so they can approach significant changes with less fear. Have them experience how social support can help when dealing with strong feelings.

Creating good communications

Teaching good communication skills, talking, and listening can help prevent protracted grieving. School is a logical place to learn how to communicate about easy and difficult topics with adults and with peers. Make sure as a teacher, counselor, or administrator that students have the opportunity to be heard and that they are invited to speak and participate. These skills can be taught at all levels. Through practice and exposure, young children can learn how to listen to adults during a crisis and older students can learn how to communicate their feelings and concerns with less anxiety.

Peer interventions

The power of peer groups is never stronger than during middle school and high school. There is great healing power released when people with common experiences can share their inner fears and beliefs. They feel less vulnerable and less isolated. Group activities are part of socialization during school. Following a crisis or loss, interaction in small groups can build a sense of community, caring, and consistency. Don't shy away from getting students together for fear that they will become more upset. If this happens they can be seen individually. Generally speaking, such groups build cohesiveness and help students formulate constructive plans that may make them feel less helpless. In the face of a death or loss, people feel powerless. Groups can give them something to do, to share, a way to help others, or to talk about how to do something to express the sad feelings they have.

Schools Must Be Prepared

Schools must be prepared for grief and loss. Personnel must be trained and a team must be in place ready to respond. Though the crisis or loss may engender feelings of disorientation and even panic, if there is a plan, energy can be used to carry out what must be done. Make sure that every school has a plan to deal with each of the dimensions of grief described earlier in this chapter. Practice them when possible with a mock event or a lively inservice discussion. Preplanning is the key to effective response. Make sure there is a chain of command in place to deal with crisis response, as well as a toolbox that includes school blueprints, phone numbers, a logistics plan, name badges for helpers, and model letters to send home with students describing grief reactions or giving referral information (Stevenson, 1999; Cornell and Sheras, 1998).

Roles for School Personnel

Everyone in the school has a role to play when dealing with grief and loss. When such an event occurs, students look to every adult for guidance and mentoring.

Teachers

Teachers are the linchpin of an effective response in school. They must feel comfortable with what they must do for students. Most teachers care deeply about their students. In-services to teach them about the process of grieving will aid them in feeling more effective with their children. The basics can be taught in a very short time. The key is often having teachers learn how to use their own feelings and experiences in supporting others. They are also likely to be mourning the loss of a student or adult friend. Sharing their own feelings constructively, showing emotions without burdening others, and talking about emotions are common elements of good classroom intervention. They must also receive support in dealing with their own issues.

Administrators

Leadership, teamwork, and responsibility are the essential characteristics of the effective response of administrators (Cornell and Sheras, 1998). They must be trained to recognize when grief and loss are issues in their school, mobilize the school-wide response, and be accountable for students, staff, and faculty alike. They also have an important role to play as liaison to parents and to the community. The most difficult decision for an administrator, however, is often how much to disrupt the regular school schedule to accommodate the needs of grieving children, and when to restore "business as usual." Students need to express their feelings when traumatic events occur, but they also are comforted by the security of continuing to live their lives as before. Learning how to recognize when and how to proceed is the responsibility of any good school administrator.

Counselors

Dealing with the specific grief reactions of students falls often to the guidance staff. School counselors often have to spend a great deal of time with scheduling and college counseling. Some are well trained as intervention agents, while others are not. School social workers and school psychologists may also have this training. All three of these groups must play a major role in developing the crisis response plan for the school and helping to carry it out. If not already familiar with grief work, they should be encouraged to gain this expertise. In addition to working with students, sometimes their most important roles are to support and debrief faculty and staff, and to conduct the inservice training for teachers and administrators.

Staff

School staff, secretaries, bus drivers, custodians, and aides all play important roles during a crisis of grief and loss. They are often the eyes and ears that know what is really going on and who is most impacted by a crisis. They need to be included in training and consulted during the aftermath of events. They often know more about the community or families than school officials and can be of immense help with logistics and preplanning. They are essential parts of the school community and need to be supported to deal with their own feelings as well.

New Roles for Schools

Schools are not separate from their neighborhoods or their communities. They are part of the lives of whole children and must learn to cooperate with all those who impact them. This includes not just their students, but families, law enforcement agencies, social service agencies, faith communities, governments, and businesses. Schools need to be responsible for making sure that there is an integrated and complete response when tragedies occur. This makes the school the center of a community, not peripheral to it.

Schools must also be more than objective centers of instruction. They must be personal and relevant. When grief or tragedy strikes, there is no better time to demonstrate the humanity of a system that is made up of people. Don't be afraid to be personal and show feelings. Stifling our own feelings to keep from "burdening" students often models denial and withholding. Schools need to model personal and democratic ideas.

As communities, schools must also remember to take care of their own. They need to model creating and supporting interactions between students and faculty, but also between faculty, staff and administrators. When loss is present, everyone may have to deal with the grief.

Conclusion

Schools play a major role in helping children and adolescents deal with grief and traumatic loss. Sometimes they are the logical place to begin interventions and to follow them up. Schools need to prepare themselves for these functions by learning about death, grief, and loss, and by having a specific plan to implement a response. At the same time, a school must know that their institution is only one of a number of places where loss is being addressed. Schools must play a role in providing services to students to help them work through their responses to traumatic loss, but they must also, increasingly, help integrate the support functions of other helpers, families, and communities as well.

Peter L. Sheras, PhD, is an associate professor in Clinical and School Psychology at the University of Virginia Curry School of Education. He co-directs the School Crisis Network and is Associate Director of the Virginia Youth Violence Project. He has worked with hundreds of schools and school systems on crisis planning and response, in addition to his work as a clinical psychologist for 25 years.

19

Resonating Trauma
A Theoretical Note

Jack D. Gordon and Kenneth J. Doka

In the aftermath of the events at Columbine High in Littleton, Colorado, where two adolescents systematically planned and executed a mass killing of their fellow students and teachers before themselves committing suicide, an interesting phenomenon could be observed. Throughout the nation, there were fears that this event could be repeated in other schools. In part these fears were the result of the initial investigation, a sense that the conditions at Columbine—the availability of weapons, the presence of cliques and disenchanted students—could be found in any school. In part they were clearly the result of a trauma that shakes assumptions of a benevolent world, revealing a sense of personal vulnerability. Certainly the media played a role as they continually explored and publicized the event and reported additional threats. Clearly there was the risk of "copycat" killings, a phenomenon already evident in teenage suicide. In fact, the Columbine killings were one of a series of similar school-based shootings.

Yet these fears often became crystallized, not in a vague feeling of unease, but in recurring rumors that threats against a particular school on a given day were reported on the Internet. Despite investigations and subsequent denials, schools throughout the country reported similar stories. And on the specified day many schools experienced high rates of absenteeism.

This is an example of a phenomenon we might call *resonating trauma*. Resonating trauma occurs when an initial traumatic event creates such fear and anxiety that rumors of future similar events affect many communities, even communities far away and with far different conditions. Resonating trauma can be seen as the effect of a traumatic event on collective behavior. The very nature of a traumatic event is that it challenges one's assumptive world—the basic beliefs that one has about the world. Most individuals believe that the world is relatively benevolent and events occur for a reason. The massacre at Littleton deeply challenged that sense of safety, offering a reminder that even adolescents in school are not free from the danger of random violence.

The study of collective behavior, especially that of rumor and panic, adds insight to the effects of these traumatic events. One condition for panic and rumor is a general sense of anxiety and unease. The killings at Littleton, following similar events, certainly contributed to an anxiety about, and by, the young. But other factors as well likely influenced that sense of anxiety. One factor was technology. While computers, the Internet and the realm of cyberspace are increasingly part of American life, they cause discomfort. It is interesting that rumors of impending attacks were attributed to reputed threats on the Internet. These reports were then the precipitating incident that created the panic. Rumors too are common as people try to understand an event. Rumors often arise when the frantic need to give meaning to the event is not convincingly fulfilled by media outlets.

But these rumors may have had another critical role, one that actually served to limit the sense of panic. Instead of the vague anxiety that something terrible can happen to our children, any time, any place, the rumors crystallized the fear into something more tangible—our children are in danger on *this* day. Conversely then, if nothing happens on that day, our children are safe, panic and anxiety are reduced, and we go back to our belief in a benevolent world. These specific rumors play a vital social role that counselors need to acknowledge, for they may be vital to restoring a sense of personal safety endangered by the initial traumatic event.

Senator Jack D. Gordon is the President of the Hospice Foundation of America. He was elected to the Florida State Senate in 1972 and served until his retirement in 1992. He is a member of the International Work Group on Death, Dying, and Bereavement, and serves on the Financing Task Force of the Last Acts Campaign. Senator Gordon is on the Board of Directors of The Center for Policy Alternatives and is a Member of the Carter Center Mental Health Task Force.

Kenneth J. Doka, PhD, is a Professor of Gerontology at The College of New Rochelle and the author of numerous books on grief and bereavement. Dr. Doka is both the editor of the journal, Omega, *and* Journeys, *a newsletter for the bereaved. He is past President of the Association for Death Education and Counseling and served as Chair of the International Work Group on Death, Dying, and Bereavement from 1997-1999. Dr. Doka is an ordained Lutheran clergyman.*

Using Books To Help Children and Adolescents Cope With Death:
Guidelines and Bibliography

Charles A. Corr

Guidelines

We now have at hand a large and growing body of books about issues related to dying, death, and bereavement for child and adolescent readers. These books are quite diverse in the topics they consider, their approaches or points of view, and their reading levels. For this we can be grateful. The practical problem facing a child, adolescent, or adult who would like to explore this literature is how to select a few useful titles from such a large variety of available books. Here are some useful guidelines that can be of help.

1. Evaluate the book yourself before attempting to use it with a child or adolescent. It is not enough to find just any book on loss or grief; one also wants to be comfortable with the information that it contains and the attitudes that it conveys. In most cases, it should only take a short time for an adult to determine if a particular book is appropriate and satisfactory.

2. Select titles, topics, and approaches that suit the needs of an individual child or adolescent. To be useful, any book must respond to the needs of a particular young reader. Ask what one hopes to gain from a book and then search for titles that serve those purposes.

3. Be prepared to cope with limitations. Each book has its own strengths and limitations. For example, in *The Tenth Good Thing About Barney* (Viorst, 1971), a pet cat who has died is said to be "in the ground and he's helping grow flowers." Is that a good explanation, one that is comfortable and sufficient for you and your child reader? In *My Turtle Died Today* (Stull, 1964), one child says that "you have to live a long time before you die." How would you reply if a child or adolescent questioned such a statement? When deficiencies or limitations are prominent, one must decide whether a book is nevertheless of sufficient value to still be useful or whether we can be creative in adapting it to our purposes.

4. Match materials to the capacities and concerns of an individual child or adolescent reader. Often this requires little more than determining a young person's interests and reading abilities. The groupings that follow should only be taken as preliminary clusters, not as fixed categories for all children or adolescents, even for those in a particular age bracket. Children with special needs should be assessed with great care. For example, some older children whose reading abilities do not match their age might be invited to join a project in which they help an adult assess the suitability of simpler materials for younger readers.

5. Whenever possible, be available for discussion of, or read a particular book along with, a child or adolescent. Many books afford opportunities for rewarding interactions when they are shared between a child or adolescent reader and a sympathetic adult. Discussing a book together can spark a "teachable moment" from which all can profit. Reading together a book about death and grief can sometimes make it possible for children or adolescents and adults to support each other in coping with loss and sadness.

Selected Bibliography

For Adults

Adams, D. W., & Deveau, E. J. (Eds.). (1995). *Beyond the Innocence of Childhood* (3 vols.). Amityville, NY: Baywood. Contributors to these volumes address a broad range of issues involving children and adolescents, including perceptions and attitudes toward death, coping with life-threatening illness and dying, and coping with death and bereavement.

Corr, C. A., & Balk, D. E. (Eds.). (1996). *Handbook of Adolescent Death and Bereavement.* New York: Springer. A comprehensive resource for understanding and helping adolescents in their encounters with death and bereavement.

Corr, C. A., & Corr, D. M. (Eds.). (1996). *Handbook of Childhood Death and Bereavement.* New York: Springer. A comprehensive resource for understanding and helping children in their encounters with death and bereavement.

Fitzgerald, H. (1992). *The Grieving Child: A Parent's Guide.* New York: Simon & Schuster. Useful advice for parents and other helpers from an experienced counselor.

The Dougy Center. (1998). *Helping the Grieving Student: A Guide for Teachers.* Portland, OR: Author. This 50-page booklet provides practical advice on grief in children and adolescents, developmental issues, helping grieving students, school-related deaths, and deaths involving special complications.

Gordon, A. K., & Klass, D. (1979). *They Need to Know: How to Teach Children about Death.* Englewood Cliffs, NJ: Prentice-Hall. Provides a rationale and goals for teaching children about death, plus suggested curricula, activities, and resources laid out by grade level from preschool through high school.

Grollman, E. A. (1990). *Talking about Death: A Dialogue between Parent and Child* (3rd ed.). Boston: Beacon. Principles for helping children; a passage to be read with a child; guidelines for responding to questions that might arise from the read-along section; and a list of helpful resources.

Jewett, C. L. (1982). *Helping Children Cope with Separation and Loss.* Boston: Harvard Common Press. Suggested techniques from a child and family therapist built around a phase theory of grief and mourning.

O'Toole, D., & Cory, J. (1998). *Helping Children Grieve and Grow.* Burnsville, NC: Compassion Press. Clear and practical guidance in an outline format in just 24 pages.

Rudman, M. K., Gagne, K. D., & Bernstein, J. E. (1993). *Books to Help Children Cope with Separation and Loss* (4th ed.; 1st ed., 1978, & 2nd ed., 1984, by Bernstein alone; 3rd ed., 1989, by Bernstein & Rudman). New Providence, NJ: R. R. Bowker. Contains knowledgeable guidance concerning bibliotherapy or the use of books to help children cope with loss and grief, along with informed and sensitive descriptions (and keen critical evaluations) of hundreds of books for children on a broad range of topics related to loss.

Schaefer, D. & Lyons, C. (1993). *How Do We Tell the Children* (2nd ed.). New York: Newmarket. Helpful advice for parents from a funeral director and his colleague.

Trelease, J. (1995). *The Read-Aloud Handbook* (3rd rev. ed.). New York: Penguin. The definitive guide to why and how adults should read books aloud with children.

Wass, H., & Corr, C. A. (Eds.). (1984). *Childhood and Death*. Washington, DC: Hemisphere. Sections on death, dying, bereavement, suicide, and helping children plus selected, annotated resources (books for adults, books for children, organizations, and audiovisuals).

Wass, H., & Corr, C. A. (Eds.). (1984). *Helping Children Cope with Death: Guidelines and Resources* (2nd ed.). Washington, DC: Hemisphere. Guidelines for parents and other adults, plus annotated resources (printed materials, audiovisuals, and organizations).

Wolfelt, A. D. (1996). *Healing the Bereaved Child: Grief Gardening, Growth through Grief and Other Touchstones for Caregivers*. Fort Collins, CO: Compassion Press. Advice, suggested activities, and resources for helping grieving children from a clinical psychologist.

Where to Learn About or Purchase Death-Related Literature

Boulden Publishing, P.O. Box 1186, Weaverville, CA 96093-1186; 800-238-8433; fax 530-623-5525; www.bouldenpub.com. Offering Boulden products exclusively as single items, packs, or kits, including age-graded activity books, videos, and CD-ROMs on serious illness, bereavement, and a variety of related topics.

Centering Corporation, 1531 N. Saddle Creek Road, Omaha, NE 68104; 402-553-1200; fax 402-553-0507; e-mail to J1200@aol.com. In business over 20 years offering over 100 of their own works and many works from other publishers, as well as caring cards, videotapes, and audiotapes.

Compassion Books, 477 Hannah Branch Road, Burnsville, NC 28714; 828-675-5909; fax 828-675-9687; www.compassionbooks.com; e-mail to Heal2grow@aol.com. In business for fifteen years offering over 400 of their own and other publishers' books, audios, and videos.

Picture and Coloring Books for Preschoolers and Beginning Readers

Bartoli, J. (1975). *Nonna*. New York: Harvey House. A boy and his younger sister, with good memories of their grandmother, are permitted to participate in her funeral, burial, and the division of her property among family members so that each receives some memento of her life.

Blackburn, L. B. (1987). *Timothy Duck: The Story of the Death of a Friend*. Omaha, NE: Centering Corporation. Timothy Duck tries to understand his own reactions to the death of a friend and the ways in which the needs of his friend's sister are being overlooked by the adults around her. Sharing his questions and concerns with his mother and with his best friend is helpful.

Boulden, J. (1989). *Saying Goodbye*. Weaverville, CA: Boulden Publishing. This activity book tells a story about death as a natural part of life, the feelings that are involved in saying goodbye, and the conviction that love is forever, while allowing the child-reader to draw pictures, color images, or insert thoughts on its pages.

Brown, L. K., & Brown, M. (1996). *When Dinosaurs Die: A Guide to Understanding Death*. Boston: Little, Brown. A cartoon format introduces young children to issues of death and loss.

Brown, M. W. (1958). *The Dead Bird*. Reading, MA: Addison-Wesley. Some children find a wild bird that is dead, touch its body, bury it in a simple ceremony, and return to the site each day to mourn ("until they forgot"). The moral is that sadness need not last forever; life can go on again.

Carlstrom, N. W. (1990). *Blow Me a Kiss, Miss Lilly*. New York: Harper & Row. Young Sara's best friend is Miss Lilly, an old lady who is her neighbor across the street. When Miss Lilly is taken to the hospital and dies, Sara cries, looks for the light in her house, and is lonely. In spring, Sara finds happiness in Miss Lilly's garden and in her conviction that Miss Lilly is blowing her a kiss.

Clardy, A. E. (1984). *Dusty Was My Friend: Coming to Terms with Loss*. New York: Human Sciences. Benjamin is eight when his friend Dusty is killed in an automobile accident. As Benjamin struggles to understand his reactions to this tragic event, his parents give him permission to articulate his thoughts and feelings, mourn his loss, remember the good times that he shared with Dusty, and go on with his own life.

Cohn, J. (1987). *I Had a Friend Named Peter: Talking to Children About the Death of a Friend*. New York: Morrow. The children's section of this book describes Beth's reactions when her friend Peter is killed by a car, along with the helpful ways in which Beth's parents and teacher respond to her needs, the needs of her classmates, and the needs of Peter's parents. An adult section tries to prepare adults to assist children in coping with death.

Dean, A. (1991). *Meggie's Magic*. New York: Viking Penguin. After eight-year-old Meggie's illness and death, her mother, father, and sister feel sad and lonely. But one day when Meggie's sister goes to their special place, she finds it still filled with the magical qualities of the games they used to play and she realizes that Meggie's magic still remains inside each of them.

De Paola, T. (1973). *Nana Upstairs and Nana Downstairs*. New York: Putnam's. One day, young Tommy is told that his beloved great-grandmother ("Nana Upstairs") is dead, but he does not believe this until he sees her empty bed. A few nights later, Tommy sees a falling star and his mother explains that it represents a kiss from Nana who is now "upstairs" in a new way. Later, an older Tommy repeats the experience and interpretation after the death of "Nana Downstairs." A charming story about relationships, whose interpretations should be addressed with caution.

Dodge, N. C. (1984). *Thumpy's Story: A Story of Love and Grief Shared by Thumpy, the Bunny*. Springfield, IL: Prairie Lark Press. In picture book, coloring book, and workbook formats (in both English and Spanish), a rabbit tells a simple story about the death of his sister, Bun, and its effects on their family.

Fassler, J. (1971). *My Grandpa Died Today*. New York: Human Sciences. Although David's grandfather has tried to prepare the boy for his impending death, when it actually happens David still needs to mourn his loss. But he does finds comfort in a legacy of many good memories from his relationship with his grandfather and in the knowledge that his grandfather does not want him to be afraid to live and enjoy life.

Fassler, D., & McQueen, K. (1990). *What's a Virus, Anyway? The Kids' Book About AIDS*. Burlington, VT: Waterfront Books. This book is designed to help parents and teachers begin to talk about AIDS with young children, using just a few words or pictures on each page so as to leave lots of room for coloring, drawing, and shared discussion.

Fox, M. (1994). *Tough Boris*. New York: Harcourt Brace & Co. Boris von der Borch is a tough, massive, scruffy, greedy, fearless, and scary pirate—just like all pirates. But when his parrot dies, Boris cries and cries—just like all pirates, and just like everyone else.

Gaines-Lane, G. (1995). *My Memory Book*. Gaithersburg, MD: Chi Rho Press. A good example of a workbook providing suggestions, guidelines, and space for children to draw or write out their memories of someone who has died.

Hazen, B. S. (1985). *Why Did Grandpa Die? A Book About Death*. New York: Golden. When Molly's beloved Grandpa dies suddenly, Molly cannot accept that harsh fact. She feels frightened, awful, and misses Grandpa very much, but cannot cry. Only after a long time is Molly able to acknowledge that Grandpa will not come back, to cry, and to realize that Grandpa still is available to her through pictures, in her memories, and in stories shared with her family.

Heegaard, M. E. (1988). *When Someone Very Special Dies*. Minneapolis, MN: Woodland Press. A story line about loss and death provides inspiration and opportunity for children to illustrate or color and thus to share thoughts and feelings.

Johnson, J. & Johnson, M. (1982). *Where's Jess?* Omaha, NE: Centering Corporation. A good book to use in helping young children cope with infant sibling loss.

Jordan, M. K. (1989). *Losing Uncle Tim*. Niles, IL: Albert Whitman. When Uncle Tim becomes infected with HIV, develops AIDS, and dies, his nephew looks for solace through an idea they had once discussed: "Maybe Uncle Tim is like the sun, just shining somewhere else."

Kantrowitz, M. (1973). *When Violet Died*. New York: Parents' Magazine Press. After the death of their pet bird, Amy, Eva, and their friends have a funeral with poems, songs, punch, and even humor. It is sad to think that nothing lasts forever, but then Eva realizes that life can go on in another way through an ever-changing chain of life involving the family cat, Blanche, and her kittens.

London, J. (1994). *Liplap's Wish*. San Francisco: Chronicle Books. As Liplap builds the winter's first snowbunny, he remembers his Grandma and misses her. He finds comfort in an old Rabbit's tale about how, long ago, when the First Rabbits died, they became stars in the sky who even now come out at night, watch over us, and shine forever in our hearts.

Mellonie, B., & Ingpen, R. (1983). *Lifetimes: A Beautiful Way to Explain Death to Children*. New York: Bantam. Through many examples, this book affirms that "there is a beginning and an ending for everything that is alive. In between is living. . . . So, no matter how long they are, or how short, lifetimes are really all the same. They have beginnings, and endings, and there is living in between."

Numeroff, L., & Harpham, W. (1999). *Kid's Talk: Kids Speak Out about Breast Cancer*. Dallas, TX: Susan G. Komen Breast Cancer Foundation. This book uses animal drawings to depict common situations experienced by children whose mothers are diagnosed with breast cancer. Death is not directly addressed, but the book conveys children's confusion when confronted by difficult situations and offers guidelines to open communication and help parents talk to children on their level.

O'Toole, D. (1988). *Aarvy Aardvark Finds Hope*. Burnsville, NC: Compassion Books. Designed to be read aloud, this is a story about how Aarvy Aardvark comes to terms with the loss of his mother and brother. Many animals offer unhelpful advice to Aarvy; only his friend, Ralphy Rabbit, is truly helpful.

Rylant, C. (1995/1997). *Dog Heaven* and *Cat Heaven*. New York: Blue Sky Press. Vivid illustrations and charming story lines in these two books describe the delights that dogs and cats might find in their own special heavens.

Stickney, D. (1985). *Water Bugs and Dragonflies*. New York: Pilgrim Press. This little book focuses on transformations in life as a metaphor for transformations between life and death. One key point is that the water bug who becomes transformed into a dragonfly is no longer able to return to the underwater colony to explain what has happened. Each individual must wait for his or her own transformation in order to appreciate what it entails.

Stull, E. G. (1964). *My Turtle Died Today*. New York: Holt, Rinehart & Winston. When a pet turtle dies, a boy and his friends bury it and talk about what all of this means. They conclude that life can go on in another way through the newborn kittens of their cat, Patty. Much of this is sound, but the book also poses two questions that need to be addressed with care: Can you get a new pet in the way that one child has a new mother? and Do you have to live—a long time—before you die?

Varley, S. (1992). *Badger's Parting Gifts*. New York: Mulberry Books. Although Badger is old and knows that he must die, he is not afraid. He worries about his friends, who are sad when he dies but who find consolation in the special memories that Badger had left with each of them and in sharing those memories with others.

Viorst, J. (1971). *The Tenth Good Thing About Barney*. New York: Atheneum. When a pet cat dies, a boy tries to think of ten good things to say about Barney at the funeral. At first, he can only think of nine things until he argues with a friend about whether or not cats go to heaven. Out in the garden, he realizes the tenth good thing is that "Barney is in the ground and he's helping grow flowers."

Warburg, S. S. (1969). *Growing Time*. Boston: Houghton Mifflin. When his aging collie, King, dies, Jamie's father gets him a new puppy. At first, Jamie is not ready for the new dog, but after he is allowed to express his grief, he finds it possible to accept the new relationship.

Weir, A. B. (1992). *Am I Still a Big Sister?* Newtown, PA: Fallen Leaf Press. This simple story follows the concerns of a young girl through the illness, hospitalization, death, and funeral of her baby sister, and the subsequent birth of a new brother.

Wilhelm, H. (1985). *I'll Always Love You*. New York: Crown. A boy and his dog, Elfie, grow up together, but Elfie ages and dies while her master is still young. Afterward, family members regret that they did not tell Elfie they loved her. But the boy did so every night and he realizes that his love for her will continue even after her death. He doesn't want a new puppy right away, even though he knows that Elfie will not come back and that there may come a time in the future when he will be ready for a new pet.

Zolotow, C. (1974). *My Grandson Lew*. New York: Harper. When six-year-old Lewis wonders why his grandfather has not visited lately, his mother says that Lewis had not been told that his grandfather had died because he had never asked. The boy remarks that he hadn't needed to ask; his grandfather just came. Sharing warm memories of someone they both miss leads his mother to conclude, "Now we will remember him together and neither of us will be so lonely as we would be if we had to remember him alone."

Storybooks and Other Texts for Primary School Readers

Alexander, S. (1983). *Nadia the Willful*. New York: Pantheon Books. Nadia's older brother dies and her father decrees that no one may speak of his death. Nadia helps her family, particularly her father, deal with their grief by willfully talking about her brother.

Arnold, C. (1987). *What We Do When Someone Dies*. New York: Franklin Watts. This book provides information about death-related feelings, concepts, and beliefs, but gives most attention to disposition of the body, funeral customs, and memorial practices.

Buck, P. S. (1948). *The Big Wave*. New York: Scholastic. After a tidal wave kills his family and all the fishing people on the shore, Jiya chooses to live with his friend Kino's poor farming family instead of being adopted by a rich man. Years later, Jiya marries Kino's sister and decides to move back to the seaside with his new bride.

Bunting, E. (1982). *The Happy Funeral*. New York: Harper & Row. Two young Chinese-American girls are puzzled when their mother says they will have a "happy funeral" for their grandfather. In the end, the children realize that although no one was happy that their grandfather died, his good life and everyone's fond memories of him did make for a happy funeral.

Carrick, C. (1976). *The Accident*. New York: Seabury Press. Christopher's dog, Bodger, is accidentally killed when he runs in front of a truck. Christopher is angry at the driver, at his father for not getting mad at the driver, and at himself for not paying attention and allowing Bodger to wander to the other side of the road as they walked. Christopher's parents bury Bodger too quickly the next morning before he can take part, but anger dissolves into tears when he and his father are able to join together to erect a marker at Bodger's grave.

Chin-Yee, F. (1988). *Sam's Story: A Story for Families Surviving Sudden Infant Death Syndrome*. Available from the Canadian Foundation for the Study of Infant Deaths, Toronto, Ontario. A rare book that tells a story (with pictures) about the confusing experiences of a child in a family that has experienced the sudden death of his infant brother.

Coburn, J. B. (1964). *Annie and the Sand Dobbies: A Story About Death for Children and Their Parents*. New York: Seabury Press. When young Danny encounters the deaths of both his toddler sister from a respiratory infection and his dog after it ran away from home, a neighbor uses imaginary characters to suggest that the deceased are safe with God.

Coerr, E. (1977). *Sadako and the Thousand Paper Cranes*. New York: Putnam's. This book is based on a true story about a Japanese girl who died of leukemia in 1955 as one of the long-term results of the atomic bombing of Hiroshima (which occurred when Sadako was two years old). While in the hospital, a friend reminded Sadako of the legend that the crane is supposed to live for a thousand years and that good health will be granted to a person who folds 1,000 origami paper cranes. With family members and friends, they began folding. Sadako died before the project was finished, but her classmates completed the work and children all over Japan have since contributed money to erect a statue in her memory.

Coleman, P. (1996). *Where the Balloons Go*. Omaha, NE: Centering Corporation. When Corey asks where balloons go as they fly up into the sky, Grandma suggests that perhaps their destination is a lovely Balloon Forest. Later, after Grandma becomes sick and dies, Corey wishes that his balloons could carry him up to the Balloon Forest to see Grandma, but settles for attaching a message of his love to a balloon and releasing it.

Corley, E. A. (1973). *Tell Me About Death, Tell Me About Funerals*. Santa Clara, CA: Grammatical Sciences. This book depicts a conversation between a young girl whose grandfather has recently died and her father. In ways that avoid euphemisms, they discuss guilt, abandonment, and choices about funerals, burial, cemeteries, and mausoleums. At one point, we encounter a child's delightful misunderstanding about the "polarbears" who carry the casket.

Donnelly, E. (1981). *So Long, Grandpa*. New York: Crown. Michael at 10 witnesses his grandfather's deterioration and eventual death from cancer. We learn about his reactions to these events and about the way in which Michael's grandfather had helped to prepare the boy by taking him to an elderly friend's funeral.

Douglas, E. (1990). *Rachel and the Upside Down Heart*. Los Angeles: Price Stern Sloan. After Rachel's daddy died when she was four, she was sad and had to move from a house with a yard, green grass, and two dogs in Kentucky to a noisy apartment in New York City. Mommy said Daddy would always be in Rachel's heart, so she began to draw hearts but could only make them upside down. Later, Rachel began to find some new friends and some of the hearts that she drew were upside up. Finally, when his father died, Rachel was able to talk to a new friend and help him with his loss.

Erling, J., & Erling, S. (1986). *Our Baby Died. Why?* Maple Plain, MN: Pregnancy and Infant Loss Center. A little boy shares his story about the death of his stillborn brother and the subsequent birth of sibling twins.

Goldman, L. (1997). *Bart Speaks Out: An Interactive Storybook for Young Children About Suicide.* Los Angeles: Western Psychological Services. Provides words for children to use to discuss the sensitive topic of suicide.

Goodman, M. B. (1990). *Vanishing Cookies: Doing OK When a Parent Has Cancer.* Available from the Benjamin Family Foundation, Downsview, Canada. This book's goal is to bridge the gap between adults and children by helping them share feelings in situations when an adult is coping with cancer. Children are encouraged to ask questions and are offered information about cancer, treatments, coping with feelings, friends and school, and death. The title refers to the vanishing cookies that some children shared with their mother when they visited her in the hospital.

Graeber, C. (1982). *Mustard.* New York: Macmillan. Mustard is an elderly cat with a heart condition who needs to avoid stress. But one day Mustard runs outside and gets into a squabble with another animal, leading to a heart attack and to Mustard's death. After Father buries Mustard, Alex goes along to donate the cat's dishes and some money to the animal shelter where they had gotten Mustard. Because he is preoccupied with sadness, Alex wisely declines (for now) a well-meaning offer of a new pet.

Greene, C. C. (1976). *Beat the Turtle Drum.* New York: Viking. Mostly, this book describes thirteen-year-old Kate and eleven-year-old Joss' loving, warm family. When Joss is abruptly and unexpectedly killed in a fall from a tree, the family is flooded with grief. Conveying this sense of the many dimensions of bereavement is the book's strong point.

Gryte, M. (1991). *No New Baby.* Omaha, NE: Centering Corporation. A caring Grandma explains the sadness and loss of miscarriage to her grandchild, reminding her that she's not to blame and that it's okay to ask questions and express her feelings.

Johnson, J., & Johnson, M. (1978). *Tell Me, Papa: A Family Book for Children's Questions About Death and Funerals.* Omaha, NE: Centering Corporation. Using the format of a discussion between children and a grandparent, this slim book provides an explanation of death, funerals, and saying good-bye.

Krementz, J. *How It Feels When a Parent Dies* (1981) and *How It Feels to Fight for Your Life* (1989). Boston: Little, Brown; paperback by Simon & Schuster, 1991. Short essays by children and adolescents (seven to sixteen years old) describe individual reactions to the death of a parent and to a variety of life-threatening illnesses. An author's photo accompanies each essay.

Marshall, B. (1998). *Animal Crackers: A Tender Book About Death and Funerals and Love.* Omaha, NE: Centering Corporation. A young girl describes her Nanny who hid animal crackers all over her house for her grandchildren. After Nanny became forgetful and went to live in a nursing home, she eventually died. But the children always remember Nanny fondly through the good times they shared with her and through her "Nanny crackers."

McNamara, J. W. (1994). *My Mom is Dying: A Child's Diary.* Minneapolis: Augsburg Fortress. The illustrated diary format of this book presents an imaginary record of Kristine's conversations with God while her mother is dying. Notes from the author identify Kristine's reactions and suggest how they could provide a basis for discussions with children.

Miles, M. (1971). *Annie and the Old One.* Boston: Little, Brown. A ten-year-old Navajo girl is told that it will be time for grandmother to return to Mother Earth when her mother finishes weaving a rug. Annie tries to unravel the weaving in secret and to distract her mother from weaving, until the adults realize what is going on and her grandmother explains that we are all part of a natural cycle. When Annie realizes that she cannot hold back time, she is ready herself to learn to weave.

Powell, E. S. (1990). *Geranium Morning.* Minneapolis: CarolRhoda Books. Two young children—Timothy, whose father died suddenly in an accident, and Frannie, whose mother is dying—struggle with strong feelings, memories, guilt ("if onlys"), and some unhelpful adult actions. In sharing their losses, the children help each other; Frannie's father and her mother (before she dies) also are helpful.

Saltzman, D. (1995). *The Jester Has Lost His Jingle.* Palos Verdes Estates, CA: The Jester Co.. This is the tale of a Jester who wakens one morning to find laughter missing from his kingdom. The Jester and his helper, Pharley, search high and low to find it. Ultimately, they discover that laughter—the best tonic for anyone facing seemingly insurmountable obstacles—is buried deep inside each of us.

Shriver, M. (1999). *What's Heaven*. New York: Golden Books. When little Kate's Great-grandma dies, she explores with her mother questions like what is heaven, how come you can't see it, how do you get to heaven, what is a person's soul, what's a funeral, and why do we bury dead bodies?

Simon, N. (1979). *We Remember Philip*. Chicago: Whitman. When the adult son of an elementary school teacher dies in a mountain climbing accident, Sam and other members of his class can observe how Mr. Hall is affected by his grief. In time, the children persuade Mr. Hall to share with them a scrapbook and other memories of his son, and they plant a tree as a class memorial.

Sims, A. (1986.) *Am I Still a Sister?* Albuquerque, NM: Big A & Company. A young girl writes about her real-life experiences when her baby brother died from cancer.

Smith, D. B. (1973). *A Taste of Blackberries*. New York: Scholastic. After the death of Jamie as a result of an allergic reaction to a bee sting, his best friend (the book's unnamed narrator) reflects on this unexpected event. Did it really happen or is it just another of Jamie's pranks? Could it have been prevented? Is it disloyal to go on eating and living when Jamie is dead? He concludes that no one could have prevented this death, "some questions just don't have answers," and life can go on.

White, E. B. (1952). *Charlotte's Web*. New York: Harper. This book is now a classic with its story of friendship on two levels: that of a young girl named Fern who lives on a farm and saves Wilbur, the runt of the pig litter; and that of Charlotte, the spider, who spins fabulous webs that save an older and fatter Wilbur from the butcher's knife. In the end, Charlotte dies of natural causes, but her achievements and her offspring live on.

Whitehead, R. (1971). *The Mother Tree*. New York: Seabury Press. Where do eleven-year-old Tempe and her four-year-old sister, Laura, turn for comfort in the early 1900s when their mother dies and Tempe is made to assume her mother's duties? To a temporary spiritual refuge in the large, backyard tree of the book's title and eventually to good memories of their mother that live on within them.

Literature for Middle School Readers

Arrick, E. (1980). *Tunnel Vision*. Scarsdale, NY: Bradbury. After Anthony hangs himself at fifteen, his family, friends, and teacher cope with feelings of bewilderment and guilt. There is no easy resolution for such feelings, but important questions are posed: What should be done in the face of serious problems? and Where should one turn for help?

Bernstein, J. E. (1977). *Loss: And How to Cope with It*. New York: Clarion. This book provides knowledgeable advice for young readers about how to cope with loss through death, for example, how to handle feelings and how to deal with traumatic deaths such as suicide or murder.

Blume, J. (1981). *Tiger Eyes*. Scarsdale, NY: Bradbury. After her father is killed during a holdup of his 7-Eleven store in Atlantic City, Davey (fifteen), her mother, and her younger brother all react differently and are unable to help each other in their grief. They attempt a change of location to visit Davey's aunt, but eventually decide to move back to New Jersey to rebuild their lives.

Boulden, J., & Boulden, J. (1994). *The Last Goodbye*. Weaverville, CA: Boulden Publishing. This is a memory book, designed to be a stimulus for recording personal reactions to a death and memories of the person who died.

Cleaver, V., & Cleaver, B. (1970). *Grover*. Philadelphia: Lippincott. When Grover was eleven his mother became terminally ill and took her own life in order (she thought) to "spare" herself and her family the ravages of her illness. His father and other adults around Grover surround this death in mystery. Issues posed include whether one must endure life no matter what suffering it holds; whether religion is a comfort; and how one should deal with grief.

Dragonwagon, C. (1990). *Winter Holding Spring*. New York: Macmillan. At first, nothing is the same for eleven-year-old Sarah and her father after her mother dies. Each is in pain, but gradually they begin to share their experiences and their memories of Sarah's mother. Eventually, they realize together that "nothing just ends without beginning the next thing at the same time"; each season somehow contains its successor (winter always holds spring). And Sarah knows that "love is alive in me and always will be."

Farley, C. (1975). *The Garden Is Doing Fine*. New York: Atheneum. While her father is dying of cancer, Corrie searches for reasons to explain why a good person like her father would die. A wise neighbor helps Corrie see that even though there may be no reasons for her father's death, he has left an important legacy (his "garden") in the form of his children. The seeds that he has planted in them will live on and she can let go without betraying him.

Fox, P. (1995). *The Eagle Kite*. New York: Orchard Books. Liam Cormac struggles to make sense of things when his father develops AIDS, moves out of their home to a rented cabin, and ultimately dies. Liam is confused, puzzled by the half-truths that he is told, and unable to understand his mother and his aunt's very different reactions. Ultimately, Liam realizes that his father is gay and comes to terms with this by sharing it with his father and later telling his mother what he knows.

Girard, L. W. (1991). *Alex, the Kid with AIDS*. Morton Grove, IL: Albert Whitman. Alex, the new kid in the fourth grade class, is at first treated differently and left out of some activities because he has AIDS. Gradually, Michael comes to appreciate Alex's sense of humor and they become friends. Their teacher realizes that Alex needs to be treated as a member of the class, not as someone odd or special.

Grollman, S. (1988). *Shira: A Legacy of Courage*. New York: Doubleday. Shira Putter died at the age of nine in 1983 from a rare form of diabetes. This book tells Shira's story based on her own writings and personal accounts from family members and friends in a way that celebrates courage, love, and hope in a life containing much hardship.

Heegaard, M. E. (1990). *Coping with Death and Grief*. Minneapolis: Lerner Publications. This book describes change, loss, and death as natural parts of life, provides information and advice about coping with feelings, and suggests ways to help oneself and others who are grieving.

Jampolsky, G. G., & Murray, G. (Eds.). (1982). *Straight from the Siblings: Another Look at the Rainbow*. Berkeley, CA: Celestial Arts. Brothers and sisters of children who have a life-threatening illness write about the feelings of siblings and ways to help all of the children who are involved in such difficult situations.

Jampolsky, G. G., & Taylor, R. (Eds.). (1978). *There Is a Rainbow Behind Every Dark Cloud*. Berkeley, CA: Celestial Arts. Eleven children, eight to nineteen years old, explain what it is like to have a life-threatening illness and the choices that youngsters have in helping themselves, for example, when one is first told about one's illness, in going back to school, in coping with feelings, and in talking about death.

LeShan, E. (1976). *Learning to Say Good-by: When a Parent Dies*. New York: Macmillan. This book offers advice to bereaved children and the adults around them on a broad range of topics, including: what grief is like; the importance of honesty, trust, sharing, and funerals; fear of abandonment, anticipatory grief, and guilt; accepting the loss of the deceased, maintaining a capacity for love, and meeting future changes.

Little, J. (1984). *Mama's Going to Buy You a Mockingbird*. New York: Viking Kestrel. Jeremy and his younger sister, Sarah, only learn that their father is dying from cancer by overhearing people talk about it. They experience many losses, large and small, that accompany his dying and death, often compounded by lack of information and control over their situation.

Mann, P. (1977). *There Are Two Kinds of Terrible*. New York: Doubleday/Avon. Robbie's broken arm is one kind of terrible, but it ends; his mother's death seems to leave Robbie and his "cold fish" father an experience with no conclusion. They are together, but each grieves alone until they begin to find ways to share their suffering and their memories.

Maple, M. (1992). *On the Wings of a Butterfly: A Story about Life and Death*. Seattle: Parenting Press. Lisa, a child dying of cancer, and Sonya, her caterpillar friend, share insights and experiences as Lisa approaches her death and Sonya prepares for her transformation into a Monarch butterfly.

Paterson, K. (1977). *Bridge to Terabithia*. New York: Crowell. Jess and Leslie have a special, secret meeting place in the woods called Terabithia. But when Leslie is killed one day in an accidental fall, the magic of their play and friendship is disrupted. Jess mourns the loss of this special relationship, is supported by his family, and ultimately is able to initiate new relationships that will share friendship in a similar way with others.

Richter, E. (1986). *Losing Someone You Love: When a Brother or Sister Dies*. New York: Putnam's. Fifteen adolescents describe in their own words how they feel in response to a wide variety of experiences of sibling death.

Rofes, E. E. (Ed.), and the Unit at Fayerweather Street School. (1985). *The Kids' Book About Death and Dying, by and for Kids*. Boston: Little, Brown. The result of a class project, this book describes what these young authors have learned about a wide range of death-related topics, making clear what children want to know about these subjects and how they want adults to talk to them. One main lesson is that "a lot of the mystery and fear surrounding death has been brought about by ignorance and avoidance." Another lesson is expressed in the hope "that children can lead the way in dealing with death and dying with a healthier and happier approach."

Romond, J. L. (1989). *Children Facing Grief: Letters from Bereaved Brothers and Sisters*. St. Meinrad, IN: Abbey Press. In the form of letters to a friend, the author records the observations of eighteen children (ages six to fifteen) who have each experienced the death of a sibling. Helpful comments from young people who have been there in grief.

Shura, M. E. (1988). *The Sunday Doll*. New York: Dodd, Mead. This is a complex story of a thirteen-year-old girl whose parents exclude her from something terrible involving her older sister (the suicide of a boyfriend) and who is frightened by her Aunt Harriet's life-threatening "spells" (transient ischemia attacks). Like the Amish doll without a face, Emily learns that she has her own strengths and can choose which face to present to the world.

Sternberg, E., & Sternberg, B. (1980). *If I Die and When I Do: Exploring Death with Young People*. Englewood Cliffs, NJ: Prentice-Hall. This book is the result of a nine-week middle-school course on death and dying. The text mainly consists of drawings, poems, and statements by the students on various death-related topics, plus a closing chapter of 25 suggested activities.

Traisman, E. S. (1992). *Fire in My Heart, Ice in My Veins: A Journal for Teenagers Experiencing a Loss*. Omaha, NE: Centering Corporation. The aim here is to provide a vehicle to be used as a journal by teenagers who have experienced a loss. A line or two of text on each page and many small drawings offer age-appropriate prompts for this purpose.

Traisman, E. S., & Sieff, J. (Comps.). (1995). *Flowers for the Ones You've Known: Unedited Letters from Bereaved Teens*. Omaha, NE: Centering Corporation. This is a support book for grieving teens mainly consisting of unedited letters and poems written by bereaved peers and reproduced here in various handwritten and print formats.

Wiener, L. S., Best, A., & Pizzo, R. A. (Comps.). (1994). *Be a Friend: Children Who Live with HIV Speak*. Morton Grove, IL: Albert Whitman. The vivid colors, drawings, and layout in this book are intended to permit children who are living with HIV infection to speak in their own voices.

Literature for High School Readers

Agee, J. (1969). *A Death in the Family*. New York: Bantam. This Pulitzer Prize-winning novel unerringly depicts the points of view of two children in Knoxville, Tennessee, in 1915 when they are told of the accidental death of their father. Agee skillfully portrays ways in which the children experience unusual events, sense strange tensions within the family, struggle to understand what has happened, and strive to work out their implications.

Bode, J. (1993). *Death is Hard to Live with: Teenagers and How They Cope with Death*. New York: Delacorte. Teenagers speak frankly about how they cope with death and loss.

Craven, M. (1973). *I Heard the Owl Call My Name*. New York: Dell. This novel describes a young Episcopal priest with a terminal illness who is sent by his bishop to live with Native Americans in British Columbia who believe that death will come when the owl calls someone's name. From them, the bishop hopes that the young priest will learn to face his own death.

Deaver, J. R. (1988). *Say Goodnight, Gracie.* New York: Harper & Row. Jimmy and Morgan have been close friends since birth. When Jimmy is killed by a drunken driver in an automobile accident, Morgan is so disoriented by the extent of her loss that she is unable to face her feelings, attend Jimmy's funeral, or speak to his parents. Her own parents offer support and tolerate Morgan's withdrawal from the world, but it is not until a wise aunt intervenes that Morgan is able to confront her feelings in a way that leads her to more constructive coping and to decide to go on with living.

Geller, N. (1987). *The Last Teenage Suicide.* Auburn, ME: Norman Geller Publishing. Text and pen-and-ink drawings describe the death by suicide of a high school senior, together with reactions from his family, friends, and acquaintances. The death mobilizes citizens to develop a program to identify and respond to the needs of those who are potentially suicidal or hurting emotionally with the goal of making this death the last teenage suicide in their community.

Greenberg, J. (1979). *A Season In-Between.* New York: Farrar. Carrie Singer, a seventh grader, copes with the diagnosis of her father's cancer in spring and his death that summer. She draws on the rabbinical teaching: turn scratches on a jewel into a beautiful design.

Gunther, J. (1949). *Death Be Not Proud: A Memoir.* New York: Harper. An early biographical account of a lengthy struggle with a brain tumor by the author's fifteen-year-old son.

Hughes, M. (1984). *Hunter in the Dark.* New York: Atheneum. A boy with overprotective parents sets out to face life and death on his own by confronting threats at different levels: his leukemia and the challenge of going hunting in the Canadian woods for the first time.

Lewis, C. S. (1976). *A Grief Observed.* New York: Bantam. The author, a celebrated British writer and lay theologian, recorded his experiences of grief after the death of his wife. The published result is an unusual and extraordinary document, a direct and honest expression of one individual's grief that has helped innumerable readers by normalizing their own experiences in bereavement.

Martin, A. M. (1986). *With You and Without You.* New York: Holiday House; paperback by Scholastic. Family members (parents and four children) struggle to cope when the father is told that he will soon die as a result of an inoperable heart condition. Before his death, each member of the family tries to make the father's remaining time as good as possible; afterwards, they each strive to cope with their losses. One important lesson is that no one is ever completely prepared for a death; another is that each individual must cope in his or her own way.

O'Toole, D. (1995). *Facing Change: Falling Apart and Coming Together Again in the Teen Years.* Burnsville, NC: Compassion Books. This little book is intended to help adolescents understand loss, grief, and change, and to think about how they might respond to those experiences.

Pendleton, E. (Comp.). (1980). *Too Old to Cry, Too Young to Die.* Nashville, TN: Thomas Nelson. Thirty-five teenagers describe their experiences in living with cancer, including treatments, side effects, hospitals, parents, siblings, and friends.

Scrivani, M. (1991). *When Death Walks In.* Omaha, NE: Centering Corporation. This little booklet was written for teen readers to explore the many facets of grief and how one might cope with them in productive ways.

Tolstoy, L. (1960). *The Death of Ivan Ilych and Other Stories.* New York: New American Library. The title story is an exceptional piece of world literature in which a Russian magistrate in the prime of his life is afflicted with a grave illness that becomes steadily more serious. As his health deteriorates, Ivan suddenly realizes that glib talk in college about mortality does not just apply to other people or to humanity in general. He also discovers that only one servant and his young son treat him with real compassion and candor.

Charles Corr, PhD, is Professor emeritus in the Department of Philosophical Studies at Southern Illinois University Edwardsville, a member of the Executive Committee of the National Donor Family Council, and a former Chairperson (1989-1994) of the International Work Group on Dying, Death, and Bereavement. Dr. Corr was seen on the Hospice Foundation of America's second annual National Bereavement Teleconference, Children Mourning, Mourning Children. *This bibliography draws on material in Corr, C. A., Nabe, C. M., and Corr, D. M.,* Death and Dying, Life and Living *(3rd ed., 2000). Belmont, CA: Wadsworth.*

Resource Organizations

Hospice Foundation of America is pleased to offer this list of national organizations that provide resources to assist children and adolescents facing a wide range of losses. There are many excellent organizations that provide assistance on the local level. To find out more about groups in your area, please contact us at (800) 854-3402.

American School Counselor Association
801 N. Fairfax Street, Suite #310, Alexandria, VA 22314
(800) 306-4722 Fax: (703) 683-1619
http://www.schoolcounselor.org
e-mail: asca@erols.com

American School Counselor Association, with a membership of over 13,000 school counseling professionals, focuses on providing professional development, enhancing school counseling programs, and researching effective school counseling practices. ASCA's mission is to help to ensure excellence in school counseling and the development of all students. Since its founding in 1952, ASCA has provided publications, educational programs, and conferences, professional development workshops, and other programs for school counselors at all levels of public and private educational systems.

Americans for Better Care of the Dying
2175 K Street, NW, Suite 820, Washington, DC 20037
(202) 530-9864 Fax: (202) 467-2271
http://www.abcd-caring.com
e-mail: caring@erols.com

Americans for Better Care of the Dying (ABCD) is a not-for-profit charity dedicated to development of service systems that meet the special needs of the last phase of life. ABCD aims to: enhance the experience of the last phase of life for all Americans; advocate for the interests of patients and families; improve communication between providers and patients; involve society in end-of-life care; control pain and other symptoms; demand continuity in service systems for the seriously ill; limit the emotional and financial toll on families; and support quality improvement initiatives by front-line providers.

Association for Death Education and Counseling
342 N. Main Street, West Hartford, CT 06117-2507
(860) 586-7503 Fax: (860) 586-7550
http://www.adec.org
e-mail: info@adec.org

The Association for Death Education and Counseling is a multi-disciplinary professional organization dedicated to promoting excellence in death education, bereavement counseling, and care of the dying. Based on theory and quality research, ADEC provides information, support, and resources to its membership and, through them, to the public.

Avanta/The Virginia Satir Network
2104 SW 152nd Street, Suite #2, Burien, WA 98166
(206) 241-7566 Fax: (206) 241-7527
http://www.avanta.net
e-mail: avanta@foxinternet.net

Avanta, The Virginia Satir Network, is an international educational organization whose individual members are committed to supporting, connecting, and empowering people and organizations to achieve their full potential. Dedicated to developing a professional training network, Avanta sponsors national and international seminars, conferences, and workshops. These workshops present applications of the Satir Process in areas such as anti-racism and trauma. Resources available through Avanta include the works of Virginia Satir and other Avanta members.

Camp Matumaini
University of Maryland School of Social Work
525 West Redwood Street, Baltimore, MD 21201
(410) 706-0814 Fax: (410) 706-6046
e-mail: ctyler@ssw.umaryland.edu

Camp Matumaini is provided through a unique partnership between the Hope Support Center, an African-American AIDS outreach program in Baltimore, and the University of Maryland School of Social Work. The goals of Camp

Matumaini are to alleviate the pain of loss and facilitate the grief process, to provide a safe environment in which to address the emotional aspects associated with HIV/AIDS, to facilitate open family communication, and to build informal networks of support.

Candlelighters Childhood Cancer Foundation
3910 Warner Street, Kensington, MD 20895
(800) 366-2223 Fax: (301) 962-3521
http://www.candlelighters.org

Candlelighters Childhood Cancer Foundation provides support, information, and advocacy to families of children with cancer (at any stage of the illness or who are bereaved), to professionals in the field, and to adult survivors, through local groups, newsletters, and other services.

The Compassionate Friends
P.O. Box 3696, Oak Brook, IL 60522-3696
(630) 990-0010 Fax: (630) 990-0246
http://www.compassionatefriends.org

The Compassionate Friends is a self-help organization whose purpose is to offer friendship and understanding to families following the death of a child. They have 580 chapters nationwide which provide monthly meetings, phone contacts, lending libraries and a local newsletter. The national organization provides a quarterly magazine, distributes grief-related materials, hosts an annual national conference, provides training programs and resources for local chapters, and answers requests for referrals and information.

The Dougy Center
P.O. Box 86582, Portland, OR 97286
(503) 775-5683 Fax: (503) 777-3097
http://www.dougy.org
e-mail: help@dougy.org

The Dougy Center provides support groups for grieving children that are age specific (three to five, six to twelve, teens) and loss specific (parent death, sibling death, survivors of homicide/violent death, survivors of suicide). Additional services include national trainings, consultations to schools and organizations, crisis-line information, and referrals. The Dougy Center's National Center for Grieving Children and Families is in the process of publishing a series of guidebooks based on what they've learned from the children they've served. Titles include: *Helping Children Cope With Death*, *Helping Teens Cope With Death*, *Helping The Grieving Student: A Guide For Teachers*, and *35 Ways to Help a Grieving Child*.

Growth House, Inc.

http://www.growthhouse.org
e-mail: info@growthhouse.org

The mission of Growth House, Inc., is to improve the quality of compassionate care for people who are dying, through public education about hospice and home care, palliative care, pain management, death with dignity, bereavement, and related issues. This award-winning web site offers the net's most extensive directory of reviewed resources for life-threatening illness and end-of-life care. Growth House offers a free monthly e-mail newsletter covering new and noteworthy net resources for terminal care, life-threatening illness, and bereavement. Growth House provides the Inter-Institutional Collaborating Network on End-of-Life Care (IICN), which links major professional organizations internationally.

Hospice Foundation of America

2001 S Street, NW, Suite 300, Washington, DC 20009
(800) 854-3402 Fax: (202) 638-5312
777 17th Street, Suite 401, Miami Beach, FL 33139
(305) 538-9272 Fax: (305) 538-0092
http://www.hospicefoundation.org
e-mail: hfa@hospicefoundation.org

Hospice Foundation of America is a not-for-profit organization that provides leadership in the development and application of hospice and its philosophy of care. The Foundation produces an annual award-winning National Bereavement Teleconference and publishes the *Living With Grief* book series in conjunction with the teleconference. In addition to the annual teleconference, HFA offers a number of other resources. *A Guide to Recalling and Telling Your Life Story* is a tool to assist people in writing their autobiographies. *Clergy to Clergy: Ministering to Those Facing Illness, Death, and Grief* is an audiotape series developed to help clergy members of all faiths minister to their communities and see to their own needs as caregivers. HFA publishes *Journeys*, a monthly newsletter for the bereaved, as well as special issues for adolescents, the newly bereaved, and those facing the anniversary of a death. HFA serves as the Managing Editor for *Omega, Journal of Death and Dying*. HFA offers brochures on *Choosing Hospice, Volunteering for Hospice*, and *Living With Grief: At Work, At School*, and *At Worship*; has published a series of educational ads; and provides resources to hospices, schools, military service centers, and other organizations. HFA is a member of the Combined Federal Campaign through Health Charities of America.

Last Acts Campaign
c/o Barksdale Ballard, 1951 Kidwell Dr., Suite 205, Vienna, VA 22182
(703) 827-8771 Fax: (703) 827-0783
http://www.lastacts.org
e-mail: lastacts@aol.com

Last Acts is a national campaign to engage both health professionals and the public in efforts to improve care at the end of life. Last Acts is made up of more than 400 partner organizations that believe that every segment of society, employers, clergy, voluntary health organization leaders, medical and nursing professionals, and counselors, among others, has a role to play as a part of a larger movement that addresses end-of-life concerns at the national, state and community levels. The three guiding principles of Last Acts are to identify models that improve end-of-life care; to examine systems of end-of-life care that may be improved; and to improve the culture of dying in America. The Last Acts Campaign's Family Task Force has developed a position paper on children to make sure children's needs are not forgotten in the death and dying process.

National Hospice Organization
1700 Diagonal Road, Alexandria, VA 22314
(703) 243-5900 Fax: (703) 525-5762
http://www.nho.org
e-mail: drsnho@cais.com

The National Hospice Organization (NHO) is the oldest and largest non-profit organization in the US devoted exclusively to hospice and palliative care. NHO operates the Hospice Helpline (800-658-8898) to provide the general public and healthcare professionals with information about hospice and palliative care, reimbursement sources, and referrals to local hospice programs throughout the US. NHO publishes a variety of brochures on hospice care, grief in the workplace, and bereavement.

Project on Death in America
Open Society Institute
400 W. 59th Street, New York, NY 10019
(212) 548-0150 Fax: (212) 548-4613
http://www.soros.org/death/index.html
e-mail: pdia@sorosny.org

The experience of dying has changed over the past several decades, with many more people enduring prolonged deaths as a consequence of chronic, progressive disease. Needless suffering physically, emotionally, existentially, and spiritually too often accompanies these deaths, for both dying persons and survivors.

The mission of the Project on Death in America is to understand and transform the culture and experience of dying and bereavement through initiatives in research, scholarship, the humanities, and the arts, and to foster innovations in the provision of care, public education, professional education, and public policy.

The St. Louis Bereavement Center For Young People

692 Wyndham Crossing Circle, Des Peres, MO, 63131
(314) 965-5015 Fax: (314) 965-8466
e-mail: rebeccab07@aol.com

The St. Louis Bereavement Center For Young People is a community-based non-profit organization whose mission is to provide comprehensive support services for children, teens, and their families who are grieving the death of someone significant. Any child or teenager, between the ages of three and eighteen, and their families are eligible for involvement. Center services include support groups, retreats, social events, resource libraries, speaker series events, and peer-based school support.

Teen Age Grief, Inc. (TAG)

P.O. Box 220034, Newhall, CA 91322-0034
(661) 253-1932 Fax: (661) 245-2536
http://www.smartlink.net/~tag/
e-mail: tag@smartlink.net

Teen Age Grief (TAG) is a non-profit organization that provides education and practical techniques to individuals working with teens individually or in a support group setting. Workshops are available for children ages eight through thirteen. TAG also creates customized curriculums and consultations for children, families, educators, and schools who may have specific needs due to special circumstances or illnesses. Training manuals, activity books, audiocassettes and videos are some of the materials available for purchase.

References

Part I: Theoretical Overview

Coles, R. (1990). *The Spiritual Life of Children*. Boston: Houghton Mifflin Company.

Kastenbaum—*Chapter 1*

Anthony, S. (1948/1972). *The discovery of death in childhood and after*. New York: Basic Books.

Bluebond-Langner, M. (1996). *In the shadow of illness*. Princeton, NJ: Princeton University Press.

Cain, A.C., & Fast, I. (1964). Children's disturbed reactions to the death of a sibling. *American Journal of Orthopsychiatry, 34,* 873-880.

Hall, G.S. (1922). *Senescence*. New York: Appleton.

Heckler, R.A. (1994). *Waking up, alive*. New York: Ballentine Books.

Kastenbaum, R. (2000). *The psychology of death*. Third edition. New York: Springer Publishing Co.

Kenyon, B. (In press). Current research in children's conceptions of death: A critical review. *Omega, Journal of Death and Dying*.

Maurer, A. (1966). Maturation of concepts of death. *British Journal of Medicine and Psychology, 39,* 35-41.

Moriarty, M. (1967). *The loss of loved ones*. Springfield, IL: Charles C. Thomas.

Nagy, M. (1948). The child's theories concerning death. *Journal of Genetic Psychology, 73,* 3-27.

Opie, I., & Opie, R. (1969). *Children's games in street and playground.* London: Oxford University Press.

Piaget, J. (1973). *The child and reality: Problems of genetic psychology.* New York: Grossman.

Corr—*Chapter 2*

Adams, D.W., & Deveau, E.J. (Eds.). (1995). *Beyond the innocence of childhood* (3 vols.). Amityville, NY: Baywood.

Corr, C.A., & Balk, D.E. (Eds.). (1996). *Handbook of adolescent death and bereavement.* New York: Springer.

Corr, C.A., & Corr, D.M. (Eds.). (1996). *Handbook of childhood death and bereavement.* New York: Springer.

Corr, C.A., Nabe, C.M., & Corr, D.M. (2000). *Death and dying, life and living* (3rd ed.). Belmont, CA: Wadsworth.

Doka, K.J. (Ed.). (1989). *Disenfranchised grief: Recognizing hidden sorrow.* Lexington, MA: Lexington Books.

Doka, K.J. (Ed.). (1995). *Children mourning, mourning children.* Washington, DC: Hospice Foundation of America.

Furman, R.A. (1973). A child's capacity for mourning. In E.J. Anthony & C. Koupernik (Eds.), *The child in his family: The impact of disease and death* (225-231). New York: Wiley.

Lazarus, R.S., & Folkman, S. (1984). *Stress, appraisal, and coping.* New York: Springer.

Rando, T.A. (1984). *Grief, dying, and death: Clinical interventions for caregivers.* Champaign, IL: Research Press.

Rando, T.A. (1993). *Treatment of complicated mourning.* Champaign, IL: Research Press.

Silverman, P.R. (1999). *Never too young to know: Death in children's lives.* New York: Oxford University Press.

Silverman, P.R., & Worden, J.W. (1992). Children's reactions in the early months after the death of a parent. *American Journal of Orthopsychiatry, 62,* 93-104.

Silverman, P.R., Nickman, S., & Worden, J.W. (1992). Detachment revisited: The child's reconstruction of a dead parent. *American Journal of Orthopsychiatry, 62,* 494-503.

Webb, N.B. (Ed.). (1993). *Helping bereaved children: A handbook for practitioners.* New York: Guilford.

Worden, J.W. (1996). *Children and grief: When a parent dies.* New York: Guilford.

Balk—*Chapter 3*

Avison, W.R. & Gotlib, I.H. (Eds). (1994). *Stress and mental health: Contemporary issues and prospects for the future.* New York: Plenum.

Balk, D.E. (1981). *Sibling death during adolescence: Self concept and bereavement reactions.* Unpublished doctoral dissertation, University of Illinois at Urbana-Champaign, Champaign, IL.

Balk, D.E. (1983). Adolescents' grief reactions and self-concept perceptions following sibling death: A study of 33 teenagers. *Journal of Youth and Adolescence, 12,* 137-161.

Balk, D.E. (Ed.). (1990). The self-concept of bereaved adolescents: Sibling death and its aftermath. *Journal of Adolescent Research, 5,* 112-132.

Balk, D.E. (1991). Death and adolescent bereavement. *Journal of Adolescent Research, 6(1).* (Special issue).

Balk, D.E. (1995a). *Adolescent development: Early through late adolescence.* Pacific Grove, CA: Brooks/Cole.

Balk, D.E. (1995b). Bereavement research using control groups: Ethical obligations and questions. *Death Studies, 19(2),* 123-138. (Special issue: Ethics and bereavement research).

Balk, D.E. (1997). Death, bereavement, and college students: A descriptive analysis. *Mortality, 2,* 207-220.

Balk, D.E. (1999). Spirituality and bereavement. *Death Studies, 23(6).* (Special issue).

Balk, D.E. & Cook, A.S. (Eds.). (1995). Ethics and bereavement research. *Death Studies, 19(2).* (Special issue).

Balk, D.E., Lampe, S., Sharpe, B., Schwinn, S., Holen, K., Cook, L., & Dubois, R. (1998). TAT results in a longitudinal study of bereaved college students. *Death Studies, 22,* 23-41.

Balk, D.E., Tyson-Rawson, K., & Colletti-Wetzel, J. (1993). Structure of a social support intervention for bereaved college students. *Death Studies, 17,* 427-450.

Balk, D.E. & Vesta, L.C. (1998). Psychological development during four years of bereavement: A longitudinal case study. *Death Studies, 22*, 23-41.

Coleman, J.C. (1978). Current contradictions in adolescent theory. *Journal of Youth and Adolescence, 7*, 1-11.

Corr, C.A. & Balk, D.E. (Eds.). (1996). *Handbook of adolescent death and bereavement.* New York: Springer.

Corr, C.A., Nabe, C.M., & Corr, D.M. (1997). *Death and dying, life and living* (2nd ed.). Pacific Grove, CA: Brooks/Cole.

Coyne, J.C. & Downey, G. (1991). Social factors and psychopathology: Stress, social support, and coping processes. *Annual Review of Psychology, 42*, 401-425.

Fleming, S.J. & Adolph, R. (1986). Helping bereaved adolescents: Needs and responses. In C.A. Corr & J.N. McNeil (Eds.), *Adolescence and death* (97-118). New York: Springer.

Fleming, S.J. & Balmer, L. (1996). Bereavement in adolescence. In C.A. Corr & D.E. Balk (Eds.), *Handbook of adolescent death and bereavement* (139-154). New York: Springer.

Frankl, V.E. (1962). *Man's search for meaning: An introduction to logotherapy.* (Trans. I. Lasch). Boston: Beacon Press.

Hogan, N.S. & DeSantis, L. (1992). Adolescent sibling bereavement: An on-going attachment. *Qualitative Health Research, 2*, 159-177.

Hogan, N.S. & DeSantis, L. (1996). Adolescent sibling bereavement: Toward a new theory. In C.A. Corr & Balk, D.E. (Eds.), *Handbook of adolescent death and bereavement* (173-195). New York: Springer.

Hogan, N.S. & Greenfield, D.B. (1991). Adolescent sibling bereavement: Symptomatology in a large community sample. (Special issue). *Journal of Adolescent Research, 6*, 97-112.

Holahan, C.J. & Moos, R.H. (1994). Life stressors and mental health: Advances in conceptualizing stress resistance. In W.R. Avison & I.H. Gotlib (Eds.), *Stress and mental health: Contemporary issues and prospects for the future* (213-238). New York: Plenum.

Kaplan, H.B. (Ed.). (1996). *Psychosocial stress: Perspectives on structure, theory, life-course, and methods.* San Diego, CA: Academic Press.

Kessler, R., Price, R.H., & Wortman, C.B. (1985). Social factors in psychopathology: Stress, social support, and coping processes. *Annual Review of Psychology, 36*, 531-572.

Lynch, W.F. (1965). *Images of hope: Imagination as healer of the hopeless.* Baltimore: Helicon.

Marrone, R. (1997). *Dying, mourning, and caring.* Pacific Grove, CA: Brooks/Cole.

Monroe, S.M. & McQuaid, J.R. (1994). Measuring life stress and assessing its impact on mental health. In W.R. Avison & I.H. Gotlib (Eds.), *Stress and mental health: Contemporary issues and prospects for the future* (43-73). New York: Plenum.

Moos, R.H., Fenn, C., & Billings, A. (1988). Life stressors and social resources: An integrated assessment approach. *Social Science and Medicine, 27,* 999-1002.

Moos, R.H. & Schaefer, J.A. (1986). Life transitions and crises: A conceptual overview. In R.H. Moos (Ed.), *Coping with life crises: An integrated approach* (3-28). New York: Plenum.

Moos, R.H. & Schaefer, J.A. (1993). Coping resources and processes: Current concepts and measures. In L. Goldberger & S. Breznitz (Eds.), *Handbook of stress: Theoretical and clinical spects* (2nd ed., 234-257). New York: Free Press.

Offer, D. (1969). *The psychological world of the teenager.* New York: Basic Books.

Offer, D., Ostrov, E., & Howard, K.I. (1977). *The Offer self-image questionnaire for adolescents: A manual.* Chicago: Michael Reese Hospital.

Oltjenbruns, K.A. (1996). Death of a friend during adolescence: Issues and impacts. In C.A. Corr & D.E. Balk (Eds.), *Handbook of adolescent death and bereavement* (196-215). New York: Springer.

Pascarella, E.T. & Terenzini, P.T. (1991). *How college affects students: Findings and insights from twenty years of research.* San Francisco: Jossey-Bass.

Pargament, K.I. (1997). *The psychology of religion and coping: Theory, research, practice.* New York: Guilford.

Perry, W.G. (1970). *Forms of intellectual and ethical development during the college years.* New York: Holt, Rinehart & Winston.

Silver, R.C. & Wortman, C.B. (1980). Coping with undesirable life events. In J. Gardner & M.E.P. Seligman (Eds.), *Human helplessness: Theory and applications* (279-340). New York: Academic Press.

Silverman, P.R., Nickman, S. & Worden, J.W. (1992). Detachment revisited: The child's reconstruction of a dead parent. *American Journal of Orthopsychiatry, 62,* 494-503.

Silverman, P.R. & Worden, J.W. (1992). Children's reactions in the early months after the death of a parent. *American Journal of Orthopsychiatry, 62,* 93-104.

Stroebe, W. & Stroebe, M.S. (1987). *Bereavement and health: The psychological and physical consequences of partner loss.* Cambridge, UK: Cambridge University Press.

Stroebe, W. & Stroebe, M.S. (1993). Determinants of adjustment to bereavement in younger widows and widowers. In M.S. Stroebe, W. Stroebe, & R.O. Hansson (Eds.), *Handbook of bereavement: Theory, research, and intervention* (208-226). Cambridge, UK: Cambridge University Press.

Tyson-Rawson, K.J. (1996). Adolescent responses to the death of a parent. In C.A. Corr & Balk, D.E. (Eds.), *Handbook of adolescent death and bereavement* (155-172). New York: Springer.

Wass, H. & Neimeyer, R.A. (Eds.). (1995). *Dying: Facing the facts* (3rd ed.). Washington, DC: Taylor and Francis.

Worden, J.W. (1996). *Children and grief: When a parent dies.* New York: Guilford.

Worden, J.W. & Silverman, P.R. (1993). Grief and depression in newly widowed parents with school-age children. *Omega, 11,* 355-361.

Work Group on Palliative Care for Children. (1999). Children, adolescents, and death: Myths, realities, and challenges. *Death Studies, 23,* 443-463.

Suarez—*Chapter 4*

Davidson, J.D., and Doka, K.J. (Eds.). (1999). *Living with grief: At work, at school, at worship.* Washington, DC: Hospice Foundation of America.

Ford, C.F. (1994). *We can all get along: 50 steps you can take to help end racism at home, at work, in your community.* New York: Dell.

Loeschen, S. (1994). *The magic of Satir: Practical skills for therapists.* Long Beach, CA: Halcyon.

McFeaters, S.J. (1999). *Experiences of African-American families at an AIDS bereavement camp: A descriptive study.* Doctoral Dissertation in Progress, University of Maryland, Baltimore.

Satir, V. (1975). *Self Esteem.* Berkeley, CA: Celestial Arts.

Suarez, M.M. (1986). *Living thru loss I & II* (Video tape teaching series). Burien, WA: M. Suarez.

Worden, W. (1991). *Grief counseling and grief therapy.* New York: Springer.

Part II: Clinical Approaches

MacPherson, M. (1999). *She came to live out loud: An inspiring family journey through illness, loss and grief.* New York: Scribner.

Grollman—Chapter 6

Adams, D. & E. (Eds.). (1995). *Helping children and adolescents cope with death.* Amityville, NY: Baywood

Blackburn, L. (1991). *The class in room 44: When a classmate dies.* Omaha, NE: Centering Corporation.

Cassini, K. & Rogers, J. (1989). *Death and the classroom: A teachers guide to assist grieving students.* Cincinnati, OH: Griefwork of Cincinnati.

Corr, C.A. & D.M. (Eds.). (1996). *Handbook of childhood death and bereavement.* New York: Springer.

Doka, K. (Ed.). (1995). *Children mourning, mourning children.* Washington, DC: Hospice Foundation of America.

Gilbert, R. (1999). *Responding to grief: A complete resource guide.* Point Richmond, CA: The Spirit of Health.

Gilko-Braden, M. (1992). *Grief comes to class: A teachers guide.* Omaha, NE: Centering Corporation.

Glassock, G. & Rowling, L. (1993). *Learning to grieve: life skills for coping with losses for high school classes.* Newton, Australia: Millennium.

Grollman, E. (Ed.). (1995). *Bereaved children and teens: A support guide for parents and professionals.* Boston: Beacon Press.

Grollman, E. (1993). *Straight talk about death for teenagers.* Boston: Beacon Press.

Grollman, E. (1990). *Talking about death: A dialogue between parent and child.* Boston: Beacon Press.

O'Toole, D. (1991). *Growing through grief: A K-12 curriculum to help young people through all kinds of loss.* Burnsville, NC: Rainbow Connection.

St. Exupery, A. (1948). *Flight to Arras.* New York: Harcourt, Brace and World.

Stevenson, R. (Ed.). (1994). *What will we do? Preparing a school community to cope with crises.* Amityville, NY: Baywood.

Underwood, M. & Dunne-Maxim, K. (1997). *Managing sudden traumatic loss in the schools.* Piscataway, NJ: University Behavioral Health Care.

Zalanik, P. (1992). *Dimensions of loss and death education: Curriculum and resource.* Minneapolis, MN: EDU-PAC Publishing.

Ward-Wimmer—*Chapter 7*

Blackwell Jones, S., Ward-Wimmer, D., & Bieschke, K. (1996). Facilitating loss groups for inner-city at-risk children victimized by violence. *Journal for Specialists in Group Work.* (Accepted for publication).

Crenshaw, D. (1992). Reluctant grievers: Children of multiple loss and trauma. *The Forum, 17 (4)*, 6-7.

Figley, C.R., Birde, B.E. & Mazza, N. (Eds.). (1997). *Death and trauma: The traumatology of grieving.* Washington, DC: Taylor and Francis.

Oaklander, V. (1988). *Windows to our children: A Gestalt approach to children and adolescents.* New York: The Gestalt Journal.

Pynoos, R. (1992). Grief and trauma in children and adolsecents. *Bereavement Care, 11(1)*, Spring, 2-10.

Terr, L. (1990). *Too Scared To Cry.* New York: Basic Books.

Wolfelt, A.D. (1991). Ten common myths about children and grief. *Bereavement, Vol. 1& 2(1)*, 38-40.

Worden, J.W. (1991). *Grief counseling and grief therapy: A handbook for the mental health practitioner.* (2nd ed.). New York: Springer.

Zambelli, G.C., & DeRosa, A.P. (1992). Bereavement support groups for school-age children: Theory, intervention and case examples. *American Journal of Orthopsychiatrics, 62(4)*, 484-492.

Webb—*Chapter 9*

American Psychiatric Association (1994). *Diagnostic and statistical manual of mental disorders* (4th ed.). Washington, DC: APA.

Bevin, T. (1999). Multiple traumas of refugees—Near drowning and witnessing of maternal rape: Case of Sergio, age 9 and follow-up at age 16. In N.B. Webb (Ed.), *Play therapy with children in crisis*, 2nd ed. (131-163). New York: Guilford Press.

Gardner, R.A. (1988). *The storytelling card game.* Creskill, NJ: Creative Therapeutics.

Goldman, L. (1996). *Breaking the silence. A guide to help children with complicated grief.* Philadelphia, PA: Taylor and Francis.

Pearlman, L.A., & Saakvitne, K. (1995). *Trauma and the therapist.* New York: Norton.

Rando, T.A. (1991). *How to go on living when someone you love dies.* New York: Bantam. (Original work published in 1988).

Rando, T.A. (1993). *Treatment of complicated mourning.* Champaign, IL: Research Press.

Raphael, B. (1983). *The anatomy of bereavement.* New York: Basic Books.

Ryan, K. (1999). *Self-help for the helpers: Preventing vicarious traumatization.* In N.B. Webb (Ed.), *Play therapy with children in crisis,* 2nd ed. (471-491). New York: Guilford Press.

Speece, M.W. & Brent, S.B. (1996). The development of children's understanding of death. In C.A. Corr & D.M. Corr (Eds.). *Handbook of childhood death and bereavement* (29-50). New York: Springer.

Terr, L.C. (1989). Treating psychic trauma in children: A preliminary discussion. *Journal of Traumatic Stress, 2(1),* 3-20.

Webb, N.B. (1993). (Ed.). *Helping bereaved children. A handbook for practitioners.* New York: Guilford Press.

Webb, N.B. (1999). (Ed.). *Play therapy with children in crisis, 2nd Ed. Individual, family and group treatment.* New York: Guilford Press.

Webb, N.B. (2000). Death of a parent. In A. Gitterman (Ed.). *Handbook of social work practice with vulnerable and resilient populations* (2nd ed.) (in press).

Doka—*Chapter 10*

Gennep, A. (1960). *The rites of passage.* Chicago: University of Chicago Press.

Martin, T. & Doka, K.J. (1999). *Men don't cry, women do: Transcending gender stereotypes of grief.* Philadelphia: Brunner-Mazel.

Rando, T.A. (1984). *Grief, dying and death: Clinical interventions for caregivers.* Lexington, MA: Lexington Press.

Rando, T.A. (1993). *The treatment of complicated mourning.* Champaign, IL: Research Press.

Schuurman—*Chapter 11*

Butler, K. (1997). Can resilience be consciously created? *The Family Therapy Networker.* March/April, 29.

Corr, C.A. & Wass, H. (1984). *Helping children cope with death.* New York: Hemisphere Publishing Corp.

The Dougy Center Staff (1990). *Waving goodbye: An activities manual for grieving children and teens.* Portland, OR: The Dougy Center Press.

Fitzgerald, H. (1992). *The grieving child.* New York: Fireside.

Goldman, L. (1994). *Life and loss: A guide to help grieving children.* Muncie, IN: Accelerated Development.

Grollman, E. (Ed.). (1995). *Bereaved children and teens.* Boston: Beacon Press.

Malone, M. (1998). *Newsweek, Oct. 26,* 64-66.

Silverman, P.R. (2000). *Never too young to know.* New York, NY: Oxford University Press.

Wolfelt, A.D. (1996). *Healing the bereaved child.* Fort Collins, CO: Companion Press.

Worden, W J. (1996). *Children and grief: When a parent dies.* New York, NY: Guilford Press.

Byrne—*Chapter 12*

Cantarella, G. (1999). *National guide to funding for children, youth and families* (5th ed.). New York: The Foundation Center.

Chronicle of Philanthropy Web Site, http://www.philanthropy.com.

Covey, S.R. (1989). *The 7 habits of highly effective people.* New York: Simon & Schuster.

Foundation Center Web Site, http://www.fdncenter.org.

The Foundation Center. (1999). *FC Search: The Foundation Center's Database on CD-ROM* (version 3.0). New York: The Foundation Center.

The Foundation Center. (1998). *The Foundation Center's Guide to Grantseeking on the Web.* New York: The Foundation Center.

Geever, J.C., & McNeill, P. (1997). *The Foundation Center's Guide to Proposal Writing* (Rev. ed.). New York: The Foundation Center.

Hummel, J.M. (1996). *Starting and Running a Nonprofit Organization* (2nd ed.). Minneapolis, MN: University of Minnesota Press.

Internet Nonprofit Center Web Site, http://www.nonprofits.org.

IRS Web Site, http://www.irs.ustreas.gov.

Mancuso, A. (1996). *How to Form a Nonprofit Corporation* (3rd Ed.). Berkeley, CA: Nolo Press, Inc.

Metropolitan Association for Philanthropy, http://www.mapstl.org.

National Center for Charitable Statistics, http://nccs.urban.org.

Philanthropy Journal On-line, http://www.pj.org.

PhilanthropySearch.com, http://www.philanthropysearch.com.

Robert, H.M. (1986). *Robert's rules of order*. New York: Bantam Books.

The St. Louis Bereavement Center For Young People, http://www.bereavementctr.org. (In progress.)

United Way of Greater St. Louis, Inc. *Through the Maze to Incorporation and Tax-Exempt Status—A How-To Guide for Not-For-Profit Organizations.* St. Louis.

Watters, M.R., Esq. (Ed.). (1996). *How to plan and organize a nonprofit corporation*. Indianapolis, IN: The United Way of Central Indiana, Inc.

Silverman—*Chapter 14*

Baker, J.E. & Sedney, M.A. (1996). How bereaved children cope with loss: An overview. In C.A. Corr & D.M. Corr (Eds.), *Handbook of childhood death and bereavement* (109-129). New York: Springer.

Bluebond-Langner, M. (1997). *In the shadow of illness: Parents and siblings of the chronically ill child*. Princeton, NJ: Princeton University Press.

Boerner, K. & Silverman, P.R. (1999). *Gender differences in parenting styles in widowed families*. Presentation at annual meeting of Association for Death Education and Counseling, San Antonio, TX.

Cook, J.A. (1988). Dad's double bind: Rethinking father's bereavement from a men's studies perspective. *Journal of Ethnography, 17,* 308-385.

Kegan, R. (1982). *The evolving self.* Cambridge, MA: Harvard University Press.

Kegan, R. (1994). *In over our heads: The mental demands of modern life.* Cambridge, MA: Harvard University Press.

Koocher, G. (1974). Talking with children about death. *American Journal of Orthopsychiatry, 44(3),* 404-411.

Martin, T.L., & Doka, K.J. (1998). Revisiting masculine grief. In K.J. Doka and J.D. Davidson (Eds.), *Living with grief: who we are, how we grieve* (133-142). Washington, DC: Hospice Foundation of America.

Nickman, S.L., Silverman, P.R. & Normand, C. (1998). Children's construction of their deceased parent: The surviving parent's contribution. *The American Journal of Orthopsychiatry, 68(1),* 126-141.

Normand, C., Silverman, P.R., & Nickman, S.L. (1996). Bereaved children's changing relationships with the deceased. In D. Klass, P. R. Silverman and S. Nickman (Eds.), *Continuing bonds: A new understanding of grief.* Washington, DC: Taylor and Francis.

Selman, R.L. & Schultz, L.H. (1990). *Making a friend in youth: Developmental theory and pair therapy*. Chicago: University of Chicago Press.

Silverman, P.R. (1980). *Helping women cope with grief.* Beverly Hills, CA: Sage.

Silverman, P.R. (1988). In search of new selves: Accommodating to widowhood. In L.A. Bond and B.M Wagner (Eds.), *Families in transition: Primary prevention programs that work.* Newbury Park, CA: Sage Publications.

Silverman, P.R. (1987). Impact of parental death on college age women. In *Psychiatric Clinics of North America, 10(3),* September 1987.

Silverman, P.R. (2000). *Never too young to know: Death in children's lives.* New York: Oxford University Press.

Silverman, P.R., Baker, J., Boerner, K., & Chait, C. (1999). *Family and developmental issues in children at risk.* [Work in progress].

Silverman, P.R. & Gross, E. (1996). *Parental perception of children's needs in widowed families.* Presentation at annual meeting of the Association for Death Education and Counseling.

Silverman, P.R., & Nickman, S.L. (1996). Children's construction of their dead parent. In D. Klass, P.R. Silverman and S. Nickman (Eds.), *Continuing bonds: A new understanding of grief.* Washington, DC: Taylor and Francis.

Silverman, P.R., & Worden, J.W. (1992). Children's reactions in the early months after the death of a parent. *American Journal of Orthopsychiatry, 62(1),* 93-104.

Silverman, P.R., & Worden, J.W. (1992a). Children's understanding of the funeral. *Omega 25(4),* 319-331.

Silverman, P.R., Nickman, S.L. & Worden, J.W. (1992). Detachment revisted: Children's construction of their deceased parent. *American Journal of Orthopsychiatry 62(4),* 494-503.

Silverman, P.R. & Worden, J.W. (1993). Children's Reactions to the Death of a parent. In M. Stroebe, W. Stroebe and R. Hansson, (Eds.), *Bereavement: A sourcebook of research and intervention.* England: Cambridge University

Smilansky, S. (1987). *On death: helping children understand and cope.* New York: P. Lang.

Speece, M.W. & Brent, S.B. (1996). Development of children's understanding of death. In C.A. Corr & D.M. Corr, (Eds.), *Handbook of childhood death and bereavement,* (29-50). New York: Springer.

Worden, J.W. & Silverman, P.R. (1993). Grief and depression in newly widowed parents with school-age children. *Omega 27(3),* 251-261.

Worden, J.W. & Silverman, P.R. (1996). Parental death and the adjustment of school-age children. *Omega 31(4),* 275-293.

Davies—*Chapter 15*

Birenbaum, L. (1989). The relationship between parent-sibling communication and coping of siblings with death experience. *Journal of Pediatric Oncology Nursing, 6,* 56-91.

Birenbaum, L.K., Robinson, M.A., Phillips, D.S., Stewart, B.J., & McCowan, D. E. (1990). The response of children to the dying and death of a sibling. *Omega, 20,* 213-228.

Brett, K.M., & Davies, E.M.B., (1988). What does it mean? Sibling and parental appraisals of childhood leukemia. *Cancer Nursing, 11,* 329-338.

Davies, E. (1983). The reaction of an early latency boy to the sudden death of his baby brother. *Psychoanalytic Study of the Child, 48.*

Davies, B. (October, 1985). Behavioral responses of children to the death of a sibling. Final report submitted to Alberta Foundation for Nursing Research, Edmonton, Alberta.

Davies, B. (1993). Sibling bereavement: Research based guidelines for nurses. *Seminars in Oncology Nursing, 9(2),* 107-113.

Davies, B. (1999). *Shadows in the sun: Experiences of sibling bereavement in childhood.* Philadelphia, PA: Brunner-Mazel.

McClowry, S., Davies, B., Martinson, I., May, K. & Kulenkamp, E. (1987). The long-term effects of sibling death on self-concept. *Journal of Pediatric Nursing, 2(4),* 227-235.

McCowan, D.E., & Pratt, C. (1985). Impact of sibling death on children's behavior. *Death Studies, 9,* 323-335.

Martin—*Chapter 17*

Abramson, L.Y., Seligman, M.E., & Teasdale, J. (1978). Learned helplessness in humans: Critique and reformulation. *Journal of Abnormal Psychology, 87,* 49-74.

Barry, B. (1989). Suicide: The ultimate escape. *Death studies, 13,* 185-190.

Bender, L., & Schilder, P. Suicidal preoccupations and attempts in children. *American Journal of Orthopsychiatry, 7,* 225-234.

Brent, D.A., Perper, J.A., Moritz, G., Liotus, L., Schweers, J., Roth, C., Balach, L., & Allman, C. (1993). Psychiatric impact of the loss of an adolescent sibling to suicide. *Journal of Affective Disorders, 28,* 249-256.

Brent, D.A., Perper, J.A., Moritz, G., Liotus, L., Schweers, J., & Canobbio, R. (1994). Major depression or uncomplicated bereavement? A follow-up of youth exposed to suicide. *Journal of the American Academy of Child and Adolescent Psychiatry, 33,* 231-239.

Brent, D.A., Moritz, G., Bridge, J., Perper, J. & Canobbio, R. (1996). The impact of adolescent suicide on siblings and parents: A longitudinal follow-up. *Suicide and Life-Threatening Behavior, 26,* 253-259.

Cable, D.G., Cucchi, L., Lopez, F., & Martin, T.L. (1992). Camp Jamie. *American Journal of Hospice and Palliative Care, 9,* 18-21.

Cain, A.C., & Fast, I. (1972). *Survivors of suicide.* Springfield, IL: Charles C. Thomas.

Cerel, J., Fristad, M.A., Weller, E.B., & Weller, R.A (1999). Suicide-bereaved children and adolescents: a controlled longitudinal examination. *Journal of the American Academy of Child and Adolescent Psychiatry, 38,* 672-680.

DeSpelder, L.A., & Strickland, A.L. (1996). *The last dance* (4th ed.). Mountain View, CA: Mayfield Publishing Company.

Doka, K.J. (1989). *Disenfranchised grief: Recognizing hidden sorrow.* Lexington, MA: Lexington Books.

Erikson, E.H. (1950). *Childhood and society.* New York: Norton.

Eth, G., & Pynoos, R. (1985). Developmental perspective on psychic trauma in childhood. In C. Figley (Ed.), *Trauma and its wake.* New York: Brunner-Mazel.

Fleming, S.J., & Adolph, R. (1986). Helping bereaved adolescents: Needs and responses. In C.A. Corr and J.N. McNeil (Eds.), *Adolescence and death.* New York: Springer.

Marcia, J.E. (1980). Identity in adolescence. In J. Adelson (Ed.), *Handbook of adolescent psychology.* New York: Wiley.

National Center for Health Statistics (1995). *Health risk behaviors among our nation's youth.* (PHS Publication No. 95-1414).

Orbach, I. (1988). *Children who don't want to live.* San Francisco: Jossey-Bass.

Pfeffer, C.R. (1986). *The suicidal child.* New York: Guilford Press.

Pfeffer, C.R., Martins, J.M., Mann, J., Sukenberg, M., Ice, A., Damore, J.P. Jr., Gallo, C., Karpenos, H., & Jiang, H. (1997). Child survivors of suicide: Psychosocial characteristics. *Journal of the American Academy of Child and Adolescent Psychiatry, 35,* 65-75.

Rubey, C.T., & McIntosh, J.L. (1996). Suicide survivors groups: Results of a survey. *Suicide and Life-Threatening Behavior, 26,* 351-358.

Shepherd, D.M., & Barraclough, B.M. (1976). The aftermath of parental suicide for children. *British Journal of Psychiatry, 129*, 267-276.

Shneidman, E.S. (1973). *Deaths of man.* New York: Quadrangle/ New York Times.

Stillion, J.M. (1996). Survivors of suicide. In K.J. Doka (Ed.), *Living with grief: After sudden loss.* Washington, DC: Hospice Foundation of America.

Stillion, J., McDowell, E., & May, J. (1989). *Suicide across the life span: Premature exits.* Washington, DC: Hemisphere.

Wise, A.J., & Spengler, P.M. (1997). Suicide in children younger than age fourteen: Clinical judgment and assessment issues. *Journal of Mental Health Counseling, 19*, 318-336.

Sheras—*Chapter 18*

Cornell, D.G. & Sheras, P.L. (1998). Common errors in school crisis response: Learning from our mistakes. *Psychology in the Schools, 35*, 297-307.

Goldberg, F.R. & Leyden, H.D. (1998). Left and left out: Teaching children to grieve through a rehabilitation curriculum. *Professional School Counseling, 2(2)*, 123-127.

Komar, A.A. (1994). Adolescent school crisis: Structures, issues and techniques for postvention. *International Journal of Adolescence & Youth, 5(1-2)*, 35-46.

Leenaars, A.A. & Wenckstern, S. (1996). Postvention with elementary school children. In Corr, C., & Corr, D. (Eds.), *Handbook of childhood death and bereavement* (265-283). New York: Springer.

Matthews, J. D. (1999). The grieving child in the school environment. In J.D. Davidson & K.J. Doka (Eds.), *Living with grief: At work, at school, at worship* (95-113). Washington, DC: Hospice Foundation of America.

Nader, K.O. (1997). Treating traumatic grief in systems. In C. Figley & B. Bride (Eds.), *Death and trauma: The traumatology of grieving* (159-192). Washington, DC: Taylor and Francis.

Perschy, M.K. (1997). *Helping teens work through grief.* Washington, DC: Accelerated Development.

Peterson, S., & Straub, R.L. (1992). *School crisis survival guide.* West Nyack, NY: The Center for Applied Research in Education.

Pitcher, G.D. & Poland, S. (1992). *Crisis intervention in the schools.* New York: Guilford Press.

Stevenson, R.G. (1995). The role of the school: Bereaved students and students facing life-threatening illness. In K.J. Doka (Ed.), *Children mourning, mourning children* (97-111). Washington, DC: Hospice Foundation of America.

Stevenson, R.G. (1996) The response of schools and teachers. In K. Doka (Ed.), *Living with grief: After sudden loss* (201-213). Washington DC: Hospice Foundation of America.

Wass, H., Miller, M.D., & Thornton, G.(1990). Death education and grief/suicide intervention in the public schools. *Death Studies, 14(3)*, 253-268.

Wilson, P.G.H. (1988). Helping children cope with death. In J. Sandoval (Ed.), *Crisis counseling, intervention, and prevention in schools*. Hilsdale, NJ: Lawrence Erlbaum.

Hospice Foundation of America Order Form

Journeys — *subscriptions are pre-paid for one year*
_____ $12.00 / 1 year individual subscription
_____ Bulk quantities of 10 or more copies @ 25¢ per copy each month
Bulk orders please indicate:
_____ Folded: 8½ x 11, or _____ Envelope: #10 fold

Special Issues of *Journeys* are also available for 25¢ per copy:
_____ Newly Bereaved issue _____ Children's Issue
_____ Anniversary issue _____ Adolescent Issue

Clergy to Clergy:
Helping You Minister to Those Experiencing Illness, Loss and Grief
_____ set of audiotapes and guide, $20.00

Living With Grief Teleconference
Videos: One-hour, $15.00 each:
Full set of seven one-hour tapes $75.00
_____ 1994 – Living With Grief: Personally and Professionally
_____ 1995 – Living With Grief: Children Mourning, Mourning Children
_____ 1996 – Living With Grief: After Sudden Loss
_____ 1997 – Living With Grief: When Illness is Prolonged
_____ 1998 – Living With Grief: Who We Are, How We Grieve
_____ 1999 – Living With Grief: At Work, At School, At Worship
_____ 2000 – Living With Grief: Children, Adolescents, and Loss

2½-hour, $25.00 each:
Full set of five 2½-hour tapes $80.00
_____ 1996 – Living With Grief: After Sudden Loss ($25.00)
_____ 1997 – Living With Grief: When Illness is Prolonged ($25.00)
_____ 1998 – Living With Grief: Who We Are, How We Grieve ($25.00)
_____ 1999 – Living With Grief: At Work, At School, At Worship ($25.00)
_____ 2000 – Living With Grief: Children, Adolescents, and Loss ($25.00)

Books: $16.95 each; 20 or more copies, $7.00 each;
Full set of five books, $60.00
_____ After Sudden Loss
_____ When Illness is Prolonged
_____ Who We Are, How We Grieve
_____ At Work, At School, At Worship
_____ Children, Adolescents, and Loss

Audiotape: Full teleconference $19.95
_____ 2000 – Living With Grief: Children, Adolescents, and Loss

A Guide For Recalling And Telling Your Life Story
_____ $15.00

Practical Guides and Brochures
one sample copy free, 50¢ each, see chart for pricing

	Quantity	Cost
_____ Living With Grief: At Work		
_____ Living With Grief: At School	25	$12.00
_____ Living With Grief: At Worship	50	$23.00
_____ Choosing Hospice: A Consumer's Guide	100	$35.00
_____ Hospice Volunteers	200	$65.00

Free
☐ sample copy of _Journeys_
☐ Hospice Care and the Military Family

Payment must accompany order — Sales are final
All prices include shipping and handling

DONATION AMOUNT _____

TOTAL ORDER AMOUNT _____

NAME _____

PHONE (   ) _____

ORGANIZATION _____

ADDRESS _____

CITY _____ STATE _____ ZIP _____

VISA / MC / AMEX number _____ Exp. _____

Cardholder Name _____

Signature _____

Make checks payable to:
Hospice Foundation of America
2001 S St. NW #300
Washington, DC 20009
Phone: 1-800-854-3402
Fax: (202) 638-5312
e-mail: hfa@hospicefoundation.org
http://www.hospicefoundation.org